D0459251

DISCARD

6 Steps to Songwriting Success

The Comprehensive Guide to
Writing and Marketing Hit Songs

6 Steps to Songwriting Success

The Comprehensive Guide to

Writing and Marketing Hit Songs

Jason Blume

Billboard Books

An imprint of Watson-Guptill Publications

New York

Senior Editor: Bob Nirkind
Editor: Margaret Sobel
Book design: Marie Mundaca
Production Manager: Hector Campbell

Copyright © 1999 Jason Blume

First published in 1999 by Billboard Books, an imprint of Watson-Guptill Publications, a division of BPI Communications, Inc., 1515 Broadway, New York, NY 10036

Library of Congress Cataloging-in-Publication Data for this title can be obtained by writing to the Library of Congress, Washington D.C. 20540

ISBN: 0-8230-8422-1

Printed in the U.S.A.
First printing, 1999

1 2 3 4 5 6 7 8 9/04 03 02 01 00 99

DEDICATION

This book is dedicated to the memories of my mother Thelma Blume and my Aunt Syb who believed I could accomplish anything, and showed me the power of unconditional love—and to my father Ned Blume who gave me the gift of music. I also dedicate this book to my students who continue to teach me every day.

Acknowledgments

There are several individuals without whom this book could never have been written. I'd like to express my heartfelt gratitude to my editor Bob Nirkind and to my associate editor Margaret Sobel for making it possible for me to write the book I always wanted to write, to my literary agent Rita Rosenkranz for her expertise and belief in this project, and to Neil Rice for his inestimable assistance and support.

Thank you to all of my teachers and to Brendan Okrent, Barbara Cane, Barbara Rothstein, Gloria Sklerov, Harlan Howard, Collin Raye, Steve Cox, Karen Taylor-Good, Randy Goodrum, Carol Elliott, Buddy Mondlock, David Friedman, Gemma Corfield, Wade Kirby, Roger Sovine, Mike Sistad, Wayne Perry, Butter, Justin Wilde, Craig Wiseman, Gary Baker, Frank Myers, Mark Mason, Michelle Stilts, Bryan Cumming, David Roth, Gina Gamble, Lee Groitzsch, Barry Sanders, Janice Cook, Virginia Rice, Patti and Tom at County Q, Bart Herbison, Donna Michael, Evon McKay, Phil Goldberg, Emily and staff at NSAI, Wayne Tester, Robert K. Oermann, Tommy LiPuma, Jeff Fenster, Judy Phelps, Allan Rich, Ira Greenfield, Thom Schuyler, Billy Steinberg, Lou Heffernan, Aaron Meza, Nick Martinelli, Franne Golde, Frank Liddell, Marty Wheeler, Judy Stakee, Kathleen Carey, Debbie Zavitson, Jeff Carlton, Sandy Carothers and Phyllis Austin of Bull's Creek Music, John Van Meter, Steve Weaver, Lynn Gann, Steve Lunt, Rick Chudacoff, Steve Gibson, and all of the talented songwriters and music industry professionals who contributed so generously to this book—and especially to Jane Snyder. And thank you to Jim Cooper for providing the musical notation.

I owe a special debt to Clive Calder and Michael Hollandsworth who believed in my talents and taught me how to be a songwriter, and to Don and Gayle Goodman, Adam Sandler, Liz Rose, A.J. Masters, Lis Lewis, Thad Tarleton, Tom Luteran, Stephanie Cox, John and Robin Berry, Steve Diamond, Teri Muench, Deborah Jones, and all of the others who've contributed so much to my career.

I'd like to acknowledge Dave Olsen and Cheryl Swack of Warner Bros. Publications; Rosa Morris and Rochelle Greenblatt of Zomba; and Donna Rader and Lee Hubner of Sony/ATV Music for their patience and cooperation (beyond the call of duty) in helping me to secure permissions to reprint the lyrics contained in this book. Thank you to Karen Will Rogers, Heather Fowler, and Jan Furman for doing their best to make me look like Brad Pitt in the photo, and to David Vincent and Takamine guitars for their generous support.

A very special thank you to my Uncle Moon, Ilene Krems, Barbara Lamb, Wayne Moore, Marvin Werlin, Andrea Horstman, Mark Werlin, Coreen Davis, Maris, Mark, Adam and Jamie Goldberg, Todd Serinsky, Leslie Brenner, Laura Powers, Hal Holzer, Katy Garvey, and to my first collaborator and biggest supporter Maureen Custer, who listened to my struggles and encouraged me to follow my dream. And to Opie, Duncan, and Coin (the cats) who sat on my lap, my desk, and my computer, providing free editorial advice.

And a final heartfelt thank you—to the source from which all creativity flows.

Contents

Introduction

Being presented with my ASCAP Award honoring John Berry's recording of my song "Change My Mind" as one of "The Most Performed Songs for 1996" will always be a highlight of my life. As I heard my name being called and when I walked up on that Nashville stage in the company of some of country music's greatest stars, including Garth Brooks, Wynonna, Trisha Yearwood, and Deana Carter, it felt like the culmination of everything I had worked so hard for during the previous seventeen years. The black tie dinner and award presentation was so extravagant that I felt as if I had gone to the Academy Awards. I could easily have floated home with my award in hand and my feet several inches above ground, with only the gold medal around my neck to keep me on terra firma . . . but the best was yet to come.

As I left, carrying my award down the Opryland Hotel's red-carpeted hallway, there were hundreds of screaming and cheering fans on either side of the ropes. I assumed they were only there for a glimpse of Garth Brooks and the other celebrities, but they were craning their necks to see the name of my song printed on the award I was so proudly carrying. Cameras flashed and hundreds of hands reached out across the ropes to shake my hand and wish their congratulations. Thankfully it was a very long hallway and I allowed myself to bask in my brief, but wonderful, moment of fame. I don't think it gets much better. But it hasn't always been that way.

I've felt the frustration of working at a day job I hated, while knowing in my heart that I was meant to be writing songs and enjoying success. I've known the pain of feeling that there's an invisible wall between me and what I wanted more than anything in the world to achieve. In the days when I was an aspiring songwriter, it seemed as though the successful writers must have been born lucky, or that maybe they'd had some magic fairy dust sprinkled on them somewhere along the way. It felt as if no matter how close I came to success, there was no way to get there from where I was.

Now, I've learned it wasn't magic that I needed—it was specific skills *that can be acquired.*

My story begins when I left Philadelphia in 1979 for Los Angeles with $400 and everything I owned packed into my Datsun Honeybee. It was crammed so full that I drove three thousand miles with my favorite framed print, *View from Carmel,* wedged between my hip and the driver's side door. I was bursting with dreams and knew that within a year (okay, *maybe* two) I'd be a rich and famous songwriter, driving around in my new Mercedes convertible. It didn't matter that it had taken Elton John and Billy Joel years and years to achieve their successes. Nothing anyone could have said or done would have convinced me otherwise. I had no shortage of confidence. What I was lacking was the craft and tools to turn my dreams into a reality.

Almost immediately after arriving in LA, I was accepted into an ASCAP (American Society of Composers, Authors and Publishers) Songwriters Workshop. Luckily ASCAP footed the bills because I was so poor that I remember fantasizing about having enough money to eat at the McDonald's around the corner. (Hey, you have to dream big!) At the time, the cost of a burger, fries, and a coke was more than my food budget for the week. There would be no Big Mac until I got my Big Break (which I knew was going to come any day now).

During that period, my friend Andrea convinced me to try eating cat food. She explained that kitty tuna was made of tuna—and "tuna is tuna." Well, generic kitty tuna was on sale at the market across the street for 15 cents a can and I was getting really tired of eggs, macaroni, hotdogs, and day-old bread. It sounded like a good idea, but even with extra mayo, it was disgusting—dark brown and intensely fishy. It may have been tuna, but I suspect it included parts of the tuna that most humans never want to even think about, let alone eat. Thanks a lot, Andrea! I couldn't eat tuna for almost a decade.

Anyway, back to that first ASCAP Workshop. It was held in the Beverly Hills home of songwriters Annette Tucker and Arthur Hamilton. Arthur was best known as the writer of "Cry Me A River," which had already been recorded 111 times at that point! Driving up into those hills, it felt as if I were a million miles away from the tiny room I shared with mice and cockroaches, and the bathroom down the hall that I shared with the junkies and hookers who lived in the twelve other rooms of the apartment building. Seeing the way Arthur and Annette lived gave me hope and inspired me to write that first big hit even faster. They were wonderfully encouraging and supportive, while giving me the basics I needed so desperately. When I began their workshop, I had no idea that songs are supposed to have any particular structure, or that the title is supposed to be *in* the song. I needed to learn the rules—*and I didn't even know there were any*. Ten weeks (and ten songs) later, I left with the basic tools that would allow me to begin crafting songs that had verses and choruses, rhymes, repetition, hooks, and singable melodies. I was on my way!

From then on I took every class and workshop I could find, and my life revolved around one thing—writing songs. I learned a lot during those first few years in Los Angeles, but looking back, I can see that there was one specific moment that actually changed the course of my career and my life. It was in October 1983.

I had once again been accepted into an ASCAP Songwriters Workshop (my third), that consisted of weekly panels of music business professionals who critiqued several songs. It was finally going to be my turn to have a song critiqued. Although the panel was there to critique my song, I knew better. I *knew* that my life would change that night, because when they heard my song, the panelists would literally fight over who would get to work with me. (I told you, it wasn't confidence that I was lacking!)

On this particular evening, one of the panelists, producer/writer/artist George Duke, was going directly from our class to the recording studio where he was producing the mega-successful R & B/pop group Earth, Wind and Fire. I decided that I would let him be the lucky one to record my song. That way, I wouldn't have to wait even one more day to tell my boss that I was a rich and famous songwriter and that he could keep his miserable job.

There was no doubt in my mind that this was the night when my life would change forever. After four years of honing my craft in Los Angeles, I had begun publishing songs with an amateur, fledgling publisher and although no one had cut any of my songs yet, I now had someone who was paying to produce professional demos of my work. The song I had chosen to play for the panel was a step above anything I had previously written. My friends Wayne & Brenda performed this song in little piano bars and it always got a great response. More importantly, my publisher assured me that this one was a hit!

My life really was about to change that night—but not in the way I'd anticipated. I thought I was going to burst as I sat there while my song was being played, and when it was finished I waited for the words that would alter my life forever. But rather than hearing, "This song will be a Grammy winner," or "This song is a smash hit," or "This song will be a Number One," instead I heard "This song would *never* be on the radio."

I knew I must have been mistaken. My heart was pounding and my hands were shaking. Perhaps I was hallucinating from all of the excitement. Surely the panelist could not possibly have said what I thought I'd heard, and certainly the next panelist would have the "ears" and the brains to know this song was a hit! But what I heard from the second panelist was, "Well, I wouldn't have put it so bluntly, but now that you've mentioned it, this song *is* a very good example of a song that would *never* be on the radio."

I knew this couldn't be happening. Everything I'd lived and dreamed for was crashing down around me. This was the very best I could do. If it was so horrible that it "would *never* be on the radio," what hope did I have? Surely the last panelist would come to his senses and recognize a great song. However, through a haze of humiliation, I vaguely heard the third panelist heartily concur.

As if that wasn't enough torture, the panelists then proceeded to list all the reasons why this song would *never, never, never* be on the radio. They pointed out the "lack of any fresh imagery," the "sappy, syrupy melody," the "trite, over-used cliches," and the myriad other flaws that made the song that I had poured my soul into and was so proud of, "a great example of all the things amateurs commonly do wrong."

During my fifteen-minute drive home I wanted to die. I kept reliving that horrible scene and hearing those panelists say that the dreams I'd cherished and sacrificed for would *never, never, never* come true. I'd been so sure that my life would change that night—and around 2:00 a.m., it did.

As I lay awake, replaying every negative comment made about my song, I realized for the first time that the panelists were right. It was like a lightning bolt when it hit me: I had been writing from my heart, *with no consideration of the commercial market.*

Somehow, through the pain, came the realization that there really were differences between my songs and the hits on the radio. It isn't just about luck, who you know, or that big break. Up until that moment, my writing had been a means of self-expression, a catharsis I had hoped would also, by pure coincidence, just happen to be something that millions of others would relate to. Until that night, when I wrote, it was solely to please myself. There was no consideration (or even awareness) of the listener's response. I just assumed that if it meant so much to me, others would like it as well. But somehow, something that had been said that night broke through the wall and it was suddenly clear that the inspiration that comes from my heart is crucial, but it is only a part of the equation.

My life really did change that night because I realized three things:

1. There are specific elements that are consistently found in the melodies, lyrics, and structures of hit songs.

2. These elements could be learned and incorporated into my songs.

3. The fact that I was writing songs at that point in my develop-
    ment that were not up to the professional standard did *not* mean
    I was incapable of writing hit songs in the future.

At first, I was resistant to fitting my songs into a commercial format. It felt
like selling out, and I thought it would weaken my work. I thought "commercial" was a dirty word, synonymous with having no heart, no genuine emotion,
and no creativity. I couldn't imagine ever writing anything that had any real
meaning for me (or anyone else) by using some recommended structure or formula. That seemed like the antithesis of creativity to me.

Nonetheless I slowly came to see that "commercial" simply meant what listeners were drawn to buy—and "commercial" included most of my favorite
artists. That didn't sound so bad. I did want people to like what I was writing,
and I did want to write songs that would be hits. But even if I could learn the
techniques that made some songs hits, I couldn't imagine employing those
principles without sacrificing the soul of my songs. But I was wrong. I never
dreamed that there would come a time when I would so fully absorb the "rules"
that my songs would spontaneously emerge in the proper structures—but now
they do.

With lots of practice these tools, techniques, and principles can be assimilated to such a degree that you won't even have to think about them—so that
the spark of inspiration that starts deep in your heart can express itself in a way
that can touch millions of listeners.

What are the common denominators? What are the factors that separate the
good songs from the hit songs, and the merely talented writers from the
successful ones?

The six steps to songwriting success are:

✔ **Developing successful song structures**

✔ **Writing effective lyrics**

✔ **Composing memorable melodies**

✔ **Producing successful demos**

✔ **Taking care of business**

✔ **Developing persistence**

A last word: While most of the tools and techniques addressed in this book will apply to all genres of music, they are most appropriate for the types of pop, rock, adult contemporary, Christian, and country songs that are recorded by artists who do not exclusively write their own songs. Chapter 4 addresses the issues facing writers who are writing for specialty markets.

Thankfully, there are writers who stretch the boundaries. It would get awfully boring if every song followed each of the rules outlined in this book. No doubt, there are exceptions to every rule and suggested technique discussed here. Some songs may become hits based on the strength of the artist or the production. But since the vast majority of hit songs that are not written by the artist do adhere to most of the techniques in this book, you will have a much better chance of achieving your goals if you learn these techniques before you make the conscious choice to deviate from them.

Step 1
Developing Successful Song Structures

Learn the techniques and structures so well that when the great idea or inspiration comes, your technical ability doesn't hinder your creativity. Learn and practice the basics so they become second nature. Then when you are ready to create something new or the inspiration hits you, the building blocks will already be in place. We all like to think that there are shortcuts to life and sometimes they do work for a while, but I feel it is better to learn the trade so that you can understand the tricks of the trade.

Mike Sistad (Director, Artists & Repertoires, Arista Nashville)

Chapter 1
Identifying the Most Successful Song Structures— and Why They Work

---

Songwriting seems to start with an introspective base as a stage. From there, serious songwriters need to step outside of themselves to develop their craft. Ideally, somewhere down the road the two meet again to combine resources in more well-crafted unique songs.

Brendan Okrent (Senior Director of Repertory, ASCAP)

I wrote my first song, "Eternal August," at age twelve by strumming the three chords I'd taught myself on my father's mandolin and singing whatever I felt. If any sections repeated or if the title appeared in the song, it was by pure chance. It never crossed my mind that the songs I loved and sang along with had been constructed using only a handful of specific structures. Although I'd heard those structures at least a thousand times, like most listeners I was never aware of them.

At the first workshop I ever attended I quickly discovered that my rambling, stream-of-consciousness style of songwriting was not going to get me on the radio. However the good news was that:

1. There are a limited number of song structures commonly heard in hit songs. These structures could be learned and used effectively.

2. It is possible to take an idea that starts in my heart and communicate it within the confines of one of these structures and without compromising the integrity or the essence of the song.

My first teachers explained that songwriting is an art that is based upon successful communication. Using one of the most commonly heard song structures is analogous to using punctuation in a sentence. It allows the listener to more readily understand and feel what the writer is trying to communicate.

Learning song structures is not the most exciting, creative, or interesting part of the songwriting process, but it is important. Whether we're conscious of it or not, we've been trained by years of listening to the radio to expect one of the forms that follow. With very few exceptions, the vast majority of hit songs that are written by "outside" writers (writers who are neither the artist, the producer, nor otherwise involved in the project) employ one of the following four basic structures or a variation on one of them.

♪ Verse - Chorus - Verse - Chorus

♪ Verse - Chorus - Verse - Chorus - Bridge - Chorus

♪ Verse - Chorus - Verse - Chorus - Verse - Chorus

♪ Verse - Verse - Bridge - Verse

IDENTIFYING THE COMPONENTS OF A SONG

"Radio-friendly" songs are built by combining the following elements:

♪ Verses

♪ Pre-Choruses

♪ Choruses

♪ Bridges

Each of these components has a specific function within the song. Let's examine each of the building blocks before attempting to put them together into a complete song.

The Verse

The primary function of the verse is to provide the exposition—the information that will lead to the song's hook or title. The verse is the place where the listener is introduced to the characters. It tells the story and sets the emotional tone. The verse contains the plot, the details, and the action.

♪ Each verse of a song has the same melody and new lyrics.

The first line of the first verse should have the same number of syllables as the first line of the second and (if applicable) third verses. The same applies to all lines of the verses. Although there is a little room for variation, a drastic difference in the length of corresponding lines in various verses will make it impossible to sing the same melody for each verse.

Most often, lyrically, each verse is eight lines long, expressed in either eight or sixteen musical bars. (Readers who require additional understanding of musical bars or measures would likely benefit from a study of basic music theory.) There have also been successful songs with verses that had four, six, or twelve lines. It is extremely rare for a popular song to contain an odd number of lines in its verses.

It is also acceptable to have a first verse that is twice the length of the verses that follow (i.e., the first verse might be sixteen lines—a "double" first verse—while later verses are eight lines). However, having all verses consist of sixteen bars is not recommended. It can become boring because verses are not designed melodically or lyrically like the chorus to be the catchiest portion of the song.

In songs that include choruses, the song title usually does not appear in any of the verses. However, there are exceptions. For example, in traditional country songs, each verse may end with the title, which is then repeated at the beginning of the chorus.

The Pre-Chorus

Within a verse there may also be a "pre-chorus"—a two or four-line section, rarely exceeding four bars musically, immediately preceding the chorus. It is crafted to propel the listener, both melodically and lyrically, into the chorus. The pre-chorus is optional. However, if the first verse includes a pre-chorus, all subsequent verses typically also include a pre-chorus section. The pre-chorus is sometimes referred to as the lift, channel, climb, or B-section. (In some countries outside the U.S. this section is called the bridge.)

♪ All pre-choruses in a song have the same melody.

♪ It is acceptable for each verse's pre-chorus to repeat the same lyric or introduce a new lyric.

The Chorus

Melodically, the chorus is the catchy, repetitious part of a song that you sing along with. Lyrically, the chorus' job is to summarize the idea of the song in a general way and to hammer home its title. Ideally, the chorus lyric is constructed so that it sounds natural to have it repeated following each verse and the bridge, if the song includes a bridge. The chorus should be easy to remember and is not the place to introduce new, detailed information, which belongs in the verses.

Lyrically, the chorus is typically four or eight lines long, which most often translates to eight musical bars. However, like everything else in songwriting, this is not a precise science and there have been many hit songs with a twelve- or sixteen-bar chorus.

♪ The chorus has the same melody and almost always has the same lyrics each time it is repeated.

♪ The title always appears at least once in the chorus.

There are no rules as to where the title of a song should appear within the chorus. For example, the song title can appear in the first line of the chorus and nowhere else within the chorus:

She's Not The Cheatin' Kind
She's been cheated one too many times
She's never fooled around
He's still lyin'—She's through cryin'
She's not foolin' now
(Written by Ronnie Dunn, Recorded by Brooks & Dunn)

The song title can also appear in both the first and second lines of the chorus:

What if God was **One Of Us**
Just a slob like **One Of Us**
Just a stranger on a bus
Trying to find his way home
(Written by Eric Bazilian, Recorded by Joan Osborne)

The song title can also appear as the first and last lines of the chorus. This technique, sometimes referred to as "book-ending," can be very effective, but the lyric must be crafted to logically lead the listener back to the title:

I Can Love You Like That
I would make you my world
Move heaven and earth
If you were my girl
I would give you my heart
Be all that you need
Show you you're everything that's precious to me
If you give me a chance
I Can Love You Like That
(Written by Steve Diamond/Jennifer Kimball/Maribeth Derry,
Recorded by All-4-One and John Michael Montgomery)

In some instances, the song title begins the chorus, is repeated one or more times within the chorus, and ends the chorus. This technique can add a powerful emotional punch if the last line of the chorus brings the listener back to the title from a new angle or perspective:

> ***Change My Mind***
> *Say you couldn't live without me*
> *Say you're crazy about me*
> *With a look—With a touch*
> ***Change My Mind***
> *I'm looking in your eyes*
> *For the love we left behind*
> *It's not too late to **Change My Mind***
> **(Written by Jason Blume/A.J. Masters, Recorded by artists including**
> **John Berry and the Oak Ridge Boys)**

The song title might even be the only lyric in the chorus, except for the last line. When using this form, the last line should tie the chorus together and provide an emotional "payoff":

> ***Hit Me With Your Best Shot***
> *(Come on and)* ***Hit Me With Your Best Shot***
> ***Hit Me With Your Best Shot***
> *Fire Away*
> **(Written by Eddie Schwartz, Recorded by Pat Benatar)**

Another option is for the song title to be saved until the last line of the chorus. To be effective, the lines of melody and lyric that precede the last line of the chorus need to be exceptionally catchy in order to sustain the listeners' attention all the way through the verse and chorus before giving them the title:

> *We've still got it good*
> *No matter how bad it gets*
> *Even after all this time*
> *The slipper still fits*
> *Hey, just look at how far we've come*
> *By choosin' to stay*
> *Baby don't go there*
> *Love don't get no where **Walkin' Away***
> **(Annie Roboff/Craig Wiseman, Recorded by Diamond Rio)**

A last option is for the chorus to simply repeat the title lyric and contain no words other than the title. While this is a very unusual structure, Dolly Parton's

"I Will Always Love You" has been a huge hit four times employing this form (twice for Dolly Parton as a solo artist, with duet partner Vince Gill, and on Whitney Houston's mega-selling soundtrack album *The Bodyguard*).

The Bridge

The bridge serves as a departure, or a release, from the rest of the song. It usually consists of two or four lines of lyric, and four or eight musical bars. The bridge's job is to add a new dimension to the song, take it to the next level, and lead the listener back to the chorus, title, and hook from a new angle. If that's not enough of a challenge, the bridge needs to accomplish all of this while still managing to sound consistent with the rest of the song.

When using a structure that includes verses and choruses, the bridge can occur in only one place—between the second and third choruses (Verse - Chorus - Verse - Chorus - *Bridge* - Chorus). When utilizing the A-A-B-A song form discussed later in this chapter, the bridge will be between the second and third verses (Verse - Verse - *Bridge* - Verse). The bridge is a release or departure, both lyrically and melodically, from the sections that surround it. Note that outside the U.S. the bridge is sometimes referred to as "the middle eight."

Lyrically, the bridge presents an opportunity to add a new dimension, a new perspective to your story. It is your last chance to lead the listeners back to your title and make it pay off one final time. The tools that can help differentiate your bridge lyrically from the rest of the song are:

♪ Revealing an added element to the story that ties it all together.

♪ Changing the "person" (i.e., from "I" to "she" or "he").

♪ Switching from specific, detailed imagery to general or philosophical statements (or vice versa).

♪ Alternating the time frame (i.e., looking back on the past, if the rest of the song is in present tense; or vice versa).

♪ Disclosing a surprise (if applicable).

Musically, effective bridges may add an element of contrast by:

♪ Introducing one or more chords that have not previously been used in the song.

♪ Changing the rhythm.

♪ Using notes that are either higher or lower than those used in the other sections.

Additional guidelines for crafting effective bridges:

♪ Do not include the title.

♪ Limit yourself to two or four lines of lyric (four or eight bars musically).

♪ Occasionally bridges can be instrumental.

The bridge is the last new section of your song to be introduced. It's your final chance to make the listener love your song—make it powerful.

BUILDING A SUCCESSFUL SONG

In order to create the kind of songs listeners expect to hear on the radio, you will need to join verses, pre-choruses, choruses, and bridges in specific ways. Now that you know all of the pieces of a successful song it's time to learn how to put them all together.

Verse - Chorus - Verse - Chorus

This structure begins with a first verse that tells the story, introduces the characters, and lets the listener know how the singer feels about the situation. The first verse leads the listener, both lyrically and melodically, into the first chorus. It typically does not include the title, but is crafted to guide the listener to the song's title.

In this structure the first chorus follows the first verse. The chorus includes the song title at least once and summarizes the idea of the song in a general way.

The second verse follows the first chorus. Lyrically, it continues the story, provides the listener with additional information, and leads back to the chorus. Melodically, it is identical (or almost identical) to the first verse.

The second chorus follows the second verse and is almost always identical to the first chorus.

This structure is often referred to as: A - B - A - B (A = Verse, B = Chorus). An example of this structure is:

"Carried Away"

Verse 1:
I don't take my whiskey to extremes
Don't believe in chasin' crazy dreams
My feet are planted firmly on the ground
But darlin', when you come around

Chorus:
I get Carried Away
By the look, by the light in your eyes
Before I even realize the ride I'm on
Baby I'm long gone
Carried Away
Nothin' matters but bein' with you
Like a feather flyin' high up in the sky on a windy day
I get Carried Away

Verse 2:
It might seem like an ordinary night
Same ol' stars the same ol' moon up high
But when I see you standin' at your door
Nothin's ordinary any more
(Repeat Chorus)
(Steve Bogard and Jeff Stevens, Recorded by George Strait)

Other examples of this structure that you may want to check out on your own include "You Oughta Know" (Alanis Morissette), "You're Still The One" (Shania Twain), and "Change The World" (Eric Clapton).

Verse - Chorus - Verse - Chorus - Bridge - Chorus

This structure is probably the most common song form in current use. It has a first verse, first chorus, second verse, and second chorus that follow the guidelines described in the previous example. A two- or four-line bridge which will be a musical and lyrical departure (as described previously in this section) follows the second chorus. After the bridge there is a third chorus, which is almost always identical, melodically and lyrically, to the previous choruses. If there is going to be a modulation (key change) it will typically occur following the bridge.

This structure is often designated as: A - B - A - B - C - B (A = Verse, B = Chorus, C = Bridge). An example of the A - B - A - B - C - B structure is:

"Because You Loved Me"

Verse 1:
For all those times you stood by me
For all the truth that you made me see
For all the joy you brought to my life

For all the wrong that you made right
For every dream you made come true
For all the love I found in you
I'll be forever thankful Baby
You're the one who held me up
Never let me fall
You're the one who saw me through—through it all

Chorus:
You were my strength when I was weak
You were my voice when I couldn't speak
You were my eyes when I couldn't see
You saw the best there was in me
Lifted me up when I couldn't reach
You gave me faith 'cause you believed
I'm everything I am
Because You Loved Me

Verse 2:
You gave me wings and made me fly
You touched my hand I could touch the sky
I lost my faith, you gave it back to me
You said no star was out of reach
You stood by me and I stood tall
I had your love I had it all
I'm grateful for each day you gave me
Maybe I don't know that much
But I know this much is true
I was blessed because I was loved by you

Chorus:
You were my strength when I was weak
You were my voice when I couldn't speak
You were my eyes when I couldn't see
You saw the best there was in me
Lifted me up when I couldn't reach
You gave me faith 'cause you believed
I'm everything I am

Because You Loved Me

Bridge:
You were always there for me
The tender wind that carried me
A light in the dark shining your love into my life
You've been my inspiration
Through the lies you were the truth
My world is a better place because of you
(Repeat Chorus)

(Diane Warren, Recorded by Celine Dion)

Other examples of this structure include "Don't Speak" (No Doubt) "Strawberry Wine" (Deana Carter), and "Sometimes When We Touch" (Dan Hill).

Verse - Chorus - Verse - Chorus - Verse - Chorus

In this structure there are three verses, each followed by a chorus. Each verse may or may not include a pre-chorus. Lyrically, every verse contains new information and develops the story further, but will have the same melody. All of the choruses will typically be identical to each other.

Only a small percentage of successful songs employ this structure. This is most likely because the verse is not intended to be the most memorable part of the song and unless it is exceptionally well crafted you run the risk of boring the listener. However, this structure does work especially well in "vignette" songs, songs in which the verses consist of little scenes, or self-contained stories. Songs that contain three separate vignettes that each relate back to the same chorus can be exceptionally powerful, as illustrated by the lyric to the following Grammy-nominated song:

"How Can I Help You Say Goodbye"

Verse 1:
Through the back window of our fifty-nine wagon
I watched my best friend Jamie slippin' further away
I kept on wavin' till I couldn't see her
And through my tears I asked again why we couldn't stay

(Pre-Chorus)
Mama whispered softly
Time will ease your pain

Life's about changing
Nothing ever stays the same
And she said

Chorus:
How Can I Help You Say Goodbye
It's okay to hurt and it's okay to cry
Come let me hold you and I will try
How Can I Help You Say Goodbye

Verse 2:
I sat on our bed—He packed his suitcase
I held a picture of our wedding day
His hands were trembling—We both were crying
He kissed me gently and then he quickly walked away

(Pre-Chorus)
I called up Mama
She said time will ease your pain
Life's about changing
Nothing ever stays the same
And she said
(Repeat Chorus)

Verse 3:
Sittin' with Mama
Alone in her bedroom
She opened her eyes
And then squeezed my hand
She said I have to go now
My time here is over
And with her final words she tried to help me understand

(Pre-Chorus)
Mama whispered softly time will ease your pain
Life's about changing
Nothing ever stays the same
And she said

(Repeat Chorus)

(Karen Taylor-Good and Burton Collins, Recorded by artists including Patty Loveless, Al Jarreau, and Melanie)

Although every verse in this example tells a different, complete story, note that they are each related to and clearly lead back to the same chorus. At the end of each verse it makes sense for the singer to say "How Can I Help You Say Goodbye" and repeat the chorus lyric.

Other examples of songs that successfully employed the Verse - Chorus - Verse - Chorus - Verse - Chorus structure include "Candle In The Wind" (Elton John), "Holes In The Floor Of Heaven" (Steve Wariner), and "You've Got A Friend" (Carole King).

Verse - Verse - Bridge - Verse

Note that this structure does not contain a chorus. When using a Verse - Verse - Bridge - Verse structure, the title will almost always appear in one of two places: the *first* line of each verse or the *last* line of each verse. While it is acceptable to have your title in either of these places, once that decision has been made, the title will appear in the same location of each verse (i.e., the title will either be in the first *or* last line of every verse). In practice, it is much more commonly found in the last line.

This song form begins with the first verse (which has the song title as its first or last line). The second verse follows. Lyrically, the second verse will develop the story further and introduce new information, and like the first verse it begins or ends with the song title. A two- or four-line bridge (a melodic and lyrical departure or release) follows the second verse. A third verse follows the bridge. Lyrically the third verse ties the story together, provides additional information, and, in some instances, provides resolution. It has the same melody as the previous verses and the title will once again be the first or last line of the verse. This song form is referred to as A - A - B - A (A = Verse, B = Bridge).

"Saving All My Love For You"

Verse 1:
A few stolen moments is all that we share
You've got your family and they need you there
Though I try to resist
Being last on your list
But no other man's gonna do

So I'm Saving All My Love For You

Verse 2:
It's not very easy living all alone
My friends try and tell me find a man of my own
But each time I try
I just break down and cry
'Cause I'd rather be home feelin' blue
So I'm Saving All My Love For You

Bridge:
You used to tell me we'd run away together
Love gives you the right to be free
You said "Be patient, just wait a little longer"
But that's just an old fantasy

Verse 3:
I've got to get ready, just a few minutes more
Gonna get that old feeling when you walk through the door
'Cause tonight is the night
For feeling all right
We'll be making love the whole night through
So I'm Saving All My Love
Yes, I'm Saving All My Love
Yes, I'm Saving All My Love For You
(Michael Masser and Gerry Goffin, Recorded by Whitney Houston)

Additional examples of the Verse - Verse - Bridge - Verse song form include "The Way We Were" (Barbra Streisand), "To Make You Feel My Love" (Garth Brooks/Bob Dylan), and "The Song Remembers When" (Trisha Yearwood).

Variations

A common variation of the A - A - B - A song form adds a second bridge and an additional verse. The resulting song form is Verse - Verse - Bridge - Verse - Bridge - Verse. When this structure is used, the second bridge follows the third verse. This additional bridge may or may not contain the same lyric as the first bridge. After the second bridge there is a fourth verse, which most often has a new lyric. As in the basic A - A - B - A song form, the fourth verse has the title as its first or last line. The resulting form can be expressed as A - A - B - A - B - A (A = Verse, B = Bridge).

A very small percentage of hit songs begin with the chorus. Brandy and Monica took that structure to the top of the charts with their duet, "The Boy Is Mine." If you choose to start with the chorus you can use either of the following structures:

Chorus - Verse - Chorus - Verse - Chorus
or
Chorus - Verse - Chorus - Verse - Bridge - Chorus

Starting with the chorus in a song that contains three verses will probably make the song too long for the radio (and for most listeners). If you decide to begin with a chorus, the chorus needs to stand up lyrically without the benefit of having been "set up" by any prior lyric. Sometimes writers start with the chorus to grab the listener immediately, but if your motivation is fear that your verse won't be interesting enough to sustain the listener to the chorus—rewrite the verse.

INTRODUCTIONS AND INSTRUMENTAL SOLOS

Musical introductions and instrumental solos are more a function of the arrangement than the basic song form. However, there are some guidelines to follow. On a demo, no one wants to listen to a long musical introduction. Four or eight bars are sufficient, with eight being the maximum.

I like to tell new songwriters that they need to listen, feel, and then analyze the songs that they love. See how they are put together. What kind of sections does the song have?

Rick Chudacoff (Songwriter/producer, Michael Bolton, Smokey Robinson, Judy Collins)

When a professional is evaluating a song, he or she listens primarily for the melody and the lyrics. Unless the instrumental section includes exciting new chords and melody that are essential to the song itself, it probably should not be included on the demo. There are instances when the instrumental is indeed an integral part of a song's success. The ending of Eric Clapton's classic "Layla" comes to mind. An instrumental solo can also be important for a song that is primarily geared toward the dance market.

If you do choose to include an instrumental solo section there are several options for its location. In a Verse - Chorus - Verse - Chorus structure the instrumental section is typically after the second chorus and is followed by an additional chorus. For Verse - Chorus - Verse - Chorus - Bridge - Chorus songs, the instrumental section can go either after the second chorus or after the bridge. In a Verse - Verse - Bridge - Verse song the solo section generally follows the third verse and is then followed by an additional bridge and a fourth verse.

Ask yourself if the instrumental solo is critical to the impact of the song. If the answer is "no," then instead of investing time and money producing a solo, at that point in the song you might have the singer say, "You can turn off the tape now"—because the executive who is reviewing your song most likely has a huge stack of tapes to screen and probably will stop listening to yours at that point.

You can learn how to write songs . . . it is a craft. If you have the desire, drive, and a little talent you can learn how to craft a song.

Roger Sovine (Vice President, Public Relations, BMI; writer)

Exercise:
Identifying Song Structures

Learning the craft of songwriting will not compromise or diminish your creativity. It will allow you to express your ideas in a way that can touch millions of people. Now that you are able to identify the components and structures of successful songs, write out the lyrics to three of your favorite songs and answer the following questions for each:

♪ What structure did the writer employ?

♪ Identify each of the sections of the song.

♪ Where does the title appear?

SONG STRUCTURE CHECKLIST

Photocopy this checklist and keep it where you normally write. Each time you finish a draft of a song, check to be sure that it has successfully incorporated the tools and techniques that follow:

Song adheres to one of the most successful structures, or one of the variations, discussed in this chapter (check the one that applies)

☐ Verse - Chorus - Verse - Chorus

☐ Verse - Chorus - Verse - Chorus - Bridge - Chorus

☐ Verse - Chorus - Verse - Chorus - Verse - Chorus

☐ Verse - Verse - Bridge - Verse

☐ Each verse has the same melody and new lyrics

☐ Corresponding lines in every verse contain the same number of syllables

☐ Each verse contains eight lines of lyric (eight or sixteen musical bars)

☐ If the first verse includes a pre-chorus, all subsequent verses also include a pre-chorus section

☐ The chorus contains four or eight lines of lyric (eight or sixteen musical bars)

☐ Each chorus has the same melody and the same lyrics

☐ The title appears at least once in the chorus

☐ If there is a bridge it contains two or four lines of lyric (four or eight musical bars)

☐ If there is a bridge, in a Verse - Chorus structure, the bridge is between the second and third choruses; in an A - A - B - A structure, the bridge is between the second and third verses

☐ The bridge (if applicable) does not include the song title

☐ The instrumental solo (if applicable) is no more than eight bars long

Step II

Writing Effective Lyrics

The first time I ever heard one of her records—I mean sat down and actually listened to it—I could not believe it. It was like somebody actually knew how I felt, like she could see inside my heart and say all the things I didn't know how to say.

(Tess, a fan speaking about Dolly Parton)

Chapter 2
Developing Great Song Ideas and Catchy Titles

The most successful thing I've done is to be original in a little way about love. I try to poke my head through a small window or find an angle that's not been beaten to death. I love good titles and original ideas. Lyrically I want to explain my idea in a simple fashion so people who are only half-listening can half-understand, and that works for me.

Harlan Howard (Legendary Nashville songwriter of "I Fall To Pieces," "Heartaches By The Number," "I've Got A Tiger By The Tail," and more than 100 top ten hits)

Simply put, lyrics are the words that tell the story, convey the emotion, and communicate the information from the writer to the listener. The lyricist's job is to provide listeners with the words they want to hear or the words they'd say if they could.

UNDERSTANDING WHAT CONSTITUTES A GREAT IDEA—AND HOW TO FIND ONE

The first step toward writing an effective lyric is starting with a great idea. The vast majority of songs on the radio are about some aspect of love, probably because it is a topic that everyone can relate to. The desire to love and be loved is a basic human need.

The joy of finding love, the pain of losing love, looking for the right love, complaining about the wrong love, missing a past love, hoping for a future love, fear of losing love, fear of finding love, cheating on a lover, being cheated on by a lover, wanting to be loved, wanting to be loved differently, and wanting to be loved by someone other than the one who loves you are all prevalent themes in popular songs. It's no wonder that "love" is the most commonly used word in songs—even more than "baby."

Whether the subject of a song deals with relationships, having a good time, getting ahead in life, a social issue, a politically oriented message, or a religious idea, to be commercially viable the idea must have universal appeal. The most successful songs strike a chord with millions of people.

I think what producers and artists are looking for is something unique. My stepsister Matraca Berg ("Strawberry Wine") is a very successful writer and she once told me that when she sits down to write she tries to come up with something lyrically or melodically that she's never heard before. I think that being original and unique will go a long way towards getting a song noticed.

Wade Kirby (Songwriter with cuts by artists including John Michael Montgomery and Sammy Kershaw)

I once critiqued a song written by two brothers who had been reunited as adults almost thirty years after being separated as children. The song recounted in first person their very unusual story. While the song was well crafted, the writers failed to take into account the fact that the topic itself was too personal for millions of listeners to want to sing along with.

I think there are many qualities that allow a song to transcend its own time. Whether it's a love song, lullaby, or a song of protest, they all have a certain elegance to them and simplicity and authenticity. They can't sound as if they were only appealing to a narrow group of people.

Mary Travers (Peter, Paul & Mary) as quoted in *Performing Songwriter* magazine.

It can be satisfying and cathartic to write deeply personal songs. Many writers also enjoy writing songs that may be too poetic, quirky, flowery, or vague to be considered commercial. If you enjoy writing in those styles, don't stop. But

don't confuse the songs that you write for your own personal satisfaction with "radio-friendly" songs with subjects and styles that have broad appeal.

Many developing songwriters write songs about wanting to write songs, becoming a famous recording artist, or leaving their small town and moving to a place where they can pursue those goals. While these ideas are very important to the songwriter, the vast majority of people who listen to the radio and buy records do not share those specific dreams. Nor do they express themselves by writing songs. While there are rare exceptions, songs that deal with those topics rarely have universal appeal. However, practically all people have fantasies and goals that they wish they could pursue. A song about following your heart, believing in yourself, and chasing your dreams can indeed speak to millions of listeners, while still capturing the essence of what the aspiring songwriter truly feels.

Once you've decided on your subject and determined that it's a topic with potential for wide appeal, one of the most important challenges is finding fresh ways to approach the subject. It's likely that your idea has been written about thousands of times. Finding a new twist or a different angle and expressing it with an intriguing, interesting title is crucial to set your song apart. There have been countless songs that express the familiar sentiment, "I wish you would come back and love me again." But only Diane Warren said it in a way that took Toni Braxton to the top of the charts with "Unbreak My Heart."

There are hit song titles all around us waiting to be written. According to hit songwriter George Teren ("Busy Man," "She's Sure Taking It Well," "Runnin' Out Of Reasons To Run"), "Ideas are gifts. Sometimes they are phrases pulled out of a conversation, a movie, TV show, or book. Sometimes everything I hear or read sounds like a title."

Potential song titles can be found in everyday conversations, in movies (especially romantic films), on television, and on road maps. The title for Paul Simon's "Mother And Child Reunion" came from a Chinese restaurant menu. Song titles have been known to "hide" in advertisements, newspapers, telephone books, greeting cards, T-shirts, and cartoons. Several times, when preparing for an important co-writing session, I've been less than enthusiastic about any of the titles I'd stockpiled and instead found inspiration at local bookstores. Browse the aisles. There's a good chance you'll find a hit song idea. Books of quotations, slang, and even titles of novels can be a great source of song titles. I have rarely attended a concert, movie, or play or read a good book without coming up with a song idea or title.

Go to nightclubs, attend concerts, watch videos on television, and, most importantly, listen to the radio. Other writers' songs may spark your own song titles and ideas. Ask yourself how you might have approached their idea. Many writers report having heard a great line in a song, only to realize that the line they "heard" wasn't actually what had been sung. In many instances, the line that they misheard sparked a new idea.

I'm a totally different writer than I was fifteen years ago when I would be inspired by the most lame ideas. When you start off you're just connecting words, but now the song has to have an honesty to it. There are three subjects to write about: life, love, and death. The secret is writing the same old stuff and staying inspired by the simple things. That's probably the secret to life itself—finding the happiness in everyday miracles.

Craig Wiseman (One of *Billboard*'s Top 25 Songwriters of the Year, 1994 – 1997; NSAI and *Music Row* magazine's 1997 Songwriter of the Year, with over 100 cuts and 30 charted singles)

Like all of the other skills that songwriting requires, learning to discern what constitutes a strong title and a great idea takes practice. Through a process of trial and error, the responses you get from your friends, family, and music industry professionals, as well as your own emotional reaction to your songs, you will begin to shape your instinct for what makes for an effective title and a powerful idea for a song.

I was at a wedding when one of my strongest titles hit me. It was the groom's third marriage and the fourth time the bride was saying, "Till death do us part," and "As long as we both shall live." It suddenly hit me that it's not "As long as we both shall live"—but "As Long As We Both Shall *Love*." When I pulled out the pen and paper that I always have handy, I knew that I had just begun a very special song.

I went to my publisher, Michael Hollandsworth, at Zomba Music Publishing (where I'm signed as a staff-writer) and asked his advice on how to proceed to get the maximum benefit from such a powerful title. We discussed the different potential angles. We both agreed that there would be little interest in a song whose premise was essentially: "We'll stay together as long as we both shall love—and if we stop loving each other, we'll break up." The stronger, more emotional approach to that title would be: *"Forever—is as long as we both shall love."*

According to Jeff Carlton (V.P./G.M. Hamstein Music Publishing), "The craft of writing is important, but after you've learned that, then it eventually comes down to who has the best ideas . . . and a writer today should be asking: how do I put myself in the position to get the great ideas? Writers have to learn to work at finding things to write about—that's a learned condition, finding ideas for hits. There are song gifts, no question, but you've got to be looking for them." When you start with a great title and a fresh approach to an idea that has wide appeal, you're already well on your way to a successful song. A boring, overused idea makes your job much more difficult if your goal is to create something unique. A strong, memorable, distinctive title almost writes itself.

Ask yourself, if you had a pile of tapes to review, based on the titles alone, which songs would you listen to first?

♪ "Butterfly Kisses"

♪ "Sunny Came Home"

♪ "Friends In Low Places"

or

♪ "I Love You Very Much"

♪ "Tell Me You Care"

♪ "I Miss You"

I would choose the songs in the first set. With nothing else to base my opinion on but a title, I'd expect the songs with the more creative, intriguing titles to be more engaging than the ones with titles that show little imagination or uniqueness.

One-word titles can often be very effective. They are easy for the listener to remember and often have great emotional impact. "Criminal," "Fame," "Help!" "Everywhere," "Desperado," "Thriller," "Home," "Mouth," "Nobody," "Falling," and "Please" have all been top ten hits. Occasionally, a series of nonsense syllables or a new word that the writer creates, like "Mmm-Bop," or "No Diggity," can provide a hit title as well. These titles probably resonate with listeners because they're original, catchy, and pleasing to the ear. But most importantly, they're fun to sing.

The most powerful song ideas and titles begin with emotions that come from the heart. If you're trying to fake the emotion, there is probably someone else writing a similar idea who genuinely feels it—and that's tough to beat.

The strongest titles:

✔ **Grab your attention**
("Like A Virgin," "Stop In The Name Of Love").

✔ **Evoke powerful emotions**
("Tears In Heaven," "How Am I Supposed To Live Without You").

✔ **Are unusual**
("Strawberry Wine," "Wind Beneath My Wings").

✔ **Are intriguing**
("In The House Of Stone And Light," "Kiss From A Rose").

✔ **Are clever**
("Cleopatra, Queen of Denial," "This Romeo Ain't Got Julie Yet").

KEEPING A HOOK BOOK

The "hook" is any part of a song that "grabs" the listener. It might be an instrumental riff that listeners can't get out of their minds, a memorable melodic phrase, or a catchy line of lyric, which "hooks in" the listener. The title of a song and its corresponding melody will always be a hook. A song can (and usually will) have more than one hook.

When you get that great title or idea, you'd better have a pen in your pocket, or a mini-tape recorder handy. Be sure to write it down or record it. Even those ideas that you are sure you won't forget can easily get lost along the way—and that title or melody might have been the one that would have won a Grammy!

Transfer your lyric ideas to a "hook book"—a list of titles and ideas. I keep my hook book, along with tiny scraps of paper, bank receipts, napkins, and matchbook covers filled with titles and ideas, in a file folder marked "future hits."

Under each title, jot down images, premises, or actual lines of lyric. They may or may not make it to your final draft, but they'll help you recapture the initial spark you were feeling when you first got the idea. Bring your hook book to your co-writing sessions and periodically review the titles. You never know when one of them will jump out and demand to be written.

MAKING THE SINGER LOOK GOOD

When evaluating the merits of your song's topic and story, an important question to ask is "Does it make the singer look good?" No one wants to appear in a bad light. With very few exceptions, women don't want to be represented as home-wreckers, immoral, weak, or as victims. The days of Tammy Wynette singing "Stand By Your Man" have been replaced by Tina Turner's "You Better Be Good To Me" and Lorrie Morgan's "I Didn't Know My Own Strength" and "(If you think I won't go) Watch Me." A common theme in popular songs is some variation of "I was a fool to hurt you, and now that I know what a great thing I lost I'm miserable and sorry." In that type of song the singer has learned his or her lesson and is no longer the fool he or she once was. But it's highly unlikely that any singer, male or female, will want to sing a lyric that presents him or her as hopeless, an unrepentant drunk, a cheater, or an idiot. It's proba-bly no coincidence that when Reba McEntire sang "Does He Love You," a duet with the "other woman," it was her duet partner, newcomer Linda Davis, who sang the role of the woman who was having an affair with a married man.

Honesty makes a great lyric. The willingness to be real and tell the truth.

Karen Taylor-Good (Grammy-nominated songwriter, "How Can I Help You Say Goodbye," "Not That Different")

In 1991, while in Las Vegas celebrating the release of my first major-label cut, the Oak Ridge Boys' version of "Change My Mind," I met a friendly couple from the Midwest. When they asked what I did for a living, I was proud to boast that I had written a song that the Oak Ridge Boys recently recorded. They didn't believe me at first because they assumed that the Oaks wrote all of their own material. Actually, the Oak Ridge Boys are among the many recording artists who are rarely involved in writing their own songs.

✔   Write what's real for you.
✔   Write what you feel.
✔   Write what you love.

But before you begin to write a song ask yourself:

✔   Would an artist want to say this?
✔   Would millions of listeners want to hear this?

This conversation helped me to understand that many fans don't realize that the songs artists sing are analogous to the words on a script that actors recite. The lyrics that come from artists' mouths are often perceived as "real" for those artists. This explains why so many people were offended when fourteen-year-old LeAnn Rimes sang about mature themes that she was far too young to have experienced. In reality, if Reba McEntire has had half as many broken hearts as she sings about, she'd probably be in a padded room on an intravenous drip of Prozac.

For a performance (either live or recorded) to be effective, the audience needs to *believe* the singer. Listeners want to be convinced that the artist is experiencing the emotion he or she is singing about. Therefore, the lyricist's job is to give the singer words that are consistent with the image that artist has chosen to present. While some recording artists (particularly in rap and hard rock) cultivate a "bad-boy" or "bad-girl" image that might glorify violence or sex without emotional involvement, most of the artists who record "outside" songs do not fit into this category.

USING THE THREE-STEP LYRIC WRITING TECHNIQUE

The Three-Step lyric writing technique was designed to help you focus your idea and craft lyrics that lead your listeners to your title. Both Sting and legendary songwriter Jimmy Webb have been quoted as saying that they always start with a title. I've written hundreds of songs. My co-writers have included Grammy-winners and some of the most successful and talented writers in the music business, and we always begin the lyric writing process by deciding on a title.

Before a word or a note is written, we'll generally exchange titles, ideas, and "starts" (ideas, lines, or phrases that may or may not eventually develop into a full song) until we settle on the title that excites both of us. Sometimes it can take an hour or more to discuss the merits and possible directions to proceed with each title.

I've noticed that all the hit songs that I've written have always started out with a strong concept first—or a title, like "You Give Love A Bad Name"(Child's hit for Bon Jovi).

Desmond Child (Songwriter whose credits include hits with Aerosmith, Ricky Martin, Alice Cooper, Cher, Michael Bolton, and Bon Jovi) as quoted in the *Recording Industry Career Handbook*.

The main function of the verse lyric is to lead and deliver the listener to your chorus—and specifically, the song title. Trying to lead the listener to your title if you don't know your title is like shooting arrows in the dark. You'll have a much better chance of hitting your target if you know exactly what you're aiming for.

When I write with a collaborator, we don't literally say, "Let's work on step one . . . (or two, or three)," but I've noticed that the underlying principles of the Three-Step approach to lyric writing are used by the vast majority of successful songwriters—whether they're aware of it or not.

Step 1: Start with a Title

Once you've selected your title, be certain you're very clear what your title means to you. It can help to pretend that you're explaining what your song is about to someone else by talking into a tape recorder. The bottom line is that you want to have no doubt what your song is about—what the real meaning is—*before you start writing the actual lines.* If you're working with a collaborator, this is the time to discuss the options and be sure you're in agreement about what constitutes the essence of your song. There is not necessarily one "correct" way to approach your title, but you need to determine the strongest, most accessible meaning of your title.

Distill the meaning of your title down to a phrase or two and write it on the top of your page. For example:

The multi-format smash "How Do I Live" can be summarized as:
   If you leave, how will I get along without you?

For "The Wind Beneath My Wings" you might jot down:
   You give me strength; I'm who I am because of you

For "I Can Love You Like That" you might write:
   I can give you the kind of love described in classic stories and movies

Are there exceptions—songs that are not written to specifically lead the listeners to the title? Yes. If you watch MTV, you'll see that many successful "alternative" artists (including those who cross over to the pop charts) sometimes seem to go out of their way to avoid making their title obvious. For example, I loved the Wallflowers' "Me And Cinderella" for months before I found out that the actual title of the song is "In The Middle." I had a similar experience with Savage Garden's smash hit, "Truly Madly Deeply," but that type of song is almost always written by artists who write their own material.

Step 2: Outline the Story

Decide on the ideas and general information that need to be conveyed in the first verse of your song to clearly lead to the title. This is the verse lyric's primary function. There may be many options, however, as long as the lyric that precedes the chorus supports the title. This is the point in the creative process when you decide what the "story" is—*before writing the actual lines.*

When you have determined what ideas and information to include in the first verse, decide what additional information will be included in the second verse to develop the story further and lead the listeners to the second chorus.

If there will be a bridge, this may be the time to decide what angle it will have and what additional information will be conveyed. You may not know yet whether you want to include a bridge. If you decide to add a bridge after you've crafted your verses and chorus, you can still follow this step by outlining the idea that you want the bridge to express—*prior to writing the actual lines.*

While the function of the verse lyric is to tell the story and lead to the chorus, the chorus' job, lyrically, is to provide a setting to showcase your title. The chorus is *not* the place to introduce new information into the story. It's a summation of your idea, the place to reiterate your title and hammer it home.

Step 3: Write the Actual Lines of Lyric

Now that you know, in a general sense, what information your lyric needs to convey, it's time to begin the process of crafting the strongest lines to express your idea. The tools and techniques described throughout the remainder of this section will help you get your idea across in a conversational, fresh, interesting way, utilizing detail and imagery.

Three-Step lyric writing example for "I Swear":

Step 1:   The title means: "I promise that I will always love you."

Step 2:   Verse 1 expresses the idea, "I see that you're worried. Let me reassure you."

Verse 2 says, "I'll do everything I can to make you happy and I will always feel this way."

The chorus is a summation of the idea; a place to reiterate the meaning of the title: "I promise I will always love you."

Step 3:   The actual lines of lyric are crafted to best tell the story.

"I Swear"

I see the questions in your eyes
I know what's weighing on your mind
You can be sure I know my part
Cause I'll stay beside you through the years
You'll only cry those happy tears
And though I'll make mistakes
I'll never break your heart (and)

> I see that you're worried
>
> Let me reassure you

I Swear
By the moon and the stars in the skies
I'll be there
And I Swear
Like the shadow that's by your side
I'll be there
For better or worse
Till death do us part
I'll love you with every beat of my heart
I Swear

> I promise I will always love you

I'll give you everything I can
I'll build your dreams with these two hands
We'll hang some memories on the walls
And when just the two of us are here
You won't have to ask if I still care
Cause as time turns the page
My love won't age at all (and)

> I'll do everything to make you happy and I will always feel this way

(Repeat Chorus)

(Gary Baker/Frank J. Myers)

Exercise:

Practicing the Three-Step Lyric Writing Technique

Step 1:

In a notebook, write down a title for which you have not yet written a lyric. Using one or two sentences, explain what that title means to you.

Step 2:

In a sentence or two, jot down the information that needs to be conveyed in your first verse to clearly lead the listeners to your title. Don't worry about rhymes, details, or the number of syllables. This is the time in the writing process to focus on creating your story and deciding what general information will best set up your title.

Continue to ask yourself, "Then what happened?" or "What else happened?" and write down the ideas that will be included in your second verse to once again lead the listener back to your title. (This is not the time to include rhymes or details, or to be concerned about the specific words or numbers of syllables. Just focus the meaning of your lyric so that it relates directly to your title.)

Step 3:

Now that you know what information needs to be imparted, use the tools and techniques described in the following chapters to fill in the details and write the actual lines of the lyric.

Chapter 3
Acquiring the Tools for Successful Lyric Writing

I think it was the simplicity and the universal appeal of the lyric that made "I Swear" so successful. The lyric was so simple that everybody could understand it. The message was very clear.

Gary Baker (Songwriter, "I Swear," "Once Upon A Lifetime," "T.L.C.A.S.A.P.," and cuts by artists including the Backstreet Boys, Reba McEntire, Joe, and LeAnn Rimes)

The tools of successful lyric writing are skills that can be acquired—with practice, patience, and lots of hard work. These techniques are not a substitute for a powerful idea that excites you and cries out to be written. They are methods to help you express your ideas in ways that evoke the feelings you want from your listeners.

LEARNING TO FOCUS THE LYRIC

A lyric needs to express one idea. Effective lyrics are crafted in such a way that listeners can clearly understand the story, even though they may be driving down the highway with the radio on, and not consciously paying attention. Keep in mind that the listener neither has a lyric sheet nor knows what you meant to say or what you had in your mind. You only have three, or three-and-a-half minutes, to tell your story. That leaves no room for sub-plots and extraneous details.

Ideally, you should be able to express the idea of your song in one sentence, and the lyric needs to stick to that focus. (Refer to step one of the Three-Step lyric writing technique in chapter 2.)

EVOKING ONE EMOTION

Evoking emotion in your listener is the ultimate goal of songwriting. No matter what you feel when you write a song, if that feeling is not awakened in your listener, you have not successfully communicated. To clearly convey the desired emotion, your entire song should express the same emotion. Your "canvas" is too small to contain varying emotions in different sections. From the opening lines of your first verse, the listener should have no doubt what it is the singer is feeling. It will confuse the listener and fail to elicit the desired emotional response if the singer is happy in the first verse, angry in the chorus, and ambivalent by the bridge.

What I look for in a song is quite simply something that makes me happy or sad, or something that can make me laugh; something that evokes an emotional response; something that moves me. Chances are if it moves one heart, it will move others.

Debbie Zavitson (Senior Director, Artists & Repertoires, Giant Records)

Effective lyrics clearly let the listener know how the singer feels, but without coming right out and saying it. Instead, imagery is used to help the listener vividly envision the scene and empathize with the singer. For example:

- ♪ The whiskey glass is empty except for his tears.
- ♪ Heartache is written in smeared mascara that falls down from her eyes.
- ♪ Sadness hangs over them like a storm cloud in the desert.

These examples leave no doubt what the characters in the song are feeling. Yet, the lyrics never actually say, "They are sad."

MAINTAINING ONE CONSISTENT TENSE AND TONE

If you've chosen a natural, conversational tone for a particular lyric, it is important to use it consistently throughout the song. Do not interrupt a sincere, heartfelt sentiment with an occasional humorous line or a clever twist on words. Likewise, a lyric that is essentially a series of funny twists on words will not work if one or more lines written in a deeply personal, emotionally vulnerable tone are interjected. Effective lyrics maintain one consistent style and tone throughout the lyric.

Another common pitfall is switching tenses. It's an easy mistake to make. Be sure to maintain a consistent tense throughout the lyric.

Incorrect:

*We **used to** go for walks*
Beneath the summer skies
*The sun **is** so bright*
*All I **saw** were your eyes*

In this example there's an abrupt switch from past tense (We *used to* go for walks) to present tense (The sun *is* so bright), and back to past tense (All I *saw* were your eyes).

Correct:

*We **used to** go for walks*
Beneath the summer skies
*The sun **was** so bright*
*All I **saw** were your eyes*

Mixing pronouns is also a recipe for confusion. It is crucial to refer to the subject or object of the song in a consistent manner. The following example illustrates the common problem of interchanging pronouns inappropriately:

Incorrect:

*When I first met **her***
***She** was warm and true*
Yes, the love that I wanted
*I found with **you***

Correct:

*When I first met **you***
***You** were warm and true*
Yes, the love that I wanted
*I found with **you***

or

*When I first met **her***
***She** was warm and true*
Yes, the love that I wanted
Came from out of the blue

If your lyric is written in the first person (speaking directly *to* the character in the song) be sure that all the pronouns refer to "you." If you choose to write from the third person (telling your listener *about* the person) be sure to consistently use pronouns like "he," "she," "him," or "her."

It also needs to be clear to the listener exactly to whom the pronouns refer. If there is any doubt, replace the pronoun with information that clarifies the situation.

Incorrect:

Mama and Susie went dancing last night
She *danced every dance till dawn*

It is unclear who danced every dance—Mama or Susie.

Correct:

Mama and Susie went dancing last night
Mama *danced every dance until dawn*

Reread your lyric after you've completed a first draft to be sure that you haven't confused the listener by abruptly changing tone, tense, or pronouns.

DEVELOPING STRONG OPENING LINES

*I look at the first two or three lyric lines and I know within
ten seconds of listening to the intro whether the song is
worth listening to any further. I look for a wonderful
opening line or some imagery that grabs me and moves
me.*

Justin Wilde (Publisher, Christmas & Holiday Music/writer, Barbara
Mandrell's five-million-selling "It Must Have Been The Mistletoe" as well as
cuts with artists including Kathy Lee Gifford, Vicky Carr, Ray Charles, and
Loretta Lynn)

When I was screening songs for the A & R (Artists and Repertoires) Department at RCA Records in Los Angeles, I'd often take home a box overflowing with cassettes. During the forty-five-minute drive in the inevitable bumper-to-bumper traffic, I'd try to get through as many tapes as possible. I'd pop one in the cassette deck and although I'd generally listen through about half of the first chorus, I'd usually draw my conclusions within the first fifteen seconds.

This was all the time I needed to assess the sound of the demo and the opening two lines of lyric and melody. In fifteen seconds I could pretty much decide if I was listening to something special enough to tell my boss about. Since RCA had a "no unsolicited tapes" policy, almost all of the songs I listened to came from major publishers, staff-writers, managers, or entertainment attorneys, so most of them were pretty good. But "pretty good" isn't good enough when only "exceptional" stands a chance of beating out the competition.

Songs that make it to the next level have to jump out of the pack right from the start with opening lines of melody and lyric which grab the listener immediately. Without a strong opening, the listener will not be psychologically prepared to be impressed with a song. Even if the chorus is a smash, the song will have to overcome a lukewarm initial impression.

In addition to having a melody that instantly tells the listener, "This song is about to be a hit," the first lines of lyric are your initial opportunity to set the emotional tone. By the time listeners have heard the second line of the lyric, they should know what emotion the singer is feeling. Those opening lines need to be unique, fresh, and interesting enough to separate your song from the "pretty good" songs.

In songwriting, as in life, you only get one opportunity to make a first impression. After your initial flow of inspiration, go back and rewrite your first lines, keeping in mind that someone may soon have a finger poised at the eject button giving you only fifteen seconds to convey that your song is a smash.

MAINTAINING CONTINUITY

Each line of lyric needs to advance the development of your story. There can be no gaps in information. Do not assume your listeners know what you know about the story and the characters. You need to present them with all of the pertinent information to successfully communicate your story and emotion.

Each line of lyric should flow from the line that precedes it and into the line that follows it. For example:

Correct:
I held you close and said, "I love you"
And saw my love reflected in your eyes
And in that moment when I kissed you
Baby, there was no doubt in my mind

Incorrect:
I held you close and said, "I love you"
I was late for work yesterday
The dog was barking when I woke up
This feeling just won't go away

Although this example does exaggerate the point, it is essential that each line maintain a smooth connection to the lines that come before and after. It is especially important that the last line of each verse is crafted to serve as a "springboard" to deliver listeners to the chorus. That final line of each verse is the link between the verse information and the summation about to be presented in the chorus. For example:

Correct:

Verse:

I held you close and said, "I love you"
And saw my love reflected in your eyes
And in that moment when I kissed you
There was no doubt in my mind

Chorus:

I'd found a once in a lifetime love

Incorrect:

Verse:

I held you close and said, "I love you"
And saw my love reflected in your eyes
And in that moment when I kissed you
No matter how hard I tried

Chorus:

I'd found a once in a lifetime love

Note that in the correct example, the last line of the verse dovetails seamlessly into the first line of the chorus. In the incorrect version, there is no logical connection between the meaning of the last line of the verse and the first line of the chorus.

INCORPORATING DETAIL, ACTION, AND IMAGERY INTO LYRICS

One of the basic rules of strong lyric writing is "Show—Don't Tell." This is important for all songwriting genres, but it's essential for successful country lyric writing. Pop, R & B, and other styles of music tend to include lyrics that state how the singer is feeling, but the most effective lyrics in any genre tend to involve the audience. The goal is to allow the listeners to feel as though they are witnesses to the scene, thereby allowing them to feel what the singer feels. There is no more powerful way to draw listeners into your story than through

Exercise:

Learning to "Tell the *Story—* Not the *Feelings*"

This exercise will help you to further master the technique of involving your audience, by allowing the listener to "witness" the scene and *feel* what the singer feels, instead of being told how the singer feels.

A song entitled "She's Lonely" might be expressed with the following "pictures":

♪ She stays up all night crying in that big old empty bed

♪ She plays solitaire every Saturday night

♪ She sips her wine at a table for one

♪ She sits alone in the dark, watching the same sad old movie on TV

The lines listed above make it very clear how this woman feels—without ever coming out and telling the listener. They will evoke far more empathy than lines like:

♪ Oh, she's so lonely without him

♪ She feels so blue deep inside

♪ Loneliness is all she feels

♪ Her heart is breaking with loneliness

In a notebook, list three detailed images that will allow the listener to "see" each of the following. Find ways to paint the scene so that the listener will have no doubt that:

1. He's in love
2. I miss you
3. I'm glad you're gone
4. I feel like dancing
5. He's never been happier
6. She'd give anything for one more chance
7. He's peaceful and content
8. I can't get you off my mind

the use of detailed, specific imagery.

The songs are always important (when I sign an artist) because as someone wiser than me said, "It always starts with the song." My main advice to developing writers is to try to tell a story and to create a visual, either with a narrative that the audience can relate to or through evocative imagery and metaphor. Too many writers are lazy in this area, feeling satisfied with using generic and recycled phrases and images we have all heard a thousand times before.

Jeff Fenster (Sr. V.P. of A & R, Island/Def Jam Records)

When learning how to avoid the common pitfall of *telling* how the singer feels, it can be helpful to visualize the video for your song. Then use words to "show" the listeners what the singer is "seeing."

The lyric below ("A Beverage") illustrates several problems commonly found in developing songwriters' work. It tells how the singer feels and uses very general descriptions, as opposed to unique, specific imagery.

Compare this lyric, one line at a time, with Matraca Berg and Gary Harrison's "Strawberry Wine." Note how much more effective it is to include the details and vivid, fresh descriptions.

"A Beverage"
He was at one of my relative's
I wanted to learn things and thought he could teach me
I was young back then
When one night we fell in love
We were down by the water

Paint pictures in your lyrics by using:

✔ **Action**

✔ **Color**

✔ **Detail**

And I still remember

Chorus:
The beverage we drank when I was young
There was a moon out
It was my first time
And I was inexperienced
But I still remember that fruity beverage we drank

I remember when I was young
I dreaded him leaving
We tried to stay in contact with each other
But then we somehow lost touch
Now I regularly return there
To bring back the memories
(Repeat Chorus)

It's not the same back there anymore
They haven't kept the place up
And everything's different there now
And sometimes I wonder if I miss him
Or just the way I used to be
(Repeat Chorus)

"Strawberry Wine"
(Matraca Berg/Gary Harrison)

He was working through college on my grandpa's farm
I was thirsting for knowledge and he had a car
I was caught somewhere between a woman and a child
When one restless summer we found love growing wild
On the banks of the river on a well-beaten path
Funny how those memories can last (like)

Chorus:
Strawberry Wine and seventeen
The hot July moon saw everything
My first taste of love on bittersweet
Green on the vine

Like Strawberry Wine

Yes I still remember when thirty was old
And my biggest fear was September when he had to go
A few cards and letters and one long-distance call
We drifted away like the leaves in the fall
But year after year I come back to this place
Just to remember the taste (of)
(Repeat Chorus)

The fields have grown over now
Years since they've seen the plow
There's nothing time hasn't touched
Is it really him or the loss of my innocence
I've been missing so much
(Repeat Chorus)

While both lyrics express essentially the same idea, note how much more interesting, and involving, the second lyric is:

"He was at one of my relative's" vs. *"He was working through college on my grandpa's farm"*

"We were down by the water" vs. *"On the banks of the river on a well-beaten path"*

"We tried to stay in contact with each other" vs. *"A few cards and letters and one long-distance call"*

No one else in the world shares your life experiences, or your unique way of interpreting and processing the events and images around you. Only you have experienced the specific heartaches, joys, fears, and loves that have touched your life. So, while it is true that you cannot write a Diane Warren lyric, a Babyface lyric, or a Gary Burr lyric, they can't write a lyric that expresses your distinctive way of looking at the world either.

Being vulnerable, and exposing your pain, fears, hopes, disappointments, and desires in your lyrics, is scary. But dig down deep. Avoid using tired old clichés and images that have been heard thousands of times. Draw on those experiences that are yours, and yours alone, to infuse your lyrics with honesty and individuality. That's what will make them special and give them the power to touch other hearts. John Van Meter, Director, Creative Services, Sony/ATV Tree Music Publishing, advises, "Be aware of the market, but don't try to copy what you're hearing. I encourage writers to put a part of themselves in each

Exercise:

Incorporating Detail, Action, and Imagery into Lyrics

Close your eyes and imagine a scene in which you are about to tell someone that you love him or her. After visualizing the setting in detail, grab
your notebook and do the following:

♪ Describe where you are.
   (i.e., On the front porch; Parked in front of the house in daddy's
   old blue pickup truck; Wrapped up together in a faded old Indian
   blanket on the cold, hard, basement floor; etc.)

♪ If you're indoors, describe the room, including the furniture,
   using as much detail as possible.
   (i.e., There are two old, oak rocking chairs with faded green
   paisley cushions, side by side in the living room; The last embers
   of a fire are turning cold in the white marble fireplace that
   Grandpa built in 1902; Our feet are up on that ugly glass coffee
   table Mama bought on sale at the Salvation Army thrift shop;
   etc.)

♪ If you're outside, describe the setting in detail.
   (i.e., Leaning up against Jimmy's 1972 red Mustang convertible,
   in the parking lot behind the Longhorn Grill; There's not a single
   other car left this late; A sliver of a crescent moon is lighting up
   her face and there's just one star in the sky; The neon sign that
   says "Best Steaks in Texas" has just been turned off; etc.)

♪ Is there music playing? If so, describe it in detail. Is it live,
   from a radio or jukebox? Loud or soft? What's the song? Is it
   fast or slow? What are the instruments? Who's singing?
   (i.e., I could barely hear a scratchy old recording of Nat "King"
   Cole singing "Unforgettable" coming from the jukebox in the next
   room; The bass was thumping so loud I could feel the vibrations
   in my bones; An elderly woman with skin like leather was softly
   singing a Spanish folk song; etc.)

♪ Describe the sounds you are hearing.
   (i.e., Crickets; The whisper of the north wind coming down
   through the ravine; Silence as loud as a scream; A whippoorwill

singing a love song to his lady; Ear-splitting electric guitars; Billie Holiday's voice coming out of an old TV; The sound of her breathing while she sleeps; The echo of high heels on a hardwood floor as she leaves; etc.)

♪ Describe the weather in detail. (Is it windy; rainy; warm; chilly?)
(i.e., It was hotter than July on the bayou; The ache in my bones told me the first snow of the season was on its way; A first hint of spring was in the air; The thermometer said it was 99 degrees but I knew it was a liar; The Santa Ana winds whipped down from the hills; etc.)

♪ Note the time (explaining how you know what time it is).
(i.e., The rooster crowed its morning wake-up call; The clock down the hall chimed three times; I heard the midnight train blow its whistle in the distance; The alarm clock told me it was 6:00 a.m.; etc.)

♪ Provide a detailed description of what you're sitting, standing, or leaning on.
(i.e., Sitting on the soft, warm grass; Propped up against grandma's old blue brocade couch, the one with the frayed gold tassels and the overstuffed cushions; Leaning up against a red leather barstool; Stretched out on the backseat of a silver limousine; etc.)

♪ Describe what's happening in your body.
(i.e., Hot tears started flowing from my eyes; My heart was pounding like a jackhammer; I looked down and saw that my hands were trembling; A smile spread all over my face; etc.)

Now try this exercise by imagining you're about to tell someone that "It's over."

You probably won't use the majority of the images you come up with in any one song. It would be overkill and there's not all that much room in a three-minute song. But having these details at your fingertips will help tremendously to learn how to "show" instead of "tell." You may be amazed at your ability to generate these "pictures." Until you get used to telling your story with images, it is helpful to begin each song by following the steps of this exercise, as it applies to that song.

song, so that it is their own; so that it is something I don't already have."

I once co-wrote with a writer who seemed to be doodling and drawing stick figures all over his lyric notes. When I asked him what he was doing, he said his publisher suggested that he include more "pictures" in his writing! The bad news is that writing lyrics that include colorful "pictures," action, and detail does not come effortlessly for most writers. It is much easier to tell the listeners how you feel than to evoke those feelings with the use of imagery. But the good news is that this is a skill that can be learned and improved with practice.

KEEPING IT CONVERSATIONAL

Think Wal-Mart—not Hallmark.

Jason Blume

The most effective lyrics sound natural, like something you would actually say in normal conversation—not like flowery sentiments you might find in a greeting card. A lyric is not a poem. Well-written lyrics (as opposed to poems):

♪ Have sections or specific lines that are crafted to be repeated.

♪ Are intended to be sung, not read silently or aloud.

♪ Use rhymes (poetry may or may not use rhymes).

♪ Take into account the actual sound of the words, not just their meaning.

♪ Are crafted to lend themselves to strong melodies.

KEEPING YOUR IMAGERY FRESH

Don't write generic crap.

Gemma Corfield (Vice President of Artists & Repertoires, Virgin Records)

There's a fun game called Scattergories. The players are given a printed list of categories (i.e., a boy's name, a foreign capital, etc.). A multifaceted cube that has the letters of the alphabet on it is rolled. Whichever letter it lands on is the first letter of the items the players will list for that round. A timer is set and you've got to be quick. So, for example, if the letter is "R," for a boy's name, the first thing that pops into your head might be "Robert" or "Richard." For a foreign capital, you might think of Rome. But there's a catch—if two or more of the players come up with the same answer, they don't get a point.

What I look for in a song is kind of like going on a blind date. You can describe the perfect mate and be given that but still something could be missing. So for me, it's what excites me, makes me passionate, twists my gut in knots . . . it's a feeling. More technically, (I look for) an interesting lyric. How many ways can you say "I love you" without using the word love?

Judy Stakee (Vice President of Creative Services, Warner Chappell Music Publishing)

Songwriting is similar. If you come up with predictable, obvious lyrics, thousands of other writers will likely have the same idea—and you won't get the "point" (i.e., the publishing deal, the cut, or the hit). To win at the game of songwriting stay away from trite clichés and overused phrases and dig deeper to find fresh, new ways to express yourself. If your lyric includes lines such as "Holding hands under the moon," "Make a brand new start," or "Under the stars above," why should an artist choose yours over the thousands of others that are typically submitted for a major recording project?

A word of caution: While you need to use detailed, specific, fresh images, millions of others still need to identify with your song. Your lyrics will not be effective if the images you choose are out of the realm of normal experience. For example, when deciding on a unique setting for the story of your song to unfold, the following locations might be effective: at the top of the Ferris wheel; in tenth grade chemistry class; or in the very last row of the movie theater. Avoid locations that are so unusual that no one will realistically be able to relate to them, such as sitting by the glow of the nuclear reactor in Chernobyl; albatross hunting in New Zealand; on the operating table in the cardiac ward. Find that happy medium that straddles the line of being fresh and distinctive, while still sounding natural and conversational.

Exercise:

Using Fresh Imagery

Replace the title and lyrics that follow with a new title and images that are fresh and detailed, and natural. For example:

Sitting in this place
With these thoughts
At this time
Having this feeling

might be expressed with fresh imagery and detail as:

Sitting cross-legged on the hardwood floor
Thinking of us growing old together
And as the grandfather clock chimes two
I've got a feeling it's the start of forever

Now, as above, replace the following title and lyric with detailed, specific images. You might want to repeat this exercise several times, each time using a new title and additional imagery. You may be surprised at your ability to generate "pictures" within your lyrics. I was.

"I Love You"

Verse 1:
Here in this setting
In this frame of mind
Doing this stuff
Here's what I want you to know

Chorus:
I love you
This is how much
This is how long I'll feel this way
This is how it feels
So in case you're wondering
I love you

Verse 2:
In the future
If you have any doubts
Remember this time
And you'll know
(Repeat Chorus)

CREATING A LYRIC PALETTE

As visual artists use a palette of colors to create their art, it can be helpful for songwriters to develop a "palette" of words and images applicable to each song, before beginning the process of actually crafting the lyric. Sometimes referred to as "word clustering," this process provides instant access to words and phrases that relate directly to the title. It's an effective way to ensure that your title will have maximum impact and will "pay off."

A palette of images and phrases for the title "It's Heaven" might include:

- ♪ Angels
- ♪ Golden Halos
- ♪ Hell
- ♪ Angel's Wings
- ♪ Silver Clouds
- ♪ St. Peter
- ♪ The Pearly Gates
- ♪ Harps
- ♪ Eternity
- ♪ Heavenly Songs

While you certainly won't use all of the related images you come up with, using some of them will add to your title's effectiveness by infusing it with color, detail, and imagery. But remember that the ultimate goal is to evoke emotion. Overloading your lyric with clever images and phrases can make it sound less conversational and more like a novelty song. A lyric palette is an important and powerful tool. Use it sparingly.

AVOIDING REDUNDANCY

"Department of Redundancy Department, how may I be of assistance to help you?" As silly as this phrase may seem, repeating and rehashing the same ideas and images within a lyric is a common problem. Be sure that each line:

- ♪ Makes a contribution.
- ♪ Furthers the development of the story.
- ♪ Gives the listeners greater understanding of how the singer feels.

Remember that you have a maximum of twenty-eight lines, and only about

---

Exercise:
Creating a Lyric Palette

In your notebook, create a palette of at least ten words or phrases for each of the following titles.

1. "Grandma's House"
2. "The Midnight Train"
3. "The High School Prom"
4. "Dancin' All Night"
5. "Daddy's Old Chevrolet"
6. "Louisiana Saturday Night"
7. "Sunday Picnic"
8. "Halfway to Mexico"
9. "Christmas Back Home"
10. "Sunset Beach"

---

three minutes to tell your entire story and evoke the desired emotion in the listener, so there's no room for redundancy. Make every line count.

AVOIDING PREACHING (UNLESS YOU'RE IN CHURCH)

Sometimes the desire to share a feeling or belief is so powerful that the temptation is to cut to the chase and tell your listeners what they "should" feel. But keep sight of the fact that the goal is to successfully deliver the emotion and message from your heart to the listener's. You can get your point or moral across much more effectively by allowing your story to evoke the feelings, rather than telling listeners what they should feel. Instead, draw the audience into the scene so they can empathize with your point of view and feel what you feel.

When Sandy Knox and Steve Rosen wrote Reba McEntire's hit, "She Thinks His Name Was John," they presented a heartbreaking, detailed story of a one-night stand that resulted in AIDS. The listeners felt they knew the woman in the song. They could understand why she made her choices and were able to share her sorrow. By simply telling a story, that song touched and educated millions of people without ever coming out and saying: "Don't sleep around. If you do, you could get AIDS and then you'll be sorry." No one likes to be told what to do or how to feel, and it's an arrogant stance for the singer to imply that as king (or queen) of the universe, he or she knows all the answers. Avoid preachy phrases like:

- ♪ So don't ever . . .
- ♪ You better always . . .
- ♪ I'm telling you to . . .

WRITING THE DREADED SECOND VERSE

A truly great song has a beginning, middle, and end—just like a good book. The second verse should give me some information, some continuance of the story that I didn't learn from the first verse. When I listen to songs as a producer I always at least listen through the middle or the end of the second verse just to see if the story ever develops. I want to be brought along and have something new unfold to keep my attention.

Steve Gibson (Producer of artists including Aaron Tippin, Engelbert, and Randy Travis)

Many writers find that writing the second verse is their most challenging song-writing task. The second verse's function is to:

- ♪ Continue the story.
- ♪ Add new information.
- ♪ Bring the listener back to the title.

When it's time to write a second verse, visualize yourself within the scene and allow it to unfold. A guaranteed way to avoid repeating information you've already covered is to ask yourself the questions: Then what happened? What else happened?

USING RHYMES: WHERE TO, WHEN TO, HOW TO, AND WHY TO

It has been said that rhyming began as a way to aid in memorization, prior to the written word. Rhymes are an important part of successful lyrics, because they help us to remember the words. People who listen to popular music have been unconsciously trained to anticipate rhymes in certain places, although they are probably not aware of it. If your rhymes fail to appear where the listener expects them, he or she will likely feel as though something is missing.

Effective rhyming:

♪ Helps hold the listener's attention.

♪ Contributes to making the lyrics easy to remember.

♪ Provides a sense of completion and satisfaction for the listener.

While rhymes are necessary, the *meaning* of what you say is far more impor-

Exercise:
Adding New Information to the Second Verse

For the following scenarios, craft a second verse that answers either: "Then what happened" or "What else happened."

"The Most Wonderful Night Of My Life"

Verse 1:
I picked you up at eight
We went dancing
And as I held you close
There was no doubt (It was)

Chorus:
The Most Wonderful Night Of My Life
All of my dreams came true
The Most Wonderful Night Of My Life
Is every night I spend with you

Verse 2:
(Complete in your notebook)

"Let's Try Again"

Verse 1:
When I picked up the phone
I was surprised to hear your voice

tant than the rhymes. It will not work to sacrifice the idea of the lyric or the conversational tone, in order to force a line to rhyme. The most effective rhymes sound effortless. You can almost always rewrite a line of your lyric to change the final word that will need to rhyme, without altering the meaning of the line.

In the example that follows, the writer has written himself into a corner. There are no rhymes for the word "orange."

We walked through fields together
While the sun turned to orange
And as night fell from the sky
A new love . . .

But not nearly as surprised
As when you said

Chorus:
Let's Try Again
To love one more time
Let's Try Again
And again till we get it right

Verse 2:
(Complete in your notebook)

"How Could We Hurt Each Other Like That"

Verse 1:
I tossed and turned all night
In this big old empty bed
I kept remembering
Every single word we said

Chorus:

How Could We Hurt Each Other Like That
With angry words we can't take back
Can we turn around from where we're at
How Could We Hurt Each Other Like That

Verse 2:
(Complete in your notebook)

However, the line can be restructured to end with an easier word to rhyme—without changing the basic meaning:

We walked through fields together
And watched the orange sun
And as night fell from the sky
A new love had begun

In the example below, the natural order of the words in the last line has been inverted and the word "conceal," which is not commonly used in that context, has been chosen to force the rhyme. In normal conversation you would never say, "My foolish pride I will conceal." By changing the final word of the second line you can avoid the need to settle for an unnatural sounding rhyme, while still maintaining the meaning of the line.

Incorrect:

If you would give me one more chance
To give you all the love I feel
From now until the end of time
My foolish pride I will conceal

Correct:

If you would give me one more chance
To give the love I feel inside
From now until the end of time
I'll put away my foolish pride

Types of Rhymes

There are many types of rhymes. Perfect rhymes and slant rhymes, masculine, feminine, triple rhymes, and internal rhymes are the primary types popular songwriters employ. They are the focus of this part of the chapter.

Perfect Rhymes

"Perfect" rhymes are exact rhymes. The sounds of the final accented vowel and the final consonant (if applicable) are identical, while the preceding consonants are different in each of the rhyming words. For example:

Tree - Free
Boat - Coat
Girl - Pearl

Slant Rhymes

While perfect rhymes were required in the era of Irving Berlin, Cole Porter, and the Gershwins, they are not mandatory in current, popular music. Perfect rhymes are still used regularly, but while some purists may insist on them, if you listen to any popular radio station you'll hear they are not required to have a hit song. The option is to use "slant" rhymes, words that invoke a sense of rhyme without rhyming exactly. For example:

Love - Touch
Hurt - Were
Mind - Time

It is perfectly acceptable to use a mix of perfect rhymes and slant rhymes within the same song. A common pitfall is using words that appear as though they should rhyme when they are on the written page, but do not actually rhyme when they are pronounced. For example:

Anger - Danger
Again - Rain
Love - Prove

Another common mistake to avoid is the use of pairs of "rhyming" words that are spelled differently, but sound alike. These are not rhymes, but identical sounds. For example:

Blue - Blew
Through - Threw
New - Knew

Masculine Rhymes

A masculine rhyme is one in which only one syllable rhymes. This can occur as either a one-syllable word (Boy - Toy) or as the last syllable of a multi-syllabic word (About - Without).

Feminine Rhymes

Feminine rhymes are two-syllable or "double" rhymes with the emphasis on the syllable preceding the last syllable (Lover - Discover).

Triple Rhymes

As the name implies, in triple rhymes, the last three syllables all rhyme (Vanishing - Banishing).

Internal Rhymes

Internal rhymes are rhymes that occur within the line (If you *feel* it's *real*). They can add extra appeal as long as they sound natural and do not get in the way of expressing the meaning of the lyric. Internal rhymes do not replace the rhymes at the end of lines, but are used in addition to them.

Rhyme Schemes

The most common rhyme schemes for segments containing four lines employ rhymes that occur at the ends of lines 2 and 4 *or* lines 1 and 2 *and* lines 3 and 4. Although it is not used as frequently, it is acceptable to rhyme lines 1 and 3 *and* lines 2 and 4.

If a section of your song is comprised of six lines, one option is to treat the first four lines as suggested above and rhyme line 5 with line 6. Another rhyme scheme for verses or choruses that are comprised of six lines rhymes lines 1 and 2, lines 4 and 5, and lines 3 and 6. For example:

1.   I know what's on your mind

2.   I've known it for some time

3.   But I promise it's not time for leaving

4.   I won't let you go

5.   Girl, until you know

6.   That baby, it's not time to stop believing

While it's not important that you learn the technical names of the various types of rhymes and rhyme schemes, it is important that you know how to use them. If your first verse rhymes line 1 with line 2 and line 3 with line 4, your second verse needs to follow the same pattern. Likewise, if your first verse contains rhymes lines 2 and 4, these lines should also rhyme in your second verse.

It is most effective to be consistent in the types of rhymes used in different verses (i.e., if the first verse contains masculine rhymes, the second verse should contain masculine rhymes). But it is preferable to vary the specific vowel sounds of the rhyming words you use in different sections of a song. For example, if the first verse relies heavily on rhyming "E" sounds (i.e., Free - Tree), you should probably avoid "E" sounds in the chorus. It will also make it easier to find rhyming words if you have a variety of sounds to choose from.

USING RHYMING DICTIONARIES

I initially avoided rhyming dictionaries, thinking that using someone else's ideas would compromise my artistic integrity. Then I read an interview in which Stephen Sondheim, Pulitzer Prize–winning Broadway composer and lyricist, said that he regularly uses a rhyming dictionary. If it's good enough for Sondheim . . . It's neither realistic, nor necessary to be walking rhyming dictionaries. Why not use every available tool to have the fullest range of possible rhyming words at your fingertips?

Most of the words listed in a rhyming dictionary will probably never find their way into a song. But some of them may spark an idea that leads your lyric in a new, unexpected direction. The rhymes you select and how you use them will reflect your own unique creativity. The rhyming dictionary I've found most helpful is Sue Young's *The New Comprehensive American Rhyming Dictionary.*

USING THE LIST TECHNIQUE

Many successful song lyrics are written by using a technique of "listing" a series of examples that relate to, and clearly lead the listener to, the title. This approach, sometimes referred to as the "Laundry List" technique, may be used throughout the entire lyric or in just a portion of it (i.e., the verses or the chorus). For example:

"Better Things To Do"

I could wash my car in the rain
Change my new guitar strings
Mow the yard just the same
As I did yesterday
I don't need to waste my time crying over you
I got Better Things To Do

(Tom Shapiro, Chris Waters, and Terri Clark, Recorded by Terri Clark)

This chorus lyric was crafted by listing the things the singer *could* do, followed by a "set-up" line (in boldface). The set-up line serves as a link between the items in the list and the title, and helps to prepare the listener for the title. The title summarizes the idea and the images in the list. When using this technique, every line does not need to be a part of the list.

Note that the usage of original, detailed ideas within the list adds much more interest than expressing the same idea in a more ordinary way. Compare the above lyric with the one that follows:

I could work or read a book
Watch television or listen to the radio
Call a friend on the phone
Or go for a walk . . .

"List" songs sometimes use images that are the opposite of the title. In the following lyric the verse is comprised of a list of things you *can* do, followed by a chorus that says, "But *don't* . . ."

"Achy Breaky Heart"

You can tell the world you never was my girl
You can burn my clothes up when I'm gone
You can tell your friends just what a fool I've been
And laugh and joke about me on the phone
You can tell my arms to go back to the farm
You can tell my feet to hit the floor
Or **you can** tell my lips to tell my fingertips
They won't be reaching out for you no more
But **don't** tell my heart
My Achy Breaky Heart . . .

(Don Von Tress, Recorded by Billy Ray Cyrus)

Exercise:
Practicing the List Technique

For each of the titles that follow, list ten phrases or images that will lead to that title. The lines do not need to rhyme or have any specific number of syllables. Do not settle for lines that are less than fresh and unique, and don't forget that sometimes the most effective way to set up the title is with a list of images and ideas that are the opposite of the title. (In each instance, one example is included.)

1. "I Don't Think She Loves Me Anymore"

   Example: I sent a dozen roses and called a dozen times but haven't gotten one call back

2. "It Must Be Love"

   Example: It must not be the flu 'cause I don't have a fever

3. "That's Her Idea Of Fun"

   Example: She drives her Daddy's new Corvette at ninety miles an hour

4. "Don't Say Goodbye"

   Example: Say there's one chance in a million

5. "I Think I Must Be Dreaming"

   Example: I don't think I died and went to heaven

Examples of other songs that have successfully employed the "list" technique include "If I Ever Lose My Faith In You"(Sting), "I Try To Think About Elvis" (Gary Burr), and "Fifty Ways To Leave Your Lover" (Paul Simon).

LOOKING FOR OPPOSITES AND TWISTS ON WORDS

The first year that I was signed as a staff-writer for Zomba Music I was in awe of the talent of the Nashville lyricists. They seemed to have an amazing ability to find clever twists on words. I thought that those other writers must be geniuses. I couldn't imagine I would ever acquire the ability to twist and turn phrases the way they did. I've since learned that finding those clever twists on words is not magic, but like so many other aspects of the songwriting process, it's a skill that can be developed and improved through practice.

The first step to using clever twists on words is learning to look for opposites. For example:

"You Hurt Me *Bad* In A Real *Good* Way"
"*New* Way To Light Up An *Old* Flame"
"*Don't* Tell Me What To *Do*"
"Time Has *Come* To Let You *Go*"

Look for key words in your title and in the text of your lyric. Circle those words that are crucial to the meaning of the song and ask yourself what each one's opposite is. Although using opposites and wordplay are techniques most commonly used in country music, they can also be effectively used in other types of music, as in Joan Jett's hit, "I Hate Myself For Loving You" (co-written with Desmond Child).

You can also create interesting wordplay by using the past tense. For example:

"You Really Had Me *Goin'*—Now I'm *Gone*"
"Once I *Held* What He's *Holding*"
"I Want To *Feel* What I *Felt* Back Then"

While using opposites is a powerful tool, and an important one to master, use it sparingly. Unless you are writing a novelty song, being overly clever can sometimes distract from the genuine emotion that the song ultimately needs to communicate.

USING ASSONANCE AND ALLITERATION

Since lyrics are intended to be sung, their sound is sometimes just as important as their meaning. Assonance and alliteration are fancy names for specific ways to use the sound of words to add interest to your lyrics.

Assonance is the technique of incorporating the same sounds on the

Exercise:

Looking for Opposites and Twists on Words

1. For each of the words in the list that follows write its opposite or past tense (if applicable).

2. Write a full line of lyric that includes the word and its opposite or past tense. For example: long (the opposite is *short*)

For a *long* time you've been coming up *short* on love

1. Easy
2. Will
3. Right
4. First
5. This
6. More
7. Fast
8. Day
9. Single
10. Weak

---

stressed vowels of two or more words to create added interest aurally. For example:

You *say* no *way*
Hold *on* or I'm *gone*
This *time* you'll *find* you're *mine*

Alliteration is the use of two or more consonants that have the same sound. Using this tool can help to make a lyric catchier, more memorable, and pleasing to the ear. For example:

I'm *falling forever*
Now I'll *never know*
The *Way* We *Were*

Pam Tillis had a huge hit with "Maybe It Was Memphis." Without the use of alliteration (*Maybe* - *Memphis*) the title would not have been nearly as effective.

"Maybe It Was Cleveland" just doesn't have the same impact. When alliteration and assonance are used effectively they sound so natural and organic to the lyric that they are barely noticed. These tools can add interest to your lyric when used sparingly, but overusing them can distract the listener from your message. Don't lose sight of the fact that the meaning must always be the top priority.

WRITING THE BIG PAY-OFF LINES

The function of "pay-off" lines is to provide a sense of satisfaction and completion for the listener. The "pay-off," most often found at the end of the chorus, is the line that ties the song together. It provides the emotional punch, or sur-

---

Exercise:
Using Assonance and Alliteration

Write one full line of lyric that incorporates each of the words below. In each instance, use the tool of assonance or alliteration to add interest to the line—while still maintaining a natural, conversational meaning.

Assonance

Example: Strong
I'm too str*o*ng to go *on* like this

1. Light
2. Dream
3. More
4. Ever
5. Believe

Alliteration

Example: Help
*H*elp me— I'm *h*urting

1. Kiss
2. Heart
3. Give
4. Sound
5. Baby

---

prise, and adds impact to the lines that preceded it. For example:

Effective:
I Wanna Dance With Somebody
I wanna feel the heat with somebody
I Wanna Dance With Somebody
With somebody who loves me
(George Merrill and Shannon Rubicam)

Less Effective:
I Wanna Dance With Somebody
I wanna feel the heat with somebody
I Wanna Dance With Somebody
Because I like the music

I'm very aware of sounds of words as well as what kind of sound is being sung when a note is being held. I don't go overboard. You certainly have to go with exactly what you feel, but you're not going to sing a sound like "it" over a long note. You're going to look for an open vowel sound that a singer can sing. I want to encourage people to be unique, but also to be aware of how things sing.

Steve Diamond (Emmy Award–winning songwriter, "I Can Love You Like That," "Let Me Let Go," "The Day That She Left Tulsa," and cuts by artists including Eric Clapton, Willie Nelson, and Reba McEntire)

In the example of the less effective way to complete the chorus, the listener is left with a sense of "So what?" In Whitney Houston's hit, the pay-off line at the end of the chorus raises the lyric to a whole new level by bringing in an additional element to the lyric. It is especially effective because of the double-entendre of the word "somebody."

When Houston sings, "I Wanna Dance With Somebody," in the first three lines, it means she wants to dance and *anybody* will do as a partner. But the inclusion of the pay-off line, "With somebody *who loves me,*" brings more power to the lyric.

VISUALIZING A HIT

Part of your job as a lyricist is to get inside the minds of the characters you create in your songs. You need to express what is real for them. You also need to remember that the words that come from your heart and your pen will hopefully be coming out of a performer's mouth someday. The exercise that follows will help you to craft lyrics consistent with the images projected by the artists you intend them for.

Exercise:

Visualizing a Hit

Decide which artist, in your wildest fantasy, you would most want to record your song. Be sure to choose an artist who records outside material. (Outside material refers to songs that were not written by the artist, the producer, the head of the record label, or anyone else "inside" the project.) Write down that artist's name.

Close your eyes and visualize a stage in front of an enormous crowd of cheering fans. Hear the announcer introduce your "dream artist" performing his or her number one smash hit—your song! Pay attention to the details. Notice what the artist is wearing and what kind of accompaniment there is. Then "listen" to the artist singing your song. Let these images "write" your lyric. When the performance is over, soak in the praise and adulation of the fans. Then sit down backstage and have a discussion with the singer. Ask what the artist would want to convey in this song and what words and images he or she would use to say it. Now write down everything you "saw" and "heard." Include specific details—especially any lyric ideas the "artist" suggested.

It can also be effective to imagine hearing your song coming out of the radio. In addition to helping you write a "radio-friendly" lyric, this exercise may also help you create the melody and arrangement. Your fantasy artist may not be the one who ultimately records your song, but if that artist has a proven track record of hits, and you write a song he or she could potentially record, it's likely that song would also be suitable for a variety of other artists in a similar style.

REWRITING YOUR LYRICS

When I teach songwriting classes I often start by writing "Songwriting" on the blackboard. I ask if everyone is there for the songwriting class and when they all say "yes," I tell them that they're in the wrong place. I put a big "X" through "Songwriting" and replace it with "Song *Rewriting*."

Songwriting seems deceptively easy from a distance, but even the most experienced, successful writers work hard at their craft. Jimmy Buffett says that he wrote "Margaritaville" in six minutes, and it's true that occasionally, the planets line up perfectly and a great song pops out very quickly, requiring little or no effort. It's almost as if the song has come "through" the writer, but a career cannot be based on that rare occurrence. It doesn't happen often, even for the most successful writers. When it does, it's a gift. The chances of that happening without having first mastered the craft are infinitesimally small.

Strip away all the filler. It may take three, four, five, ten rewrites. You don't need five more songs in your catalog. You don't need one more. You need one great one. It's too competitive to let yourself off the hook with lines that are just okay. Dig deep to find that part of you that makes it special and get rid of the things that you would discount if it was another person's song. It's just too competitive.

Steve Diamond (Songwriter/producer)

It's said that Picasso painted up to a dozen versions of each of his most famous works, destroying each one until he felt it was the best it could be. Having to struggle and rewrite (and rewrite and rewrite) doesn't make you a bad writer—but failure to do so might.

My entire career is based on rewriting (and re-demoing!) a song seven times. In 1983 I went to a "temp" agency to find any kind of office job that would put food on the table (preferably, food fit for humans—as opposed to felines!). Fate must have been smiling on me that day because they told me there was an opening, two days a week at RCA Records in the country promotion department. I'd be answering phones, typing, filing, and mailing out new releases to radio programmers.

I just knew this was going to be my big break. Wow, my foot in the door at a major record label—and no one slamming the door shut! My first hour on the job I was told to send out the debut single release by a brand new act signed to the label. It was a mother and daughter act—The Judds. I could hardly believe it when I heard the music. I was totally prepared to hate it since I was not at that point a big fan of country music, but I loved it. I thought it was some of the best music I'd ever heard. Wynonna's voice possessed a richness and emotion I could hardly believe and the harmonies delivered me straight to heaven. But when I listened to the entire album, over and over again, it was the songs that surprised me the most. They were powerful, rockin', fun, and poignant. They touched a place in me that few songs had ever reached, and I decided right there and then that I wanted to write like that.

I started my first country song, "I Had A Heart," with The Judds in mind, but it wasn't quite working. So, when my friend Leslie Brenner mentioned that she was collaborating with a songwriter from Georgia, I asked if she'd introduce us. (It hadn't occurred to me yet that someone could be from the South and *not* write country music!)

I met Bryan Cumming at an ASCAP annual meeting. Bryan played sax in the band "Sha-Na-Na" and was the first real "professional" I had the chance to work with. I told him my idea: "Where I had a heart—there's just a heartache." It sounded like a country song to me and Bryan agreed. We got together at his home studio and really hit it off. Not only was he the sweetest man, but he could play almost any instrument and he had a studio where we could demo songs for free—a real plus considering my financial state.

After our first writing session together, the song was infinitely stronger than the version I had written alone. We did a rough, 8-track demo and brought it to Jim Vellutato, a publisher who at that time was at Famous Music's Los Angeles office. Jim was an early supporter of my songwriting. He was encouraging, but felt the song still needed a lot of work. He pointed out specific weaknesses in the melody and lyric and sent us back to the drawing board. Well, this scenario repeated itself over and over again. It was frustrating and disappointing each time that we were told that our rewritten masterpiece still required major surgery—but it was getting closer each time and we were determined to get it right.

We rewrote and re-demoed that song seven times. The last few times, when we were *certain* that we were done, we hired professional singers. (Stuffing those envelopes at RCA was paying me enough so that I could kick in $15.00, which was my share back then.) We'd thrown out the verse lyrics at least five times and tweaked the chorus melody again and again before we heard that magic word from the publisher: "Yes."

Yes, Yes, Yes!!!

It was a Monday afternoon when Jim said he'd FedEx the song to his Nashville office. Less than twenty-four hours later, I got the call that my first country song had already been recorded in Nashville and was going to be a single! (That was 1986—and it's never happened to me like that again!) Don Goodman, a wonderful songwriter/producer with hits by artists from Alabama to Reba, recorded the song with a new female artist named Darlene Austin, on Magi Records, a tiny independent label. They changed my favorite line of lyric, and the record didn't sound quite like I had envisioned it, but the next thing I knew, I had a song on the country charts! It wasn't exactly a smash hit, but it was a big step in the right direction and it gave me the confidence and credibility to pry a few doors open.

The producer's wife Gayle was a real sweetheart and suggested that on my "next" trip to Nashville I co-write with Don. I'm sure it never occurred to her I had written only one country song and that my only experience with the South was that I had been born in South Philadelphia. I knew I'd need fourteen days to get a low price on an airline ticket, so without a moment's hesitation I told Gayle that my "next" trip to Nashville would be in two weeks . . . and I got out the credit card.

Be yourself and then keep honing your craft. I know that a great song is rarely written quickly and that it is important to learn how to go back and rework, rework, rework until good becomes great.

Kathleen Carey (Senior Vice President of Creative Affairs, Sony/ATV Music Publishing)

Then I set to work, preparing "starts"—song ideas that I could bring to co-writing sessions. Sometimes it was just a title, a rough draft of a whole lyric, or a chorus melody. Writing with such a successful writer was an incredible opportunity for me and I didn't want to leave anything to chance. I wanted to have something strong to bring to the collaboration, so even if I happened to wake up feeling like a slug on that particular morning I could still bring something worthwhile to work on. One of the "starts" I'd prepared was a first draft of a lyric titled, "Change My Mind."

When it came time for my co-write with Don Goodman, I was nervous, and more than a little intimidated, but I felt good about the "starts" I had brought along, especially "Change My Mind." I showed up at Don's office, Bull's Creek Music, at the designated time—but he didn't. Gayle couldn't find him and after about thirty minutes, she said that she'd try to find someone else for me to write with. She went down the hall and returned with another writer signed to Bull's Creek. She said, "Jason this is A.J.—A.J. this here is Jason. Now, ya'll go write a hit." And that's exactly what we did.

About forty-five minutes later, A.J. and I had finished the song that would change both of our lives. When Don Goodman finally showed up, he listened to our song and swore he'd never go out to lunch again! When A.J. played the song that night for his wife Stephanie, she cried and said, "Our kids are going to college!"

All of this happened because I did the seventh rewrite on "I Had A Heart." If I had stopped after rewrite number six, I might still be sitting behind a desk, saying how unfair the business is, and never knowing that success was waiting just a rewrite away.

The most direct route to success is to rewrite each line of lyric and melody until it's the strongest you can possibly make it. This means that even after you like it, you might still want to try several different approaches to see if you can beat the one you've already got. If not, you can always go back to your original draft.

I still need an objective ear to tell me where I'm hitting the mark, and where I'm not, and to inspire me to push myself to do yet one more rewrite, even though it's already "good." I get that from my publisher. In the absence of a publisher you can get that input from a songwriting teacher, a qualified critiquing service, or a co-writer.

I never was great at rewriting. I probably have a lot of songs that were never recorded because of that.

Harlan Howard (Legendary Nashville songwriter)

Early on in my career, I had a chance to collaborate with a great writer named Jack Conrad. Luckily for me, when we first co-wrote, I had no idea that he'd written songs I'd grown up on, by some of my favorite artists, including Heart and The Babys, or I probably would have been too intimidated to be creative. Jack and I lived in Los Angeles and he asked me if I wanted to write a lyric to a rock melody that he'd written with a Nashville writer, Todd Cerney. Todd had recently won a Grammy for Country Song of the Year, Restless Heart's "I'll Still Be Loving You," and had co-written some of Eddie Money's hits. Since I hadn't established a track record as a songwriter, the understanding was that if they weren't happy with my work, they'd give the music to another lyricist.

The melody and the track were great and I knew this was a major opportunity for me. When I was finally pleased with the lyric, I mailed it to Todd and waited nervously for my phone to ring. When it did ring, the news wasn't good. He said that while there wasn't anything _wrong_ with the lyric, he had a whole drawer full of similar ones. It just didn't knock him out, but he appreciated my giving it a try. I could feel my entire career slipping away, and quickly told him that I had several other great ideas and titles for that same music and if he'd just give me a few days to sort through them, I'd give him another option. It was a reasonable request and he agreed to wait a few days to see what else I had.

Unfortunately, the truth was that I didn't really have any other ideas and now that I was close to panic, there didn't seem to be any forthcoming. I'll never forget that Sunday afternoon, driving for hours, in circles around the parking lot of the Northridge Mall, blasting the tape of that track and praying for inspiration. It finally came. I started with a new title, "White Heat," and created a whole new concept for the song. I worked at it as if my entire career depended on it and when Todd read the new lyric he said he "thought it would work."

That song was the only "outside" song cut by a new Canadian rock band that changed their name to White Heat. The album wasn't exactly an international smash hit and I didn't make much money from the recording, but it was a big step for me to chalk up another cut and to establish my credibility with top professionals. But most importantly, I learned a new lesson—the importance of rewriting.

I once read an interview with legendary songwriter Leonard Cohen ("Suzanne"), in which he said that when he writes a lyric, he might spend the day filling an entire notebook and if one line actually makes it into the song, he's had a good day! At first that seemed incredible to me, but then I realized that most songs don't have more than eight lines in each of two verses (sixteen); a maximum of another eight lines in the chorus; and at the most, another four lines of lyric in the bridge. That's a total of twenty-eight lines (and many songs might have less). Taking twenty-eight days to write a song with

Exercise:
Rewriting a Verse Lyric

♪ In your notebook, rewrite each of the following verse lyrics three times.

♪ For each rewrite, keep the idea the same, but change the images and the specific words.

♪ Feel free to change the length of the lines and where the rhymes occur.

Remember to:

♪ Use detail.

♪ Keep it conversational.

♪ Use fresh imagery.

♪ Allow the listener to "watch" the scene unfold.

1. *I held you close*

   That first night we danced

   And when I took you home

   I took a chance

2. *There's really good music*

   Where I go on Saturday nights

   Everybody has a lot of fun

   And they're feelin' alright

3. *When you said that you were leaving me*

   The first thing I did was cry

   Then I got really angry

   And then I told you why

When you've completed the exercise, answer the following questions:

♪ Did you use detail?

♪ Is the language conversational?

♪ Does it incorporate fresh imagery?

♪ Does the lyric allow the listener to "watch" the scene unfold?

♪ Did the work get stronger with each rewrite?

each line being an extraordinary line could produce twelve incredible songs per year. It's easier to get one great song published and recorded than a hundred "pretty good" ones.

John Houston's words helped me with the craft of powerful rewriting. He believed very strongly that no matter how wonderful a scene is in a film, if it's "off the spine of the movie" it will weaken the film. Sometimes it's very hard to cut out those "darlings" but if you can't or won't do what it takes to make your film powerful, then you are not being true to your art.

A song is a three-minute movie playing to an audience with the attention span of a butterfly. Once you break the thread of your story, whether musically or lyrically, you've broken the spell and they fly away.

Barbara Rothstein (Director, MusiCONCEPTS, and songwriter with cuts in *The Barney Movie,* and by artists including Bobby Womack, Melba Moore, Kathy Lee Gifford, and Lisa Fisher)

Great songs are rarely written—they're rewritten (and rewritten and rewritten and . . .). Rewriting is one of a songwriter's most important tools. The exercises on pages 67 and 69 are designed to encourage you not to settle until each line is the strongest you can possibly make it.

Don't fall in love with your song until it's a hit. Always stay open for possible revision.

Russ Regan (Former CEO, Motown Records)

In his book, *Unlimited Power,* self-help guru Anthony Robbins writes that there is no greater predictor of success or failure in any venture than previous successes or failures of similar ventures under comparable conditions. For example, if you were considering opening a cookie store in a shopping mall in a

Midwestern city, and cookie stores like the one you were contemplating have fared well in malls in other Midwestern cities with similar populations, it would be a good indicator of likely success.

Tools, techniques, and formulas are no substitute for artistry and for expressing the unique gift that is within each writer. Craft will not take the place of an emotional song idea that starts in your heart and is bursting to get out. When you share your creativity with the world through your song, be sure that each line has been examined and is as strong as you can make it.

Remember that the tools presented within this section of the book are intended to help you express your creativity. They are not a substitute for an original, emotional idea that starts in your heart. Some of these techniques are probably new ways for you to approach the writing process and it's not realistic to expect to master them instantly. But with patience, practice, and persistence, these tools can be successfully assimilated into your own songs.

Exercise:
Rewriting the Lyric to an Existing Hit Song

Copy the lyric of a recent hit song that you love and wish you had written. Be sure to select one that was written by an "outside" writer.

In crafting your new lyric use the same:

- ♪ Basic idea (i.e., positive love song, sad love song, social issue song)
- ♪ Song structure (i.e., A - A - B - A, A - B - A - B - C - B)
- ♪ Number of lines in each section
- ♪ Rhyme scheme (i.e., rhyming lines 2 & 4 in the verses, 1 & 2 and 3 & 4 in the choruses)
- ♪ Approximate number of syllables in each line
- ♪ Tone of the lyric (i.e., clever, heartfelt, conversational, twists on words)

Create a new title, fresh images, and new ways to express the essence of the original lyric while using the same set of tools that led to success for the writer of the existing lyric.

I look for songs that set themselves apart from the pack; a different way of saying things, but something everyone can relate to. Try to bring something new to the game. Even though it is most difficult to find new ideas, that is really the key. Experience new things and see different parts of life. Find a new way to say something—not that you're going to find a new issue to cover on a regular basis, because most songs are about some type of love relationship (the good part, the bad part, or the ugly part). Express how people really feel without being contrived. I think the common factor in the songs I've gotten cut is a real direct link to human emotion: loss, true love, a good time. Find a way to tap into real emotion.

Lynn Gann (Professional Manager, Zomba Music Publishing)

Chapter 4
Writing for Specialty Markets

Be generous in granting permission for live performances of your "specialty" songs. This is still the best way for other artists to hear your songs and begin performing them.

Wayne Moore (Owner, Ducy Lee Recordings; cabaret performer; and songwriter/producer of music for television, film, and stage whose songs have been performed by artists including Michael Feinstein, Debbie Reynolds, Jill Eikenberry, Liz Torres, and Andrea Marcovicci)

In addition to writing mainstream pop, country, and R & B songs, there are many other genres songwriters might choose to explore. These include writing Christian, Latin, Christmas, folk/Americana, comedy, cabaret, and children's songs. The primary focus of this book is geared to the songwriter who wants to write mainstream radio hits. However, this chapter explores the special considerations a writer should be aware of when writing and marketing songs for auxiliary markets.

When gearing a song to any specific market it's important to remember that some lyrical and musical elements lend themselves to certain styles of songs and are quite inappropriate for others. For example, while poetic, offbeat, "nonlinear" lyrics may work well in an "alternative" pop or rock song, they'd be out of place in a children's song or a country song. It's important to use vocabulary and colloquialisms consistent with the genre you're writing for. For example, while a rap or urban song might include a phrase such as "chillin' with my homeboy," this would obviously be out of character in a country song. Likewise, some chords and melodies are better suited for particular types of songs. Dissonant melodies and complex chords may be just the ticket for writing an effective jazz song, but are not suitable for a country or folk song.

When writing for specialty markets the primary motivation needs to be a deep love of the music because these styles of music are rarely as lucrative as the mainstream markets. But, whether you write commercial pop, country, R & B, jazz, children's songs, New Age, Christmas songs, Christian songs or any other genre, if you write them because your heart draws you to the music, you'll enjoy success regardless of the amount of money you earn.

WRITING SUCCESSFUL CHILDREN'S SONGS

When my collaborator Karen Taylor-Good offered me the opportunity to co-write songs for country star Collin Raye's album of children's songs, I had never written a song for that market. We crafted our melodies and lyrics by incorporating the same tools and techniques that we'd use to write successful songs in any mainstream genre. For each song, we started with a fresh, interesting concept, an idea that we wanted to share with children. While avoiding being condescending, we were careful to choose vocabulary and concepts that would be easy for children to understand. Melodically, we strove to craft beautiful, memorable melodies that relied on simple, short phrases and repetition that a child could readily sing along with and remember. Both of our songs were included on Collin Raye's album and I learned that writing for the children's market required the same skills and considerations as writing for any other genre. The ultimate goal is to write quality songs that successfully communicate lyrically and melodically to your audience.

Think about what you want to impart to children. In this market, you have the opportunity to say things of value in a very direct way that the adult market is too hip or cynical for. Start with wanting to say something of importance; wanting to pass something on to children.

David Friedman (Composer of songs for *The Barney Movie, Aladdin and the King of Thieves,* and children's television shows *Happy Ness, Sky Dancers* and *Dragon Flyz;* conductor of Disney's "Beauty And The Beast," "Aladdin," "Pocahontas," and "The Hunchback Of Notre Dame")

The market for children's songs includes film, animated television shows, live action television shows, and musical theater pieces, as well as audio recordings. Many writers of children's songs are also performers who record and distribute their own albums. These albums are sold at artists' shows, and on the Internet, in addition to traditional methods of sales.

Animated family-oriented musical films have taken the place of live action movie musicals, such as *The King and I* and T*he Sound of Music.* Enormously popular animated musical films, such as *The Lion King, The Prince of Egypt,* and *Beauty and the Beast,* have provided outlets for songs that appeal both to children and their parents. Songs from these films, such as "A Whole New World," "Go The Distance," "Circle Of Life," and "Beauty And The Beast" have proven their appeal by becoming pop hits as well. Without talking down to children these songs use language and music that's accessible to the young audience, as well as their parents. When writing for children's films, the songs create an actual scene, driven by characters just as in any other musical theater piece. The lyric is crafted to further the story and is told from the point of view of the character.

There are melodic and lyrical considerations that must be taken into account when writing songs geared specifically for children. Simple, memorable melodies, and catchy, easy-to-sing choruses are found in most successful children's songs. Melodic lines that are crafted by using relatively few musical notes (and corresponding syllables) are easier to remember.

When you're writing for kids, just think wonderful songs. Don't think in terms of writing down to a kid. We used the same principles in writing the songs for the Barney scenes as we would in any sophisticated musical. Whatever your principles are, they're going to have to work for children, too.

Barbara Rothstein (Writer of songs for *The Barney Movie*)

Children typically sing between "middle C" and the "A" or "B" above it. For very young children (three to five years old) it's best to use a small melodic range—between five notes and one octave, and avoid melodies that include complex musical intervals. However, when writing for a project that's geared to a wide range of ages (i.e., a Disney musical) it's acceptable and advisable to include some melodies that are more sophisticated.

The subject matter and language must be accessible to children without being condescending. Choose words that your audience can readily understand. Lyrics can be both simple and powerful. When writing for this market, it can be fun and effective to sometimes incorporate "nonsense" words, or words that you've created, such as "super-duper-ific," "happy-yappiness," or "bippity-boppityboo." Successful children's lyrics typically have a specific, narrow focus. Their stories stick to one idea, follow a thread, and make sense. Likewise, it's best to be very direct in terms of expressing the emotion that's being conveyed. The children's market is not the place for impressionistic, "non-linear" lyrics. It's more effective to write: "I like hugs—I like smiles" than "Hugs and smiles are shadows of sunshine on winter snow."

Demo recordings of children's songs typically require less elaborate production than their mainstream counterparts. A well-produced piano/vocal or guitar/vocal demo that allows the listener to clearly hear the words and melody should be sufficient in most instances.

There are also important business matters to consider when working in the children's market. When approaching large film companies, such as Disney or Dreamworks, it is necessary to be represented by a publisher, or a theatrical agent who represents composers for television, film, and theatrical projects. These companies will rarely do business directly with songwriters. When writing for children's films or television shows, composers are typically paid an upfront, flat fee. They also receive the writer's share of the royalties generated by the sale of audio recordings, as well as performance royalties if the composition airs on television or radio. The writer rarely retains the publisher's portion of the royalties. Composers of music for children's television series are usually paid a weekly salary, as well as receiving performance royalties when the show airs on television.

There are occasions when a children's song, written specifically for a television show or film, is treated as a "work for hire." In these instances, the composer is paid a flat fee with no additional royalties for sales or performances. (See chapter 11 for a detailed explanation of royalties and "works for hire.")

As in all genres of music, networking plays a crucial role in successfully placing songs and generating income in the children's market. Unless your songs are placed in major films, television shows, or exceptionally successful albums, writing children's songs is not as lucrative as writing for mainstream radio formats. However, if that's where your heart leads you, it can be deeply satisfying and rewarding.

WRITING CHRISTIAN MUSIC

Many songwriters enjoy expressing their religious beliefs through their songs. The burgeoning Christian music market provides an outlet for many of these songs. "Christian music" includes styles of music from folk to heavy metal, rap to rock, and everything in between. What sets Christian music apart is its spiritual message—not the music, the melody, the instruments, the production values, or the quality of the performers. Many Christian artists, such as dc Talk and Jars of Clay, are as contemporary sounding as anything on pop radio.

Some writers make the mistake of thinking that their faith and the spiritual message of their songs override the necessity to write well-crafted songs. However, the best and most successful Christian songs present their messages with memorable melodies, catchy hooks, and well-crafted lyrics—all the same elements found in successful mainstream songs.

Faith and subject matter cannot be an excuse for substandard writing. The thing that makes Christian music unique is its message, not it's music.

Jim Van Hook (Chairman/CEO, Provident Music Group) as quoted in *Music Row* magazine.

The three largest Christian music companies are EMI Christian Music Group, Provident Music Group, and Word Entertainment. All of these companies are based in the Nashville area. EMI Christian Music Group includes Sparrow Records, Star Song Records, Forefront Records, EMI Gospel, re:think Records, Chordant Distribution Group, and EMI Christian Music Publishing. Their artists include Susan Ashton, Avalon, Steven Curtis Chapman, Andy Griffith, BeBe and CeCe Winans, Keaggy, Twila Paris, Newsboys, Charlie Peacock, and Margaret Becker.

Provident Music Group encompasses Benson Records, Diadem Music Group, Tattoo Records, Verity Records, Reunion Records, Essential Records, Brentwood Records, Ranson Records, and Brentwood-Benson Music Publishing. Their artists include Bob Carlisle, 4HIM, Jars of Clay, Dino, Clay Cross, Kathy Troccoli, Gary Chapman, and Michael W. Smith.

Word Entertainment includes Myrrh Records, Word Records, Squint Entertainment, the Gospel Music Division, Everland Entertainment, and Word International. Their artists include Anointed, Amy Grant, Sandy Patty, Petra, John Tesh, Point of Grace, Cindy Morgan, Carman, and Shirley Ceasar.

The larger Christian music publishing companies sign staff-writers, as well as artists who are also songwriters. As in any genre of music, those publishers that have a large staff of exclusive writers have less need to acquire songs that are written by outside writers. However, there are also smaller publishing companies that have success pitching songs to the Christian market. The performing rights organizations, the Gospel Music Association, and of course, networking can help you to find these companies. Christian/gospel music accounts for an estimated 4.5 percent of the domestic music market. In this genre, record sales are typically generated more from touring than from radio airplay.

———

As far as getting established as a songwriter or an artist, the Christian market is very different from the pop or country markets. The best advice I can give is to get involved in your local ministry at your church. If you're writing songs and not performing them yourself, find people who are performing in your local area and try to get them to perform your songs. Success has a lot to do with your local ministry—especially if you want to be an artist. Start working at it at a local level in your own church to get people to sing your songs. The cream rises to the top. If you're doing a great job you'll get noticed. Then enter some contests.

In the Christian market lyrics are based on one specific book—the Bible. It's hard to find a new and creative way to say the same things over and over. The writers who do break through are the ones who have an amazing talent. It takes a very poetic person to say what has already been said in new fresh ways, or come up with new ideas of how to put something in to music.

Marty Wheeler (Vice President Publishing, Brentwood-Benson Music Publishing)

———

It's very difficult for songwriters to earn their living by exclusively writing Christian songs. While a top five pop or country song may earn writers $100,000 to $300,000 in performance royalties, an equally successful Christian song may generate only $1,000 to $3,000, because there are relatively few radio stations that play Christian music. Those stations that do play Christian music tend to be smaller than the major pop and country radio stations and pay lower licensing fees to the performing rights organizations. (You'll learn more about licensing fees and performing rights organizations in chapter 11.) Those songwriters (who are not also artists) who earn their living by writing Christian songs tend to be those who procure numerous recordings of their songs on a regular basis—typically by co-writing with successful artists. Many Christian artists write or co-write some, or all, of their own material. However, some Christian artists rely on outside songs. As in other musical genres, an extraordinary song can still break through.

Any competent music publisher should be able to pitch songs for the Christian music market. However, if your primary focus is writing for this market, it is probably best to work with a publisher who is an integral part of the Christian music business. He or she will be more likely to have the personal relationships that are so important to successful song plugging, and will likely have better knowledge of which artists are currently looking for songs, as well as a better ability to discern which songs are best-suited for specific Christian artists.

Contests, like those sponsored by the Gospel Music Association, are a good way to gain exposure for Christian music. (For more about contests, see chapter 14.) It can also help to network with other songwriters and artists at Christian music festivals. (See the appendix for a listing of Christian music festivals, as well as additional resources for writers of Christian songs.)

CRAFTING COMEDY SONGS

The most important consideration in crafting a successful comedy song is that it be funny—and accomplishing that can be a serious matter. Elements that may contribute to making a song funny include a fresh, humorous point of view about a familiar situation; something unexpected; puns; twists on words; outrageous characters; and a story or situation that makes people laugh.

There are two types of comedy songs: parodies of existing songs and original humorous songs.

Parodies

Parodies are funny imitations of previously existing material. When writing song parodies, the original melody remains the same as the song the parody is based upon. However, a new, funny lyric replaces the original. For example, Cledus T. Judd turned Deana Carter's "Did I Shave My Legs For This" into "Did I Shave My Back For This," and "Weird Al" Yankovic transformed Michael Jackson's "Beat It" into "Eat It" with hilarious results.

When planning to write a song parody, it's essential to secure permission from the publishers of the song you are parodying. You must also determine the extent to which you'll be compensated for your efforts. In some instances, publishers may grant the right to allow a parody to be written and recorded; however, they may or may not consent to sharing the performance or mechanical royalties with the writer of the parody. This means that there are instances in which the writer of the comedy lyric earns nothing when the parody is played on the radio, or when recordings are sold. When recordings of the parody are sold or are performed on radio or television, the writers of the original song earn the same royalty as if their original version were being played or sold.

The same ingredients that make a ballad a hit song make a comedy song a hit song—a good story, well told.

Ray Methvin (Producer/writer of comedy album by Shane Caldwell, songwriter, with cuts by artists including Clay Walker, Chris LeDoux)

If you're a comedy artist, in addition to being the songwriter, it may benefit you to include a parody of a hit song on your own album even if you don't participate in the writer's royalties. If your parody becomes a comedy hit, you'll earn royalties *as the artist* as a result of album sales. However, you can see why it's crucial to reach an agreement regarding royalties if you do not plan to perform your own parodies. (For additional information about royalties see chapter 11.)

Original Comedy Songs

Songs in this category are original songs intended to make the listener laugh or smile. They may rely on outrageous situations, puns, twists on words, sarcasm, or other techniques to evoke humor. Some comedy songs are mildly humorous, while others can be described as slapstick—broad, boisterous comedy. Successful original comedy songs include "The Monster Mash" and "Grandma Got Run Over By A Reindeer."

There are several melodic considerations to keep in mind when writing for this market. First of all keep your melodies simple to allow the listener to focus on the lyric, which is the most important aspect of a comedy song. Secondly, performers of comedy songs are not typically known for their vocal abilities. Most comedians have a limited vocal range and may not be able to make intricate melodic moves. For this reason, it is best to restrict the melodic range of a comedy song to approximately one octave and avoid tricky intervals that may be difficult for a "non-singer" to sing.

Artists who record comedy songs sometimes enlist the help of a well-known singer to sing the choruses, while the comedy artist performs the verses—the spoken word portion. This practice accomplishes two things: it adds to the quality of the recording by letting an accomplished vocalist sing the chorus, and lends a recognizable name to add credibility to the project and encourage radio programmers to play the single. For example, Alan Jackson sang the choruses of Jeff Foxworthy's hit "Redneck Games," and Bill Engvall's country hit "The Sign" featured Travis Tritt.

Most importantly, a comedy song needs a new point of view about a familiar situation; something unexpected. And it should get quickly to the point. If you have the opportunity to write "specialty" material for a particular artist, try to write in the distinctive voice of that artist. Ask yourself how he or she would tell the joke if they were speaking rather than singing. Find something true in that performer's life to write about, whether for a comedy song or not, and that truth will resonate with both the artist and the audience. Keep the melody simple so your listeners can focus on the lyrics. It has to be funny.

Wayne Moore (Accompanist and/or writer of material for comedy performers including Joan Rivers, Debbie Reynolds, Liz Torres, and Rose Marie)

The comedy song market is extremely limited. While there are hundreds of successful mainstream recording artists, there are only a handful of well-known artists who record comedy songs. These include Adam Sandler, Jeff Foxworthy, "Weird Al" Yankovic, Cledus T. Judd, Tom Lehrer, the Capitol Steps, Ray Stevens, and Bill Engvall. Many successful performers of comedy songs write or co-write their own material and few major publishers actively seek out or pitch comedy songs. As in other musical genres, networking plays a key role in successfully placing comedy songs with performers, publishers, and recording artists. Performing your songs at writer's nights and encouraging other artists to perform your songs gives them increased exposure. The Songwriters Guild of America/National Academy of Songwriters (see appendix) sponsors "Song Mania," a monthly comedy songwriter's night and competition in Nashville. In addition to being great fun, it offers an excellent networking opportunity for writers of comedy songs.

When pitching a comedy song, an elaborately produced, full-band demo is rarely required. In most circumstances, a well-produced guitar/vocal or keyboard/vocal demo is sufficient. Since the lyric is the most important component of a successful comedy song, it's crucial that the words can be easily understood. The demo singer's comic timing and delivery will also play a major role in conveying the potential of your song.

Ideas for comedy songs can be found in jokes, films, television; on T-shirts, greeting cards, and the Internet; or anywhere else you might find ideas for mainstream songs. Writing effective comedy songs may appear deceptively simple, but it's not easy to make people laugh. If you want to write successful comedy songs, in addition to analyzing hit comedy albums, it can be helpful to study comedy-writing techniques that can be found in books for stand-up comedians and writers in other comedy fields.

WRITING FOLK/AMERICANA SONGS

Folk music encompasses a wide range of musical styles, including traditional folk, songs written by contemporary singer/songwriters, bluegrass, protest songs, Celtic, ethnic, and even polka music. Americana refers to the radio format that plays contemporary folk artists, such as Nancy Griffith, John Gorka, the Woodys, Gillian Welch, and Patty Larkin. This format also plays bluegrass music, and songs by alternative country artists such as Kim Richie, Guy Clark, and Steve Earle. Contemporary folk songs are written as forms of personal expression and aren't bound by the same rules that apply to pop, country, and R & B songs. The words, images, and stories that are included in the lyrics of successful contemporary folk songs would typically be considered too personal, poetic, or, in some instances, too controversial for other mainstream genres.

Traditional folk music is based largely on Appalachian songs. These Appalachian songs evolved from the fifteenth and sixteenth century Scottish, Irish, and English airs that immigrants later brought with them when they moved to the United States. The songs we call "traditional folk songs" have been passed down through the generations.

The 1960s saw a resurgence in the popularity of folk music, with artists including Peter, Paul & Mary, Judy Collins, the Kingston Trio, the Weavers, and

Joan Baez performing and recording traditional folk songs. However, many of these successful artists also recorded songs by contemporary folk artists such as Bob Dylan and Phil Ochs. Some of these songs, such as "Blowin' In The Wind," "Puff, The Magic Dragon," and "Where Have All The Flowers Gone," have become such an integral part of our musical milieu that they seem as though they're traditional folk songs. Easy-to-sing memorable melodies, simple straightforward lyrics, and stories that appeal to listeners of all ages and backgrounds have made these songs modern classics.

I don't sit down and set up a structure and force a song. I just write what I'm feeling inside but it seems that a lot of folk artists write because they've got to write. Although, I don't feel like I'm writing for a "market," fortunately, a market has presented itself for this kind of music, because it really has something to say. It's powerful, personal, and intelligent. Writers in this market strive to come up with uncommon metaphors and unusual lyrics that people find riveting because it's not the same trite sentiment they've heard over and over. In the folk and Americana market the best writers take a few momentous things that happen in people's lives and transform them into real poetry. They're the modern day troubadours.

Carol Elliott (Kerrville Folk Festival performer featured on *The Women of Kerrville* album; winner of the Wrangler Award for Best Western Song of the Year, recorded by Michael Martin Murphy)

The vast majority of folk singers perform their own material. The contemporary folk scene is dominated by performing songwriters who were influenced by traditional folk music and now write their own songs. It's very difficult for a writer who is not a performer to earn a living writing folk songs. Even the most successful folk recordings rarely sell more than 50,000 to 100,000 units, and many very talented artists sell as few as 10,000 units. Although artists such as Shawn Colvin and Tracy Chapman have emerged from the folk scene to win Grammys and sell hundreds of thousands of albums, most listeners now consider them as pop artists.

Many contemporary folk singer/songwriters earn a large portion of their income by recording their own albums and selling them, following performances at folk festivals, coffeehouses, and concerts in private homes (known as "house concerts").

It's very difficult to make a living in the folk genre. It involves a lot of hard work. In most cases you're doing everything yourself. You're your own booking agent, your own publisher, and manager, and that's a lot of full-time jobs for one person. So know that that's what you want to do and believe in it. Try and write the best songs that you can write—the ones that feel good to you. Don't copy other people's work or try to conform to a certain formula in your writing. While that may work in some markets, it's probably not the way to go in folk music.

I just try to write a good song; one that communicates something worth hearing, or feeling, or knowing about, in a way that people can understand—if not on a literal level, on an emotional level. Songwriting speaks to people's hearts even more than their intellects. The brain is only part of the equation. For me, when I'm writing it, a good song makes me think, "Wow—this is cool, I think I'm onto something here."

Buddy Mondlock (Performer and recording artist whose songs have been recorded by artists including Peter, Paul & Mary, Garth Brooks, Janis Ian, Nancy Griffith, and Joan Baez)

These artists are not necessarily looking for other artists to record their songs. However, some savvy pop and country artists keep a finger on the pulse of what's happening in the contemporary folk community because some of the most original, powerful songs have emerged from that genre. Bette Midler, Garth Brooks, Kathy Mattea, and Rod Stewart are just a few of the mainstream artists who have recorded contemporary folk songs. Often, these songs find their way to recording artists via unconventional routes. While they are occasionally pitched by publishers, more often these songs are stumbled upon by an artist who hears them being performed live at a coffeehouse or folk festival, or hears the song on a contemporary folk artist's CD.

Many of the major publishing companies sign one or more folk-oriented singer/songwriters to acquire songs that might be appropriate for those mainstream artists who occasionally record material that's more left of center. These companies can be found by networking with other songwriters and by referrals from songwriters' organizations.

Folk festivals offer an excellent opportunity to network with other songwriters and performers, as well as a chance to hear artists who are successful in this genre. Many of the festivals sponsor songwriting classes, song camps, and competitions that have served as stepping stones for many artists to launch or advance their careers.

The Folk Alliance website (http:www.folk.org/links/falinks.html) is a tremendous resource for songwriters and artists in the folk genre. This website offers links to folk festivals, as well as folk societies and organizations, performance venues, song camps and conferences, record companies and distributors, radio stations, print media, agents, managers, promoters, and performing artists.

CRAFTING SUCCESSFUL CHRISTMAS SONGS

Find different ways of saying the same old thing. Before Mel Torme and Bob Wells wrote "The Christmas Song" you never heard the lines "And folks dressed up like eskimos" or "Jack Frost nipping at your nose." What a wonderful way to say, "It's cold outside." With the imagery you can feel the sensation.

Justin Wilde (Publisher, Christmas & Holiday Music; writer and publisher of the five-million-selling "It Must Have Been The Mistletoe," which has been included on thirteen compilation albums and recorded by artists including Barbara Mandrell, Kathy Lee Gifford, and Vicky Carr, as well as cuts with Ray Charles and Loretta Lynn)

It's not surprising that many songwriters dream of writing the next "White Christmas." Irving Berlin's holiday classic has sold more than thirty million singles, making it the best-selling song of all time. A successful Christmas song can generate income for many years and has the potential to be recorded by multiple artists. However, there are far fewer slots for Christmas songs than for non-seasonal songs.

The majority of the songs recorded on Christmas albums are standards. Most fans purchase Christmas albums to hear their favorite artists' renditions of the Christmas standards they grew up listening to. Anne Murray has recorded three Christmas albums and out of the more than thirty cuts there was only one original song. A large percentage of the original (non-standard) songs included on Christmas albums are written by the artist, the producer, or another individual "inside" the project. Your Christmas song must be incredible enough to make the artist or producer bump one of the standards or their original songs to put yours on. The competition is fierce because only a handful of artists record Christmas songs each year. There are only so many Christmas images out there, so you have to work extra hard to craft fresh, unique lyrics in order to have your song rise above the competition. However, as in any style of music, the extraordinary songs usually find a way to break through.

What I look for in Christmas songs is the same thing any non-seasonal publisher would look for. If you want a Christmas song to become a standard, it has to have a melody that is so memorable that after you've heard it three or four times you should be able to hum the majority of the melody. It should be something that the average man or woman can sing a cappella on the front porch steps or in a rest home.

Justin Wilde (Songwriter/Publisher, Christmas & Holiday Music)

Christmas songs are typically recorded from December to July, prior to the Christmas season when they are released. Depending on schedules, some artists record their Christmas album during the Christmas holidays for the following year. If the album is one of those that is recorded live during Christmas, with a choir and orchestra, the songs are typically selected by the previous August or

September, which is fifteen or sixteen months prior to the album's release. The bulk of country Christmas albums are completed by the end of May, while pop and R & B Christmas albums are sometimes recorded up through the July prior to their Christmas season release.

I listen to everything that comes through the door and I've gotten cuts on songs from unpublished writers, but they sent me brilliant material. You have to go through 150 to 200 pieces of junk to find that gem.

Justin Wilde (Songwriter/Publisher, Christmas & Holiday Music)

Any reputable publisher should be aware of which artists are recording Christmas albums—and should be capable of getting material to those artists, or those who screen songs for them. Justin Wilde's Christmas & Holiday Music is the

Exercise:
Writing Christmas Lyrics

When writing a Christmas lyric many developing songwriters rely on cliches like:

The snow was falling
The stockings were hung in front of the fire
The presents were under the tree

This exercise is designed to help you generate interesting, fresh, unique lyrics for Christmas songs.

1. Think about a memorable or special Christmas.
2. Jot down your recollections. (You don't need to rhyme or be concerned about meter.)
3. Compose a list of words, phrases, and images that relate to those Christmas memories. Be specific and be sure to include colors, details, and actions.
4. Incorporate your personal memories into a Christmas lyric.

foremost publisher of holiday music and has placed holiday songs with artists including Anita Baker, Vince Gill, Toby Keith, Johnny Mathis, Tanya Tucker, Melissa Manchester, and the Brooklyn Tabernacle Choir. Write to Christmas & Holiday Music, Attn: Justin Wilde, 3517 Warner Blvd., Suite 4, Burbank, CA 91505, for song submission guidelines. Website: christmassongs.com.

First, if you look at all the Christmas standards like "Winter Wonderland," "Chestnuts Roasting...," "White Christmas," and all those other evergreens, they have very simplistic, memorable melodies that are easy to assimilate. Kenny Rogers used to say that he looks for songs that the common man can sing along with. So you don't want something with a range over an octave and a fourth. You want to write something that people in high schools and community centers can carry off.

Second, the lyric should function completely by itself without the benefit of melody. When people tell me, "Well, it works with the track," that's a cop out. If you look at the lyrics of all of the Christmas standards, as well as any of the standards from the golden age of songwriting, they hold up on the written page without a melody.

Third, do not write anything negative unless you are writing a blues song. In a blues song, you can say "My baby left me and I'm lonesome and blue for the holidays." Otherwise, don't bother. In my experience, people don't want to hear about people being out on the street and homeless for Christmas. They want to hear about happy, positive, inspiring stuff.

Justin Wilde (Songwriter/Publisher, Christmas & Holiday Music)

WRITING CABARET SONGS

Cabaret songs are intended primarily for performance in intimate nightclub settings. Occasionally, some of these songs may be recorded or performed in larger venues. However, they're first and foremost conceived as a vehicle for a performer to emotionally connect with his or her audience in a small cabaret, bar, or lounge.

The key to writing cabaret songs is storytelling. A successful cabaret song should be inherently theatrical (without going over the top), drawing the audience into a story that is ostensibly about the performer. For instance, instead of saying "I love you, baby," the song could be about the singer meeting the girl, stumbling over the furniture, dreaming of an impossible affair, and then—surprise!—she feels the same way. In cabaret, each song is an "act" unto itself and you have to interest the audience all over again with each new story you tell. Remember that this material will generally be performed live, so clear away the clutter. A simple, catchy melody attached to surprising, personal lyrics makes a song that people want to perform.

Wayne Moore (Owner, Ducy Lee Recordings; cabaret performer)

Cabaret songs are not bound by the rules and structures that are typically required for success in mainstream genres—the composer has free rein to express him- or herself. Songs written specifically for cabaret performance often have much in common with the Broadway standards that frequently comprise a large part of cabaret performers' repertoires. Lyrically, they cover a wide range of expression and topics. These songs may be deeply personal, poignant, happy, sad, or funny. But ideally, they evoke some strong emotion.

Cabaret shows are typically produced by the artists themselves. Therefore, if an artist falls in love with your song and wants to include it in his or her performance, there are no additional hurdles to overcome. Many songwriters in this and other specialty styles produce their own albums partly in the hopes that their song will find its way into the hands of other recording artists. The various performing rights organizations handle payment for live cabaret performances differently. If you're primarily writing material that's geared for live performance in a nightclub setting, contact the performing rights organizations to determine which society will best suit your needs. ASCAP's New York office sponsors a highly successful cabaret showcase. (For additional information about performing rights organizations, see chapter 11 and the appendix.)

In cabaret you write songs just for the love of writing and give them to people. It's a more accessible market than the pop and other mainstream markets. There's a lot of brilliant material that comes out of this market. In cabaret you can start from the true reason that we write—for the joy of it. It's different from writing from the point of view of "What do they want?" or "How do I get this cut?" We start from "What is my heart saying?" and "How do I want to say this?" You can use more range of language and emotion in this market. Cabaret can be one of the most satisfying mediums, but it's not lucrative—it's a labor of love.

David Friedman (Academy Award–nominated songwriter/producer of albums by Nancy LaMott)

WRITING FOR THE LATIN MARKET

It was 12 degrees in Nashville when I received a call, asking me to present a songwriting seminar for BMI in San Juan, Puerto Rico. Needless to say, I jumped at the chance to teach in such a beautiful (and warm) setting. It wasn't until after all the business and travel arrangements were concluded that I was informed that the songs I'd be critiquing, following my lecture, would be in Spanish!

It had been more than a few years since I'd struggled through high school Spanish, and I'd had very little exposure to the Latin music market. I had no idea what elements went into hit songs in the Puerto Rican or other Latin markets. Therefore, I sadly said that I probably was not qualified to teach the seminar. Luckily, the seminar's organizers felt differently. It didn't take too much effort to convince me that by studying the hit songs on the Latin charts, I'd be able to learn the differences from and similarities to successful songs on mainstream radio in the United States. BMI agreed to provide interpreters to help with translations, as well as copies of the six biggest hit CDs in the Latin market.

When I listened to the albums that were the current Latin top sellers, the first thing that struck me was the wide spectrum of styles that Latin music encompassed. Just as "American" music runs the gamut from traditional country songs, to gangsta rap, adult contemporary ballads, Broadway show tunes, grunge rock, folk, R & B, and heavy metal, "Latin" music includes an equally wide variety of styles. The Latin hits included teen pop songs, adult contemporary ballads, pop/rock songs reminiscent of Sheryl Crow (but sung in Spanish), funky synthesizer-driven dance music, and songs by quirky, "alternative" sounding singer/songwriters—all in addition to the sizzling tropical rhythms I had expected.

The only difference in writing for the Latin market is the language. If you have a favorite artist, study that artist's past productions. Seek contacts through the label copy information. The label copy may list the record company and management company, through which the composer could inquire where and when the next recording is taking place, who the producer is, and where to send the demo. Network, network, network and have many demos available for distribution to those contacts made from networking. If you wholeheartedly want to become a songwriter, "perseverance" is the key.

Diane Almodovar (Senior Director, Latin Music, BMI)

I began by analyzing the song structures and I found that the majority of the popular Latin songs were constructed using the same structures commonly heard on the radio in the United States: Verse - Chorus - Verse - Chorus and Verse - Chorus - Verse - Chorus - Bridge - Chorus structures seemed to heavily predominate.

Next, I examined the rhyme schemes. With a few exceptions, I found that the majority of the hit songs in the Latin market employed rhymes in the same places where I would expect to find them in their American counterparts.

One of the most interesting things I noticed was how easy it was for me to identify the titles of most of the songs—even though I couldn't understand the meaning of their words. As in so many of the successful English-language hits, the melodies were crafted in such a way that the titles seemed to "jump out" of the songs. (In chapter 5, you will learn how to accomplish this very important technique.)

When I studied the translations of the Latin hits, I found they had much in common with American songs. The ideas typically had universal appeal (mostly dealing with some aspect of love) and they seemed to possess some unique angle, an interesting title, and a fresh approach. However, in many of the Spanish-language hits there were far more syllables and words per line than would typically be heard in successful English-language songs. The Spanish lyrics I analyzed were often very passionate and poetic. They frequently incorporated images that would be considered too "flowery" and not conversational enough to be effective in the U.S. market. I suspect I learned as much as, if not more than, my students in San Juan. I was introduced to some exceptionally talented Latin artists and songwriters, and I became a fan of some wonderful music.

Most major publishers, such as Warner Chappell, Sony Music, Universal, and BMG, have Latin publishing divisions based in Miami, Florida. ASCAP and BMI also maintain Miami offices that deal primarily with Latin music. Billboard's *International Latin Music Buyer's Guide* is an excellent resource for songwriters who want to write for the Latin market (see appendix).

LYRIC CHECKLIST

Photocopy this checklist and keep it where you normally write. Each time you finish a draft of a song, check to be sure that it has successfully incorporated the tools and techniques that follow:

☐ Adheres to one of the most successful song structures

☐ Has an interesting title and idea

☐ Has a universal theme—not too personal for others to relate to

☐ Makes the singer look good

☐ Has verse lyrics that clearly lead to the title

☐ Contains one focused idea

☐ Evokes one emotion

☐ Maintains one consistent tense

☐ Uses correct pronouns

☐ Contains opening lines that "grab" the listener and set the emotional tone

☐ Maintains one consistent tone and style throughout

☐ Uses fresh imagery

☐ Sounds conversational

☐ Avoids clichés

☐ Is not redundant

☐ Second verse adds new information

☐ Doesn't preach

☐ Doesn't "tell" how the singer feels—the listener feels it

☐ Bridge (if applicable) adds a new angle

☐ Each line logically flows from the previous line and into the following line

☐ Employs rhymes in appropriate places

☐ Has a title that "pays off"

Step III
Composing Memorable Melodies

The important thing about the melody is that it has something that you can't get out of your mind. It could be two o'clock in the morning and next thing you know you're singing the chorus.

Tommy LiPuma (Chairman, The GRP Recording Company; recipient of eighteen gold and platinum records, thirty Grammy nominations, and two Grammy Awards; co-producer, Natalie Cole's *Unforgettable* LP; producer of Anita Baker, George Benson, Diana Krall, and Al Jarreau)

Chapter 5
Learning Effective Melody Writing Skills

My most successful songs were easily singable. I have a built-in acid test in my six-year-old son who winds up singing my most singable songs. I'm not encouraging people to write a nursery rhyme type of song but to ask, "Can the layman actually sing the song or is it too complicated for them to grasp?"

I want it to be singable, not only by the artist but by the people who hear it and primarily, by me. I have to enjoy singing the song myself. If I sit there and I want to hear it over and over, inevitably, that's the test that tells me if the song is going to work. With certain demos you finish, some you never want to hear again and some, you want to hear over and over. I want the song to speak to me when I've finished writing it.

Steve Diamond (Hit songwriter/producer)

I've heard too many publishers and industry professionals say, "The melody's not catchy enough," "It's not 'hooky' enough," "The melody's just not memorable"—but they have never told me *how* to make it catchier, "hookier," or more memorable. In chapters 5 to 7, you'll learn there are specific tools and techniques that you can use to craft catchy, memorable melodies that communicate the feeling you intend to evoke.

This section of the book is geared to songwriters, like myself, who have little or no musical training. I've attempted to study music theory several times, but it never quite makes sense or sinks in. Nonetheless, this lack of training has not stopped me from writing melodies to hit songs. The chapters that follow identify and explain the elements of successful, memorable melodies in non-technical, plain English.

WRITING *A CAPPELLA*

A cappella means without instrumental accompaniment. Writing *a cappella* means composing melodies in your head, without a guitar or a piano. For me (and for many of my songwriting students) it's been the ticket to crafting the strongest melodies.

When I was just beginning my career in Los Angeles, my father accompanied me to a songwriting workshop during one of his visits. The guest speakers were Jay Livingston and Ray Evans, writers of standards including "Que Sera, Sera," "Silver Bells," "Mona Lisa," and the theme from the classic television show *Mr. Ed.* After watching these two pros musically punctuate their points from their perch at the piano, my father said he didn't think I could possibly write hit songs because of my limited musical knowledge and inability to play the piano.

I couldn't deny that outside of the clarinet lessons I took as a child, I had very little musical training or knowledge of music theory. When I attended my first songwriting workshop, I was indeed one of those who raised their hands when the instructor asked, "Who writes lyrics only?" I didn't play piano or guitar, so I assumed that meant I could not write melody. I was confusing the ability to play a musical instrument with the ability to compose catchy, memorable melodies in my head. I've since learned that they are two distinct and very different skills.

Over the years, I've taken a few guitar lessons and learned some basic chords. But like so many developing songwriters, I made the mistake of composing melodies by strumming chords and allowing them to lead me to the next predictable notes that sounded good with those chords. I wrote lots of boring,

---

Exercise:
Writing *A Cappella*

♪ Write three original catchy chorus melodies by singing into a tape recorder without using any instrument. (For the purposes of this exercise, do not write an accompanying lyric unless you choose to after you have finished your melodies.)

♪ Write your next five songs *a cappella* before deciding if this is an effective way for you to strengthen your melody writing.

uninspired melodies this way. Needless to say, none of them brought me any closer to writing a hit song.

Then I tried a new approach: I accepted that I was probably never going to be a very good guitarist or keyboard player, but I wasn't willing to let that hold me back. My solution was to try writing a melody by simply singing it into a portable tape recorder. After all, most individuals do not have a piano or a guitar in their shower or their car, yet they still have the ability to sing a memorable melody in the shower, or while driving on the highway. It's melody that people sing and remember—not chords.

> *First and foremost, a great melody makes a great song; something that connects emotionally. Don't let the craft get in the way of the passion.*
>
> Steve Lunt (Senior Director of A & R for Jive Records and songwriter of hits including Cyndi Lauper's "She-Bop")

I'm not implying that finding the most effective chords is not important. But I'm not willing to let my limitations in figuring out chords and playing a musical instrument stop me from writing hit songs. I tend to collaborate with songwriters who are better than I am at figuring out the chords that will best support our melody. When writing alone, I hire a guitarist or keyboardist to bring forth the chords I hear in my head. I ask the musician to play me all of the options and when I hear them, I recognize the chords I had in mind. This process rarely takes more than thirty minutes and does not constitute a collaboration unless that is your choice.

My first success as a songwriter came when I had a song recorded by the 5th Dimension. The song was called "On Love Tonight" and I wrote 100 percent of it without ever touching a musical instrument until the melody and lyric were finished. I could clearly hear the chords in my head, but had no idea what they were or how to play them. I enlisted the help of a friend who was a step ahead of me in the chord department to translate what I heard in my head. He observed that I had employed modulations (key changes) and chords that were quite unexpected and unorthodox. I have no doubt that the freshness of the melody was a big factor in getting that song recorded. Knowledge of musical theory can be helpful, and you should study it if you're so inclined. But I've managed to have success by simply singing melodies that sounded good to me—without knowing what the next chord "should" be according to classic music theory. Remember:

- ♪ Playing a musical instrument is not a requirement for writing a hit song.
- ♪ Knowing how to read music is not a prerequisite for writing great melodies. (You just have to be able to hear them in your head and find a way to get them out.)
- ♪ Knowledge of musical theory is not necessary to compose successful songs.

I know that writing *a cappella* works. Still, I was amazed to learn that singer/songwriter Seal had composed and arranged his Grammy-winning smash hit "Kiss From A Rose" by singing all of the instrumental parts into a tape recorder. Stephen Sondheim, a proficient pianist and composer of some of the most richly textured and complex melodies on Broadway and in popular music, has said that he often chooses to compose his melodies without the aid of an instrument. Sting has also been quoted as saying that he frequently writes his melodies *a cappella*. If it's good enough for Sting, Seal, and Sondheim. . . . After attending more workshops than I can count, and writing (and rewriting) hundreds of songs, I have gone from believing I am "only a lyricist" to writing melodies for hit songs by singing them into a tape recorder. Although I've become a much better guitarist, I still never use an instrument when writing melodies.

Since writing melody (or writing melody without an instrument) may be a new experience for you, be patient with yourself. It's unrealistic to expect to master this skill with the first few attempts. The fact that you may not be an expert melody writer today does not preclude the possibility of composing hit melodies in the future—*whether you play an instrument or not.*

KEEPING IT SIMPLE AND SINGABLE (K.I.S.S.)

Remember that your goal as a songwriter is to deliver your idea from your heart to the listener—both lyrically and melodically. Your objective is to communicate. But when composing melody, the language available to us is comprised of notes, rhythms, and chords—instead of words, images, and rhymes.

Many developing songwriters make the process of melody writing more difficult than it needs to be. They make the mistake of composing complicated melodic lines that are too intricate for a non-singer to retain. It's impossible for the average listener to remember or sing melodic phrases that are excessively long and complex. For example, it's easier to remember:

"I love you"

than

"I want you to know that there's no doubt in my heart whatsoever that there's a feeling I want to share with you and you can always know that no matter where I am I love you."

It's easier for listeners to remember and sing whatever melody might accompany the simple phrase "I love you" than any melody that could correspond with the rambling second phrase.

> *The best melodies are simple, easy to remember, and easy to sing along with. However, the knack is being simple without being run-of-the mill.*
>
> Jeff Fenster (Senior Vice President of Artists & Repertoires, Island/Def Jam Records)

If your audience does not connect emotionally with your melody, your melody has not done its job—and it's easier for listeners to feel an emotional connection to a melody they can easily sing and retain. Remember the acronym, K.I.S.S. (Keep It Simple and Singable).

USING HYMNS AND CHILDREN'S SONGS FOR MELODIC INSPIRATION

> *There is no question in my mind that if a non-performer feels comfortable whistling, singing, or sharing a piece of music with their neighbor it's going to linger.*
>
> Noel Paul Stookey (Peter, Paul & Mary), as quoted in *Performing Songwriter* magazine.

I once read an interview in which Elton John said that at times, he has drawn inspiration for his melodies from hymns. I thought about why that might be the case and concluded that hymns have melodies that are intended for "non-singers" to sing. Almost anyone can sing "Amazing Grace" or "Rock of Ages."

Exercise:

Writing a Melody Based on a Hymn and a Children's Song

1. Write a melody that has the same number of syllables and uses similar rhythms and some of the same notes as a favorite hymn. (If you can't think of one, try "Rock of Ages.")

2. Repeat the exercise, modeling your melody on a famous children's song.

They have endured throughout the years largely because they are easy for millions of "non-singers" to remember and sing along with. Isn't that a primary goal of popular songwriting?

Likewise, classic children's songs from "Twinkle Twinkle Little Star" to "Mary Had A Little Lamb" and the theme song for "Barney" can be powerful melodic models. I've even written a very successful verse melody based upon the notes that children sing when teasing each other with "Na-Na-Na-Na-Na-Na."

Children's songs are easy to retain and to sing because:

♪ The phrases are short and concise.

♪ They employ melodic and/or rhythmic repetition.

♪ The melodic intervals (the space from one note to the next) tend to be close to each other and, therefore, are easy to remember

MAKING IT OBVIOUS WHERE THE TITLE GOES—WITHOUT THE LYRIC

After hearing a melody one time, there should be no doubt in the listener's mind where the title will occur within the song. The portion of melody that contains the title needs to jump out and separate itself from the rest of the melody. This can be accomplished by any of the following techniques, or by a combination of more than one of them.

Altering the Range

The title can be sung using notes that are higher or lower than the rest of the melody. An example of the title being higher than the surrounding melodic phrases can be found in "Over The Rainbow." Sing through a verse of that classic song and you'll see that the title line includes notes that are indeed higher than the notes in the rest of the song. In "Somewhere In My Broken Heart" (written by Billy Dean and Richard Leigh) the title, which is at the end of each verse, is set apart by notes that are lower than the rest of the verse.

Varying the Rhythm

A rhythm that is different from the rhythms employed in the rest of the song can effectively set your title apart. An example of a song that used this technique with great success is Gary Baker and Frank J. Myers' "I Swear" (recorded by All-4-One and John Michael Montgomery). Sing the chorus and you'll find that the notes that accompany those title words are held out longer than any other notes in the surrounding phrases.

Inserting Pauses

The title can also be set apart from the rest of the melody by employing a brief pause immediately preceding the melodic phrase that encompasses the title. A strong example of this technique can be found at the end of the chorus in Diane Warren's "How Do I Live," which was a hit for both Trisha Yearwood and LeAnn Rimes.

MARRYING THE MUSIC TO THE LYRIC: PROSODY

To achieve prosody, the melody should sound as if it is happily married to the lyric it accompanies, and vice versa. A melody that makes the listener feel happy should accompany a lyric that has a positive, pleasant message. Likewise, a lyric that conveys sadness should be expressed melodically with notes, chords, and musical phrases that evoke a similar feeling of sadness. Minor chords typically contribute to a sad-sounding melody, while major chords can have the opposite effect.

Great melodies are simple, memorable, and enhance the mood and emotions set forth in the lyric.

George Teren (Writer of country hits, "Busy Man," "She's Sure Taking It Well," "Running Out Of Reasons To Run," and cuts with artists including Trisha Yearwood, John Michael Montgomery, Tim McGraw, and Lorrie Morgan)

Tape recording your melody, without any lyric, can help you be sure that your melody and lyric work together. Either play your melody instrumentally (or have someone play it for you), or sing it *a cappella* using a nonsense syllable, like "La" or "Ooh." Listen back to the melody and ask yourself what feelings it evokes. If it's not consistent with the emotion of the lyric, it's definitely time for a rewrite.

According to Michael Hollandsworth, V.P./G.M. Zomba Music Group, "It's the total combination of lyric and melody that makes a song a hit." Although the lyric and melody may have been rewritten many times, the final version of your song should sound as though the words and music fit so perfectly together that the listener cannot imagine another melody accompanying that lyric, or another lyric working with that melody.

VARYING THE RHYTHMS

The use of different rhythms in the various sections of a song helps to maintain the listener's interest. Using similar rhythms in the verses, choruses, and bridge tends to be boring and makes it difficult for the listeners to differentiate the chorus from the verse. For example, if your verses are comprised primarily of long, held-out notes (i.e., half notes or whole notes) your song will have added contrast if your chorus takes a more rhythmic approach, using shorter notes (i.e., quarter notes and eighth notes), or vice versa.

If you do a study of the hits on the radio you'll hear that the majority of them incorporate different rhythms in the various sections of the song. Examples of songs that successfully varied the rhythms to differentiate the verses from the chorus include "Unbreak My Heart" (written by Diane Warren and recorded by Toni Braxton), "Blue" (written by Bill Mack and recorded by LeAnn Rimes), and "I Can't Live" (written by Nilsson and recorded by Celine Dion).

The same is true with bridges. When it's time to craft a bridge, explore rhythms that will set your bridge apart from the choruses or verses that surround it. For example, in "Over The Rainbow" think about how different the rhythm is in the bridge section compared to the verses. The verse ("Somewhere over the rainbow bluebirds fly") contains ten syllables (and ten corresponding notes). In that same amount of space (four bars), the bridge ("Someday I'll wish upon a star and wake up where the clouds are far behind me") contains nineteen syllables and corresponding notes. The result is a sense that the bridge provides a melodic and rhythmic departure from the rest of the song.

CHOOSING THE APPROPRIATE MELODIC RANGE

My voice instructor in college used to say that just as we have ten fingers, we should have ten notes that we can comfortably sing. Most professional singers will be able to sing at least an octave and a third without any difficulty. An example of an octave and a third would be the distance from middle "C" on a piano to the "E" an octave above. (If all of this sounds incomprehensible, don't despair. Have someone who's more comfortable with music theory plunk out the notes of your song and see if what you've written is within "normal" range.)

It is perfectly acceptable to craft a strong, catchy melody that uses less than ten or eleven notes. In fact, if a song is considerably more than an octave and a third, you risk getting into a situation where singers who want to record your song may not be capable of singing it. I learned that lesson the hard way.

When A.J. Masters and I co-wrote a song called "What Would Happen," for some inexplicable reason we wrote it in a key that was too high for either of us to comfortably sing. We were singing in our falsetto range as we wrote and the melody sounded so good that neither of us realized how "rangy" the song was until it was finished. By then, we had fallen in love with our melody and were unwilling to change it, even though it required a singer to have a strong two octaves plus one additional note. Only a handful of singers in the class of Celine Dion, Reba McEntire, Michael Bolton, or Mariah Carey are capable of singing that range.

We hired an extraordinary singer named John Wesley Ryles to sing our demo. In addition to having his own record deal, John had sung demos for countless hit songs in Nashville, including "Change My Mind." He sang the demo so effortlessly that the song seemed deceptively easier to sing than it actually was. We were ecstatic when the song went "on hold" for a major female country artist, but were concerned about her ability to hit the notes.

As the time approached for this singer to record her album we grew more and more excited, especially after we heard how much the head of the label loved our song. A friend had overheard our demo playing at the artist's managers' office and reported that there had been talk of it being "a career single." I was bursting with equal parts excitement and anxiety on the day they went into the studio, as I waited to hear that our song had been recorded.

On the final day of recording sessions I was told that they had tried to record our song, but when the artist couldn't sing it well, they discarded it and moved on to the next song in line. To say I was devastated is a gross understatement. I had already been talking to real estate agents and car salesmen. I was depressed for three months—but I learned a valuable lesson. We've since "de-ranged" the melody. Now, unless I know that I'm writing for an artist with an exceptional vocal range, I stick to an octave and a third.

On the other hand, songwriters with excessively small vocal range or limited singing ability must be careful to avoid the trap of writing only the kind of melodies that they themselves can easily sing. Remember, you are writing for professional singers who will hopefully use your melody to showcase their vocal abilities. Craft melodies that will intrigue and challenge a skilled vocalist, without being something that only Pavarotti would be comfortable singing.

Chapter 6
Using Repetition Effectively

A great rock song, a great country song, or a great folk
song are three different beasts. What makes a great song
varies from genre to genre. There are some eternal truths,
however. First the song must be memorable. When you
walk away from that record or from that radio station, a
great song is one that you remember. The song must have
something unique about it, either it's point of view, melodic
structure, or its hook—something about it has to stick out
in your mind. If it says something profound, to me that's
the best. It is important that a song touches you and makes
you feel something, whether it's hilariously silly, profoundly
sad, deeply touching, or profoundly depressing.

      Robert K. Oermann (Music journalist)

A successful melody touches listeners and stays with them. It communicates the emotion that the composer felt and wanted to convey when he or she wrote it. One of the most effective ways to connect with your listeners is by using the tool of melodic and rhythmic repetition. Nothing contributes more to a melody's being "memorable" than incorporating notes, rhythms, and phrases that repeat. It's common sense that it's easier for listeners to remember a melodic phrase that they've heard over and over again than one that they've heard only once.

Repetition can be employed by repeating a melodic phrase exactly, or by repeating a rhythm while altering some or all of the actual notes of the phrase. Melodic or rhythmic repetition may be exact or may be close enough to evoke a sense of repetition.

KEEPING YOUR PHRASES SHORT AND CATCHY

On my first visit to Nashville a friend introduced me to Carson Chamberlain, who was working as a road manager for a then-unknown country singer named Keith Whitley. (Whitley went on to tremendous success before his untimely death.) Carson is now a record label executive, as well as a songwriter with hits by artists including Alan Jackson. I played Carson a song I had written and his comment was "Y'all have enough words in this verse for a whole album!"

That meeting was a turning point in my development as a writer. The proverbial "light bulb" went on over my head. It was the first time I grasped the idea that it was virtually impossible to compose lines of catchy, memorable melodies if their lyrical counterparts had too many words and syllables.

I began analyzing the hit songs on the radio and found that an overwhelming majority of them were comprised of short, melodic (and corresponding lyric) phrases. Of course, songwriting is not an exact science and there are some exceptions. But over and over again I found that most hit songs contain melodic and/or rhythmic phrases that repeat and usually are comprised of less than ten notes (or syllables), and sometimes as few as two or three notes.

Composing melodies that have short, repeating phrases is a skill that can be acquired with practice. As you master this technique you'll be amazed at how much catchier your melodies become.

I learned another valuable lesson about melodic repetition and the impact of short melodic phrases from Kevin Richardson, a member of the multi-platinum selling pop group, the Backstreet Boys. I was co-writing a song with Kevin and Gary Baker and felt we were writing a hit when Kevin said he thought something was wrong with the melody. He said that the chorus seemed to have "too many sections" and that their previous hits had been more simple and straightforward melodically. Kevin was right. The chorus needed additional repetition.

We deleted the second half of the chorus (a rhythmic and melodic departure from the first section) and replaced it with lines that repeated the rhythm that we had established in the first half. Here is the resulting chorus lyric for the song "Back To Your Heart":

(Tell me)
The words to say
The road to take
To find a way
Back To Your Heart

What can I do
To get to you
And find a way
Back To Your Heart
(Jason Blume/Gary Baker/Kevin Richardson, Recorded by the Backstreet Boys)

Exercise:

Writing Short, Repeating Melodic Phrases

The purpose of this exercise is to get accustomed to writing short melodic phrases that repeat.

- ♪ Compose a four-line melody by singing it into a tape recorder. Each of the lines will contain only three notes. Once you have established the length of those notes and the rhythm of that first line, repeat that rhythm three more times.

- ♪ In each of the four lines, you may choose to use some notes that have the same pitch or not. You also have the option of using the identical melody for two or more of the lines. The only restriction is that each line contains three notes and that each line has the same rhythm. (For the purposes of this exercise you will not be writing lyrics, but it can be helpful to think of it as writing three syllables per line.)

Example:

(Line 1) Now　　　　　　　I　　　　　　　know

(Line 2) How　　　　　　you　　　　　　feel

(Line 3) There's　　　　　no　　　　　　doubt

(Line 4) It's　　　　　　for　　　　　　real

Note that in the example, although the pitch of the notes varies from line to line, the rhythm remains the same. Repeat the exercise using four notes per line then try the exercise one more time using five notes per line.

While you probably won't want to use repeating rhythms exclusively, incorporating short phrases that repeat into sections of your songs will make your melodies easier to remember and sing. It may take some practice to get comfortable with composing this way. But you'll notice how much catchier your melodies become.

Every line in the chorus lyric contains the same number of syllables—four. This simplicity contributed significantly to the song's success as people could not get it out of their heads—and our song was recorded by the Backstreet Boys, one of the best-selling groups in the world today.

WRITING SYMMETRICAL PHRASES

Counting the number of syllables in each line when you write a lyric will have the same effect as counting the number of individual notes in the corresponding melodic phrases. It is impossible to craft melodic or rhythmic phrases that repeat if each line contains a different number of syllables.

Some of the most effective melodies employ a technique that can be referred to as "Call and Response." When portions of melodies are crafted using this tool, the lines seem to "answer" each other melodically. The reason these lines seem to answer each other is that they are symmetrical; they mirror each other by containing the same number of syllables.

Within a song, the entire verse or chorus may use repeating phrases—or there may be rhythmic and/or melodic repetition of several lines within the verse or chorus. There are no hard and fast rules about how much or where to use repeating phrases. As you study and analyze hit melodies you will become aware of the prevalence of this tool.

Exercise:

Crafting Lyrics That Lend Themselves to Catchy Melodies

Part 1:

Here are some examples of lyrics that "answer" each other by using the same number of syllables in key lines.

How do I live without you (7 syllables)

Answer: *How do I breathe without you* (7 syllables)

Heads Carolina (5 syllables)

Answer: *Tails California* (5 syllables)

With a look (3 syllables)

Answer: *With a touch* (3 syllables)

In your notebook, write the next line of lyric, using the same number of syllables as the initial phrase. Note that for the purposes of this exercise it is not necessary to rhyme these lines. For example:

The past is past (4 syllables)

Answer: *What's done is done* (4 syllables)

1. *If that's the way you want it* (7 syllables)

2. *If this is a dream* (5 syllables)

3. *Say the words that I want to hear* (8 syllables)

4. *Hold me* (2 syllables)

5. *I never meant to hurt you like I did* (10 syllables)

Part 2:

Write the next two lines of lyric, using the same number of syllables as the two-line phrase. For this part of the exercise, be sure to rhyme the second line you write with the original second line. For example:

I love you so much (5 syllables)

And I want you to know (6 syllables)

Answer:　　*These two loving arms* (5 syllables)

　　　　　　Will never let you go (6 syllables)

1. *Tell me that you love me* (6 syllables)

   If you really do (5 syllables)

2. *Hold me close* (3 syllables)

   And swear that it's forever (7 syllables)

3. *All I want to do is dance with you* (9 syllables)

   All night long (3 syllables)

4. *Show me* (2 syllables)

   How you feel (3 syllables)

5. *There's a place down the road* (6 syllables)

   Where everybody goes (6 syllables)

6. *I wouldn't stop loving you if I could* (10 syllables)

   And I don't want to try (6 syllables)

7. *One sweet* (2 syllables)

   Hot night (2 syllables)

8. *High-heeled boots* (3 syllables)

   Skin tight dress (3 syllables)

9. *Give me a call* (4 syllables)

   If I ever cross your mind (7 syllables)

10. *Don't ever stop* (4 syllables)

    Whatever it is that you're doing (9 syllables)

Part 3:

Compose a melody for each of the four-line lyrics that you have written.

Chapter 7
Acquiring Additional Melody Writing Techniques

Just when you think you are done writing, he changes the melody ever so slightly and suddenly you have a whole new song.

Raul Malo (Lead singer of The Mavericks, speaking about Kostas, who has
written hits for artists including Dwight Yoakam, Patty Loveless, and Vince Gill)

Few songwriters would assume that every word of their first draft of a lyric is the very strongest it could possibly be. It's taken for granted that rewriting a lyric will almost always be necessary if the goal is to write the most effective, creative lines possible. The same holds true for melody writing.

The odds of every note, rhythm, and chord of your first melodic draft being the very best that you could possibly write are infinitesimally small. We've all heard it said that "songwriting is 10 percent inspiration and 90 percent perspiration." That applies just as much to composing melodies as it does for lyrics. The strongest melodies start as inspiration, but are then scrutinized and rewritten until they are the best the composer is able to write.

Although for some songs, the story contributes more to the song's success than the melody does, even "lyric-driven" songs require memorable melodies that showcase their lyrics if they are to become hits. Many songs, especially in the fields of pop, dance, and R & B, seem to become hits largely on the strength of their melody and/or groove. For some of these songs, the lyric seems almost secondary. Indeed, a good case could be made that without a catchy, memorable melody, listeners might never get an opportunity to hear the lyrics of any song—because it would not ever get on the radio. Frank Liddell (Director of Artists & Repertoires, MCA/Decca Records) has said, "I am melodically driven, so the first thing that will catch my attention is a great and unique melody. Sometimes I'll listen to a song twenty times before I know what it's about."

The bottom line is that settling for the very first melody that pops into your head sells you and your song short. Such an effort is unlikely to lead you to success. Melody is crucial to a song's success. Put at least as much time and effort into writing your melodies as you do with your lyrics. It's easy to get accustomed to a melody, and many songwriters have a hard time coming up with alternatives. What follows are specific tools that can help you explore your melodic options before deciding which is the strongest.

BREAKING THE LINES

It can be helpful to look at the various places where you might place pauses and emphases within a melodic line to alter the rhythm. For example, let's look at different ways to approach the title "If You Really Love Me."

1.   One option is to craft a melody that does not include any pauses or emphases in it. Rhythmically, each syllable of the lyric has a corresponding note of equal value (i.e., all quarter notes, or all eighth notes).

If - You - Real - ly - Love - Me

2.   A second rhythm to try when crafting a melody for this title is to assign a longer note value to the first word, "If" (i.e., a dotted quarter note, while all other notes are eighth notes). Holding it out longer will add emphasis to that word.

If   -   You - Real - ly - Love - Me

3.   Another place to break up the line would be after the word "You."

If - You   -   Real - ly - Love - Me

4.   You might emphasize the word "Really" by assigning a longer note value to its two syllables and adding a pause after that word:

If - You - Real   -   ly   -   Love - Me

5.   Another option is to emphasize the word "Love" by assigning a longer note value to that word:

If - You - Real -ly - Love   -   Me

While every note of melody is important, it's essential that your hook is the strongest melody you're capable of composing. Of course, a line of lyric that contains many syllables will present more places to break up the line than a lyric with only one or two syllables. But even a line with very few syllables can be expressed rhythmically in a variety of ways by turning one-syllable words into multi-syllabic words:

You   -   ooh - ooh - ooh - ooh

When you're rewriting your melodies, try a variety of notes with different rhythmic breaks. There are an infinite number of combinations of notes and rhythms. If you attempted to try all of them you'd never finish a song. But your songs will improve as you experiment with at least five different melodies for each section, before settling on the one that best conveys the emotion of your lyric in a catchy, memorable way.

LEARNING TO USE NONSENSE SYLLABLES

Using nonsense syllables (sounds that have no meaning) can be an effective tool to add interest to your melodies. The first line of Peter Frampton's classic hit "Baby I Love Your Way" wouldn't have nearly the same melodic impact

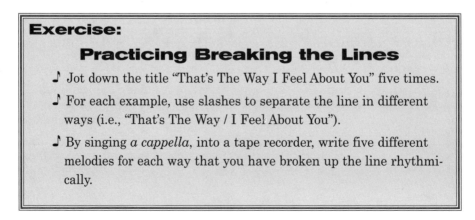

Exercise:
Practicing Breaking the Lines

♪ Jot down the title "That's The Way I Feel About You" five times.

♪ For each example, use slashes to separate the line in different ways (i.e., "That's The Way / I Feel About You").

♪ By singing *a cappella*, into a tape recorder, write five different melodies for each way that you have broken up the line rhythmically.

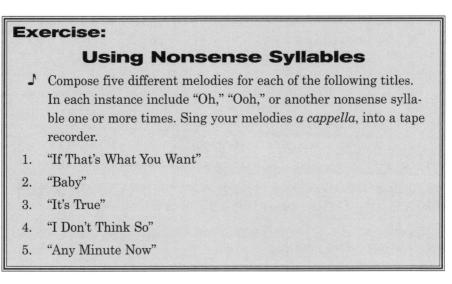

without the "Ooh" that precedes it. Blackstreet added an additional hook to their mega-hit "No Diggity" by including a section that repeats "Hey-Yo, Hey-Yo, Hey-Yo, Hey-Yo," and the hook of Anne Murray's classic "I Just Fall In Love Again" is actually sung "*Oh*—I Just Fall In Love Again." Sounds, like "Ooh" and "Oh" can be added either once or several times to help craft a catchy melody.

REPEATING WORDS OR PHRASES

Repeating a word or a phrase can also add interest to your melodies. For instance, for the example given previously in this chapter, "If You Really Love

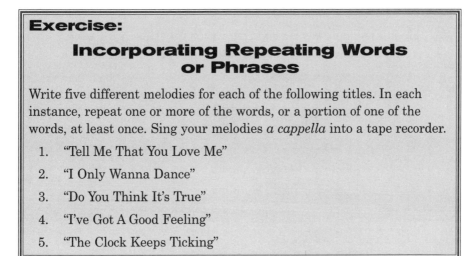

Me," you might craft a hook that sings: "If You *Really-Really-Really-Really* Love Me." David Bowie had great success by repeating just a part of a word: "*Ch-Ch-Ch-Ch*-Changes" and Van Morrison repeated the word "love" in a song that's been recorded over and over: ("She gives me *love-love-love-love*") "Crazy Love."

You certainly will not want to use nonsense syllables or repeating words or phrases in all of your songs, but it is important to remember that you have them as options. When experimenting with various melodic alternatives, inserting a nonsense syllable or repeating a word may be just the ticket to make your melody special.

LEARNING THE POWER OF SEQUENTIAL INTERVALS, ASCENDING NOTES, AND DESCENDING NOTES

Writing melodies that are memorable can be much easier when you build them by using sequential intervals—notes that are consecutive. For example, the sound of C - D - E will be easier to remember than C - F# - Bb. Notes that are close to each other on the scale seem to go together naturally. Order "makes sense" to the brain and it is easier to retain. For those readers who are as non-technically oriented as me, think of the melody of the popular tune "Mary Had A Little Lamb."

Exercise:
Incorporating Sequential Intervals, Ascending Notes, and Descending Notes

For each of the following lines of lyric:

a. Compose a melody that incorporates notes that are all either one note above or one note below each other.

b. Compose a melody that includes notes that ascend in succession.

c. Compose a melody that includes notes that descend in sequence.

1. *I don't think I love you anymore*
2. *I'm gonna fly you to the moon*
3. *Why can't we still be friends*
4. *I've got a feeling that I'm dreaming*
5. *What's going on in your heart*

Ma- ry   had a   lit-tle lamb   lit-tle lamb   lit- tle lamb

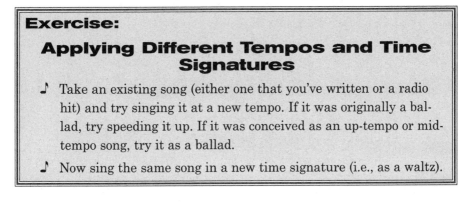

Ma- ry   had a   lit-tle lamb whose   fleece was white as snow

Notice that each note is only one note away in the scale from every other note, or is a repetition of the same note. The only exception is the interval that goes from "C" to "E" flat. Repeating notes can also help to make a melody easy to remember.

Using notes that descend in succession can help create a melody that is memorable. One notable example is "The Christmas Song." Think of the classic melody that accompanies "Chestnuts roasting on an open fire." The distance from the note sung on "Chest" to the note sung on "nuts" is an entire octave. However, the rest of the phrase is made up of notes that descend one step or musical interval at a time in a logical sequence.

It can also be quite effective to build melodies by including a series of notes that ascend in sequence. It would be terribly boring if all melodies were crafted using sequential notes, but using some notes that either ascend or descend in succession can make a melody easier to remember.

VARYING THE TEMPO AND TIME SIGNATURE

The tempo refers to the speed at which a melody is performed. When exploring different melodic options it can be helpful to try your song at various tempos.

Exercise:

Applying Different Tempos and Time Signatures

♪ Take an existing song (either one that you've written or a radio hit) and try singing it at a new tempo. If it was originally a ballad, try speeding it up. If it was conceived as an up-tempo or mid-tempo song, try it as a ballad.

♪ Now sing the same song in a new time signature (i.e., as a waltz).

The song that you thought was a terrific ballad may make an even better mid-tempo or up-tempo song.

Likewise, it can be beneficial to try your song in different time signatures. A song that you had intended as a waltz (3/4 time) may be even stronger in a more straight-ahead 4/4 time signature.

FINDING THOSE MAGIC MOMENTS: THE UNEXPECTED NOTE OR CHORD

Imagine hearing "Send In The Clowns" by Stephen Sondheim without that wonderful, distinctive, high note that accompanies the word "my" (in boldface below):

Isn't it rich
Are we a pair
Losing my timing this late
*In **my** career*

Now imagine Garth Brooks singing "I've Got Friends In Low Places" without dipping down to the very low note that corresponds to the word "low." In both instances, that single, special note provides one of the most memorable, "magical" moments in the songs.

When rewriting your melodies, consciously look for those places within your songs that might benefit from a fresh, unexpected chord, rhythm, or note that is out of the ordinary. When used effectively, those tools grab the listeners'

Exercise:
Incorporating Magic Moments

Writing the strongest melodies involves conscious decision-making and lots of rewriting. Think about the places where you can include "magic moments" to bring your melodies to the next level.

- ♪ Sing the chorus melody of a song you've written and explore where you might incorporate a special note, rhythm, or chord to add to the emotional impact of the melody. It might help to write down the lyric first and see if there are words like "up" or "down" that lend themselves to a higher or lower note.

- ♪ Try at least three different options and repeat this exercise with several of your existing songs..

attention, add interest and uniqueness to the melodies, and bolster the emotion that the composer is trying to evoke.

Generally speaking, there is something about the songs I can get cut that separates them from the other songs—a unique idea or a unique melodic passage.

John Van Meter (Director, Creative Services, Sony/ATV Tree Music Publishing)

In some instances, the lyric will dictate the most effective way to insert a "magic moment" into the melody. For example, in "Friends In Low Places" it was natural for songwriters Dewayne Blackwell and Bud Lee to give the singer a low note to sing on the word "low." Likewise, words like "top," "up," and "fly" will lend themselves to being sung on a note that is higher than the surrounding notes.

There needs to be something about your song that sets it apart if you want to rise to the top. A special melodic moment is often the ticket. You have a multitude of melodic options to explore to take your melodies to the next level—from good to WOW! But don't insert "magic moments" into your melodies with a proverbial crowbar. Use them only where they genuinely support the melody.

USING SIGNATURE LICKS

Listeners can usually identify a favorite hit song on the radio within the first few moments of the instrumental introduction. This is because the recording begins with a catchy, melodic phrase unique to that song. This instrumental hook, or *signature lick,* is often included in the song's introduction, at the turnaround (between the end of the first chorus and the beginning of the second verse), and again at the end of the song.

The signature lick is commonly the same, or very similar to, a melodic line used elsewhere in the song. This added hook often reiterates or evokes the melody that accompanies the song's title, the first line of the chorus, the last line of the chorus, or the opening line of the verse. Although not as common, it's also acceptable to have a signature lick that is a totally separate melodic entity, not appearing in any other section of the song.

THE MELODY TEST: CAN YOU WRITE EFFECTIVE MELODIES?

The ultimate test of whether a melody is powerful and memorable is its ability

---

Exercise:
Composing Signature Licks

1. Compose two different signature licks for a song you've written, but have not yet demoed. If you are unable to play these melodic phrases on an instrument, sing them *a cappella* into your tape recorder.

   ♪ Have the first lick be a melodic line that is the same or similar to a melody already within your song.

   ♪ Create an alternate signature lick using a melody that is not found elsewhere within your song.

2. Decide what instrument you want to play your signature licks when you record your demo.

---

to stand up on its own. If you want instrumental versions of your hit songs to play on "Muzak," they will need to have melodies that do not require the benefit of a lyric to sound like a hit.

Sing your melody into a tape recorder—without the lyric. Either use a nonsense syllable like "La" or try humming. When you listen back, be objective and ask yourself the following questions:

♪ Are there extra notes crammed in to make the lyric fit?

♪ Does it sound as though notes (or syllables) are missing?

♪ Is this the strongest melody you could have written—regardless of the lyric? Or does it sound like the melody was written to accommodate the lyric?

♪ Does your melody sound like it is following the chord changes—or do the chord changes support a catchy, memorable melody?

♪ Does your melody evoke an emotion all by itself?

Stay open to exploring the full spectrum of melodic possibilities before settling for one that may not be the very strongest you're capable of writing.

Let the radio be your teacher. Analyze the techniques used by the composers of the songs that you love. Note the length of the melodic phrases and how much repetition was used and where. Are there varied rhythms in different sections of the songs? How much range is required to sing them? Are there unexpected, fresh melodic intervals or chords? Learn those lessons. Then, incorporate them into your melodies.

MELODY CHECKLIST

Make a photocopy of this checklist and keep it where you normally write. Each time you finish a draft of a song, check to be sure that you've incorporated the tools and techniques that follow:

☐ Easy to remember and sing

☐ Not too "wordy" to be melodic

☐ Obvious where the title goes (without a lyric)

☐ Rhythmic and/or melodic phrases repeat

☐ Melody and lyric seems to go together

☐ Rhythms are varied in verse, chorus and bridge

☐ Not too much range for singers to sing

☐ Phrases are short and catchy

☐ Melodic phrases are symmetrical

☐ Contains a "magic" moment (fresh, unexpected note or chord)

☐ Contains sequential, logical intervals

☐ There's no doubt where the chorus is

☐ Bridge (if applicable) adds a new musical dimension

☐ Melody holds up without the lyric

Step IV
Producing Successful Demos

A great demo can get an average song cut. A poor demo

can keep a great song from getting cut.

George Teren (Writer of country hits "Busy Man," "She's Sure Taking It Well,"
"Running Out Of Reasons To Run," and cuts with artists including Trisha Yearwood,
John Michael Montgomery, Tim McGraw, and Lorrie Morgan)

Chapter 8
Learning How and When to Record a Demo

*When it's time to make the actual demo that will be used to
pitch, there are very few, great songs that can make it with
a demo that uses only a guitar and a vocal—and most of
those are written by writer/artists who have the rare ability
to sit down and play a guitar to sell a song. Being able to
do that is a much rarer talent than being a hit songwriter.
To play a song for an artist, a full demo is what's normally
needed in order to compete with what's going on out there.*

Michael Hollandsworth (Vice President/General Manager, Zomba Music Group)

"Demo" is an abbreviated form of the word "demonstration"; an effective demo
literally "demonstrates" your song's potential. Ideally, it provides the listener
with all he or she needs to hear to determine the song's hit potential and appro-
priateness for his or her needs. Different types of songs require varying types of
production to convey the song's possibilities.

When I began writing songs I had no clue what constituted an effective
demo. I couldn't imagine how I would ever acquire the skills—or the money—
to produce one. I could barely pay the rent for the tiny room I was living in,
so initially, I would look for collaborators who owned home studios where we
could demo the song for free. If they could also play all the instruments and
sing the song, that was even better.

At that point, hiring a studio, an engineer, musicians, and vocalists—and
knowing what to tell them to do—seemed as likely a possibility for me as flying.
But, like everything else in songwriting, learning how to produce successful
demos was part of a long process that included trial and error, and lots of practice.

HOW TO KNOW WHEN YOUR SONG IS READY

Few things break my heart more than hearing an elaborately produced, expensive demo of a song that I know will never stand a chance of being legitimately published or recorded. The writer has not only spent time and money unnecessarily, but will likely have grown attached to the song "as is." (There seems to be a direct correlation between the amount of money spent on a demo and the songwriter's refusal to do additional rewriting—especially if the demo sounds terrific to friends and family.)

The very first step in the demo process is being sure that the song itself is ready. But how can you be sure? Put your song under the proverbial microscope. Ask yourself if you can honestly say that each line of lyric and melody is the strongest and freshest you're capable of. Use the lyric and melody checklists provided in this book to see if you're hitting the mark.

When you're confident that your work is as strong as you can make it, it's time to get some additional opinions. In order to play the song for others and to objectively evaluate it yourself, you'll need a rough recording of your song— a "work tape." (More about recording work tapes later in this section.)

You can get song critiques from a variety of sources. There are songwriters' organizations throughout the U.S. and some of them provide critiquing services as part of their meetings (see appendix). The National Academy of Songwriters and the Nashville Songwriters Association International are among the organizations that offer their members professional song evaluations through the mail. There are also workshops and classes where you may be able to get a professional opinion. If you have already established relationships with music publishers, and you trust their ability to recognize your song's potential in a rough version, ask if they would be willing to share their opinion. But, do not send a rough work tape as your first introduction to a music industry professional. You'll want to make your best first impression with a well-produced demo recording.

If you co-write, ask your collaborators for their honest opinion of your work. You might set up a support group to review each other's songs, using the lyric and melody checklists included in this book. Using the checklists helps evaluators objectively specify your song's strengths and weaknesses, avoiding hurtful, unproductive comments like, "I just don't like it," or "It doesn't sound like a hit." Unfortunately, friends and family are not generally qualified to determine if your work is meeting professional standards. The goal is to get as much objective, professional input as possible before investing money in a demo.

A word about critiques: Not all evaluators (even professionals) are equally skilled at identifying the areas that need work, or at determining the merits of songs. They may be able to instantly spot a hit, but may be at a complete loss to express why your song doesn't meet the criteria. After receiving a critique of one of your songs, if you instantly feel, "Wow, she's right! Why didn't I see that?" or "That would make the song so much stronger," you will obviously want to make the suggested revisions. But, if you feel strongly that the critique is off-base, allow a few days to pass (to recover from being told that your "child" is not quite as perfect as you thought) and ask yourself if there are any elements of the critique that resonate as true. If you strongly disagree with what has been said, and you have a legitimate basis for your feelings, get additional opinions before making any changes.

I fully produce my demos. It seems that nobody can hear them otherwise. The days of the piano/vocal are gone.

Franne Golde (Writer of songs on Grammy-winning albums, and cuts with artists including Whitney Houston, Diana Ross, and Celine Dion)

You may need to repeat the process of rewriting, recording a work tape, and receiving critiques several times before you decide that your song is ready for a demo. Not every song warrants the time and financial commitment of a demo. Most professional songwriters do not record a demo of every song they write. You may decide that a particular song is simply one more step in your journey of honing your songwriting skills, and it is not in your best interests to produce a demo.

IDENTIFYING WHAT'S RIGHT FOR YOUR SONG

You've gotten positive feedback on your song and have decided to proceed with recording a demo. What's the next step? There are two primary considerations: What does this particular song require and how much money can you afford to spend?

A successful demo gives the listener an indication of how a song might sound if it were fully produced. Songs in various genres require different amounts of production and instrumentation. In preparing for this book, I interviewed many successful songwriters, music publishers, A & R executives, and record producers. One of the questions I asked them was what qualities they felt were important in a demo. Almost all of these music industry professionals concurred with my own experience: a demo of a ballad does not generally need more than a professionally produced guitar or piano, and an excellent vocal, but an up-tempo song usually requires additional instrumentation. That doesn't mean that a ballad might not benefit from additional embellishment, or even a full-band demo—but it's not mandatory, the way it is for most up-tempo songs. If you are writing an up-tempo, groove-oriented dance song, your demo better include those elements that will make the listener want to dance. For demos of up-tempo songs, it's almost impossible to get the feel of the song across without including a rhythm section (bass and drums), in addition to other instruments.

The demo is very important, but has to be decided upon on a song by song basis. A great ballad doesn't need as much as a full-on dance song.

Judy Stakee (Vice President of Creative Services, Warner Chappell Music Publishing)

You may be lucky enough to find an A & R person or a record producer who has the rare ability to hear your song's potential from a very rough demo. But he or she will have to play that same demo for the artist (who will play it for his or her spouse), the artist's manager (who will play it for her boyfriend), the other A & R executives, and the record label president. The chances are between slim and none that all of these people will be able to hear what a great song you've written if it's represented by a poorly produced demo.

AVOIDING "THE BIG LIE"

I think for a newer writer, the safest way to go is to make the demo sound as good as you can.

Wade Kirby (Hit songwriter)

Early on in my career, I used to tell myself over and over: "But this song is so wonderful, surely, they'll be able to hear how great it sounds even though my demo isn't very good." But it's not true.

Most music industry professionals who review songs are deluged with tapes. They have neither the time, nor the ability, to envision how your song might sound if your demo had been produced differently. It either sounds like a hit or it's on to the next tape.

While a big part of your demo's job is to get your song published or recorded, it also serves another crucial purpose. Since songwriters are rarely invited to an artist's recording sessions, your demo is your representative there. The music on that tape is your only opportunity to share with the artist and record producer your vision of how your song could sound. If you envision a specific guitar lick, a unique vocal harmony line, a particular combination of instruments, or a special string part that you feel is important to your song, it needs to be included in your demo. Music publishers, A & R executives, recording artists, and record producers are not mind readers. If those elements that contribute to your vision for your song are included on your tape, there's a good chance they will be on the finished record. If they are not on the tape, there's virtually no chance that the publisher, record producer, or recording artist will imagine what you are hearing.

The demo is very important. If people tell you they can hear it through a guitar/vocal, don't believe them. Try to make the demo as close to a record as you can. With most of my songs, the artists and producers have tried to come close to the demo. The songwriters are the "true producers." The artists and producers reproduce what we produce. If you can get a great demo you can get a great record.

Wayne Perry (Hit songwriter)

I used to resent being forced into the position of "record producer"—especially since I knew that my skills were very limited in that department. I felt it should be enough that I had written a song with a strong melody and lyric. Why should I be obligated to spend money I didn't have to present a "finished record" on a silver platter to a professional who should be able to hear my song's potential even if I sang it a cappella? In the real world it doesn't work that way and my energy is better spent honing my demo production skills than complaining about the way I wish things were. To compete with the professional competition, I've learned to produce the very best demos my budget and skills allow.

DISTINGUISHING BETWEEN SONG DEMOS AND ARTIST DEMOS

To determine what level of production your demo will require, you need to be clear about what function your demo is intended to serve. If your demo is intended as a tool to get your song published and ultimately recorded by an artist other than yourself, it is considered a "song demo." But, if the demo's purpose is to demonstrate your potential as a recording artist, it is considered an "artist demo"—and it will need to meet even higher standards. Typically, the vocals are mixed louder on a song demo than they would be on an artist demo, or on a song you might hear on the radio. This is done to ensure that a listener who is considering recording your song can clearly hear the words and melody.

The musicianship, clarity, and overall production values of an artist demo often approximate those of a finished record. But most importantly, the vocal performance in an artist demo needs to be nothing less than perfect. The pitch, tone, and emotion of the vocals must be excellent.

Many aspiring recording artists spend thousands of dollars and hire well-known record producers to help them record their artist demos. In these instances the producer helps the artist find songs and uses his or her expertise to create a demo that is indistinguishable from a master recording. This is often referred to as a "custom session." While you may not need to invest to that extent, if your goal is to produce a demo to secure a record deal as an artist, you need to present a demo that will sound like a hit record—with no excuses or apologies attached.

I like for a demo to effectively put across the "intent" of the writers. The style of music often dictates the type of demo. Many country songs can be very effective in a guitar/vocal demo, whereas an urban or R & B piece may need loops and more production techniques to translate the groove intended by the writers. In general, I'd much rather get a simple demo of a song rather than a poorly, but more produced version.

Rick Chudacoff (Hit producer/songwriter)

I can't count how many times I've heard an artist say, "But if you could just hear me play live . . . " While it's important for an artist to have the skills to present an exciting live performance, there's a problem with that thinking. Since it is a recorded product that is played on the radio and purchased by the consumer, the record label executive needs to hear how the artist sounds on tape. It's true that a handful of artists have been signed to record deals based on a live performance in a record company president's office. But it's a rare artist who has the kind of connections that can facilitate that kind of meeting without someone in the chain of music industry professionals hearing a demo that sounds like a radio hit. It's also a rare performer who can convey the full extent of his or her artistry without the trappings of a band, and the enhancements a professional recording studio can add.

As with a song demo, the amount of production and instrumentation on the artist demo depends to a large extent on the genre of music. An acoustic-oriented folk or country singer may require far less embellishment to convey his or her potential than a euro-techno rock or funk band. But even the majority of acoustic-oriented artists are signed to record deals on the strength of a demo that showcases them in their very best light.

The one instance in which it might be best to use a live recording (as opposed to a demo produced in a recording studio) is when the demo is intended exclusively to help you secure work as a live performer. According to Wind River Recording artist David Roth, "People who book folk venues have told me they often prefer live demo tapes to fully produced CD's. It makes sense because someone who books live performances is more interested in how you sound and relate to a live audience than how you can use studio musicians and studio tricks to sound good."

MEASURING UP TO THE PROFESSIONAL STANDARD

Prior to the first time I heard demos of songs that had gone on to become hits, I had no idea of the quality of the demos my competition was producing. I was amazed at how much the demos sounded like finished records. The musicians were excellent, and I couldn't believe the demo singers didn't have their own record deals. Most of the time, the catchy, instrumental hooks on the record had come straight from the demo. The final product usually had vocal harmonies in the same places the demo had used them. With the exception of the sound quality and the vocalist, sometimes it was hard to differentiate the demo from the hit record.

My first demos were recorded for free in friends' basements. The musicianship was mediocre at best, and the vocal performances were even worse. When I pitched those demos, no matter how well-written the songs might have been, from the opening notes I was sending a message loud and clear: "This tape is from an amateur." Whether you are producing a guitar/vocal song demo or a full-band artist demo, your demo needs to be a clear, professional-sounding recording with top-notch musicians and the best vocalist you can possibly hire. We'll discuss these details further later in this section.

The most important part of the demo is being able to hear the lyrics and melody, whether it is just a guitar/vocal work tape or a full demo.

Mike Sistad (Director, Artists & Repertoires, Arista Nashville)

KNOWING HOW MANY TRACKS ARE NECESSARY

Virtually all professional recordings are made on multi-track tape recorders. These machines are able to record multiple instruments and sounds, while keeping each individual sound separated on different "tracks." Different multi-track recording machines have the capability to record 4, 8, 12, 16, 24 or 32 tracks. For some albums, these machines are linked together to provide the artist and producer with 96 tracks or more, but for a demo you will rarely need more than 24 tracks. Depending on the type of demo you are producing, you may need far less.

Drums may be assigned 12 tracks or more so that each sound (hi-hat, crash cymbals, kick drum, snare, etc.) can be isolated. Having each instrument (and vocal) on its own track allows the engineer to adjust the reverb, equalization, and other effects. (If this sounds overwhelming, don't despair. You don't need to be an expert in this area—you just need to hire one.)

How many tracks do you need for your demo? The standard answer I've always heard is that what is on the tracks is far more important than the actual number of tracks. That's true. No number of tracks will turn a mediocre song into a great one. However, using multiple tracks will allow your engineer to make the instruments and vocals that are recorded sound their best.

If you are producing a demo that will consist of a guitar and a vocal (with no harmony vocals), you probably don't need more than 4 tracks. If you are recording a seven-piece band and three background vocalists, you may need 24 tracks or more. Of course, part of your decision will be based upon the size of your budget.

DETERMINING BUDGETS

Producing demos can be expensive. A professional, full-time songwriter may spend $10,000 (or more) per year on demos. Your primary costs will be for the studio, engineer, musicians, vocalists, and tape costs. The cost of each of these can vary greatly, depending upon their quality or credentials. It also depends on what part of the country you live in.

It is important to decide how many musicians you will need to hire in order to get what you hear in your head onto tape (i.e., is this particular song crying out for a saxophone, a steel guitar, or a cello?). This decision will help you determine how many tracks you will require in a studio.

It costs far less to rent studio time in a 4-track or 8-track studio than in a studio with 32-track capability. Depending on your location, a competent 8-track studio may cost as little as $25 per hour, including an engineer. The best 32 track studios cost in excess of $200 per hour. However, there's no reason to spend that much for a demo studio. Most cities have 24-track studios available for less than $50 per hour. This should be sufficient for even the most elaborately produced demo.

One of the recording engineer's responsibilities is to effectively capture the sounds of your instruments and vocals on tape. This requires selecting the most appropriate microphones and positioning them to best record each instrument and vocalist. The engineer is skilled in operating the recording console and the equipment that will add "effects" (i.e., equalization, echo, or reverb) to each sound. It's also the engineer's job to mix the instruments and vocals together, placing each in its appropriate place in relation to the other sounds.

Many small studios are owned and operated by recording engineers who include their services in the price of the studio. If you need to hire an engineer, ask the studio manager to recommend someone who is familiar with that particular studio's equipment. Then ask to hear samples of the engineer's work before making your decision. The cost of hiring an engineer can range from $10 per hour to more than $100 per hour depending on the individual's skill level and credentials. In most circumstances, a competent engineer for a demo costs in the range of $25 to $35 per hour.

It's often most cost effective to record more than one song during a recording session. Musicians who are members of the American Federation of Musicians union (AFM) are paid per hour (usually in a three-hour block), not per song. Therefore, when employing musicians who are union members, it will cost you the same amount of money for musicians whether you record one song or six songs in a three-hour recording session. However, I don't recommend recording multiple songs during one session until you gain some experience in demo production. Trying to cram in as many songs as possible with the time clock ticking is very stressful and can result in compromising the quality of all the song demos recorded.

In Nashville, it's not unusual for professional songwriters to record the music tracks for five or six country songs in one three-hour period. The vocals are then recorded and the tracks are mixed during another session. When songs are recorded this way, the complete demos generally cost in the range of $250 to $500 per song. Whether you're at the high or the low end of this range depends on how many musicians you hire, the credentials of those musicians, the quality of the studio, and how many songs are recorded in the three-hour block.

"Cartage" is an additional expense you need to calculate into your budget. It refers to having musical equipment and instruments delivered and set up. Many musicians haul their own equipment and do not charge any additional fee. However, it's quite common for successful drummers, keyboard players, and electric guitarists to have a company or individual move their instruments and equipment from one gig to the next. The fee varies from $50 to $150. When calculating your demo budget, ask the musicians you are hiring if there are additional fees for cartage, and how much those charges will be.

The cost of blank tape also needs to be included in your demo budget. The type of equipment available at the recording studio you choose will determine the format of the tape you need to purchase. Studios almost always provide blank multi-track tape, cassettes, and DATs if they know in advance that you wish to purchase them. However, most studios add a surcharge for providing that service. You will save money if you supply your own tape. Be sure to ask the studio what format is required. (For additional information about tape formats, see chapter 10.)

For urban and pop music demos, it is much more common to hire one musician to program the drums, bass, and keyboard parts on synthesizer. This is frequently all that is required to produce a full-sounding demo. Depending on the song, you may also choose to add a guitarist.

It may sound as though hiring one or two musicians should be less expensive than hiring a full band, but that is usually not the case. Building a music track by programming one sound at a time can be very time-consuming. Professional-quality demos of R & B or pop songs usually cost at least $400 per song and it is not uncommon for successful professional pop writers to spend more than $1,000 per demo. A developing, unpublished songwriter should not be spending this kind of money unless his or her last name is Rockefeller, Getty, or Trump. You certainly want to present your songs in their best light, but until you secure a publisher to absorb your demo costs, or begin generating income from your songs, you probably don't need to spend more than $300 per song demo. Excellent demos of ballads can be recorded for half that amount.

The amount of money you spend recording a demo of your song is affected by the amount of time you take to record the instruments and vocals. In preparing a budget, always factor in a "cushion." When Murphy wrote his famous law ("If something can go wrong—it will") he must have been producing song demos. There will inevitably be a vocalist who can't quite get the harmony right, a musician who needs an extra twenty minutes to nail his solo, an equipment failure, or an engineer who accidentally erases the last note of your song. Or, it may just take longer than you'd anticipated to convey what you'd like to hear to the musicians. As you produce more demos and practice the skills required for producing demos, you will get better at them and will require less time in the studio.

DECIDING BETWEEN SELF-PRODUCING AND DEMO SERVICES

Deciding whether to produce your own demo or to hire a demo service is similar to deciding to either hire a contractor to build an addition on your house

---

Exercise:
Planning to Record Your Demo

This exercise is designed to help you practice the skills necessary to produce a successful demo.

1. Select a song you've written, but have not yet demoed, and answer the following questions:

    ♪ What type of demo would be best to show your song's potential (i.e., keyboard/vocal, guitar/vocal, or full-band)?

    ♪ What instruments do you want to use?

    ♪ How many tracks will be required?

    ♪ Do you feel competent to produce the demo yourself, or will you hire a demo production service?

2. After you've answered these questions, research what it will cost to produce the demo you have in mind.

or build it yourself. Assess if you have the time, skills, and inclination to hire a studio, recording engineer, musicians, and vocalists; purchase tape; and oversee and make decisions about every aspect of the recording and mixing process. Consider also whether the quality of musicianship you need in order to be competitive is available in your hometown. If you live in an area that is not close to a major music center, it may be difficult to find studios, engineers, musicians, and vocalists at the level of those available in New York, Los Angeles, Nashville, Austin, Atlanta, Minneapolis, Orlando, Philadelphia, Muscle Shoals, Seattle, or other cities with vital music scenes. Using a top-quality demo service in one of those areas gives you access to professional musicians and vocalists who are skilled in recording for the current market, so it may be worthwhile to make periodic trips to a music center to produce demos. Due to supply and demand, studios and musicians in Nashville, New York, or Los Angeles may cost less than they would in other cities.

Because of the volume of demos they produce, demo services are often able to produce a demo less expensively than the writer could on his or her own. They can also take the guesswork out of your budget by quoting a flat fee per song. Many demo services work via the mail. Songwriters send a rough work tape and lyric sheet, and the demo service returns a finished demo. Some songwriters prefer to be included in each aspect of the creative process and are not comfortable being "out of the loop." They may choose to produce their demos themselves.

When turning your song over to a demo service, it's important to let them know what you want. Provide as much detail as possible. Be specific. Instead of saying "I want it to sound country," try "I'm looking for a contemporary, pop/country feel along the lines of Faith Hill's 'This Kiss.' I want to include electric guitars and an organ sound like they did on that song."

If you've always imagined an electric guitar playing the instrumental solo in a specific song, don't assume the demo service will know that. If you hear three-part vocal harmonies on your choruses, be sure to specify that, too. It can help to send a copy of another song that has similar instrumentation or the same "groove" or feel that you're hoping to capture on your song. Of course, it's not realistic to send a demo service a copy of a Madonna song that may have cost $20,000 to produce as your example, and expect your $200 demo to sound the same. But it will give the producer and musicians a direction to pursue.

On your work tape, include any instrumental hooks that you want on your demo. If you're unable to play them, sing them *a cappella* into a tape recorder. Let the demo service know whether you want a male or female vocalist and specify the style you want. Again, it's important to be specific. There's a world of difference between the styles of Aretha Franklin, Brandy, and Whitney Houston, yet they could all be considered female R & B singers. The more information you provide a demo service, the better the odds are of your demo sounding the way you imagined.

As in any business, the best referrals usually come as a result of networking. When you hear a demo that sounds great, ask the songwriter how he or she produced it. Was it produced by a demo service? Were live musicians used, or was it programmed on computers and synthesizers? Who is the singer? Who played those great electric guitar parts? You can often get referrals to demo services by calling songwriter organizations in the major music centers. The Nashville Songwriters Association International (NSAI) maintains a limited listing of Nashville-based demo services. They also recommend purchasing a copy of the *Nashville Red Book,* a comprehensive music business directory that is available in Nashville bookstores and at the NSAI office. There are similar directories that list musicians' services in New York and Los Angeles (see appendix.).

To write successful songs and produce effective demos, you don't have to be an expert in every aspect of the songwriting and demoing process. What you do have to do is honestly examine your strengths and weaknesses. You can then concentrate on the tasks you're good at, while working with professionals in those areas where you need help.

Chapter 9
Preparing to Record Your Demo

When a writer is prepared, it makes everything easier and more efficient in the studio. Some people are continuing to write when they bring the song into the studio. Part of the creative process includes possible rewrites at any time, but you should have had enough critiquing to know that the song is finished. The lyrics should be typed and you should have plenty of copies. You need a work tape that is in tune and in tempo so that it's possible to decipher what is intended. It doesn't have to be polished, but if it doesn't have a consistent meter and a consistent pitch then it's going to be a real guessing game to decipher what the song really is.

Bryan Cumming (Studio 23, Nashville demo production studio)

The more time you spend preparing for your demo, the less aggravation and expense you're likely to encounter in the studio. Always reconfirm your appointment with the studio, engineer, vocalist, and musicians several days prior to the recording session. It's important to listen to your song repeatedly and either jot down notes or tape record your melodic ideas so you won't forget them. Expressing your ideas to the musicians as clearly as possible avoids the risk that they won't know what you have in mind.

Producing demos takes a lot of time and involves many individual tasks. At a workshop I attended at the beginning of my journey as a songwriter, I met songwriter/recording artist Peter McCann ("The Right Time Of The Night," "Do You Wanna Make Love?"), who was the guest speaker. When we spoke after the seminar, I confided to Peter that I had never produced a demo before. He was kind enough to allow me to observe one of his demo recording sessions. I learned more that day than if I had read a dozen books. Try to find a songwriter who is willing to let you attend one of his or her demo sessions.

It's not uncommon for me to finish a song in only a few hours, and then spend twenty hours preparing for and recording the demo. When producing your own demo, you need a work tape, charts, lyric sheets, an arrangement, and the proper key all prepared before the recording session.

RECORDING WORK TAPES

A work tape is a rough, bare-bones recording of a song. Its purpose is simply to allow the listener to hear the words and music. A guitar or piano and a vocal will be sufficient. Your work tape may be recorded onto a portable, hand-held tape recorder at home. This tape won't be used to pitch the song. The only ones who will hear it are you and whomever you decide to trust to help you determine if your song needs additional revision. If you are unable to play an instrument or sing the song well enough to accurately get the melody on tape, hire someone to do that for you. If you do employ someone else to record your work tape, the process should not take more than an hour, or cost more than $25 to $50 per song.

The instrumental and vocal performances do not need to be perfect on a work tape. But, it is important that the melody, chords, and timing be accurate, because in the event you decide your song is ready for a demo, this is the tape the musicians and singers will listen to in order to learn the song.

WRITING CHORD CHARTS

The chord chart of a song is usually referred to as simply "the chart." This is the music your musicians read in order to know what to play. Chord charts are not to be confused with leadsheets. A chord chart shows the chords for each measure of a song. Lyrics and actual notes are not included. A leadsheet includes every note of the melody, as well as the corresponding chords and lyrics. (Sheet music is an example of a leadsheet.) A leadsheet is neither required nor expected by the musicians or vocalists at your demo session.

Prior to your recording session, clearly write out the chord chart for each song or arrange to hire someone to do that for you. For an individual to write a chord chart for you, he or she needs to hear either a live performance or a work tape that includes the chords. If you employ musicians who are members of the musicians' union, it is standard for the musician who is designated as "leader" on the session to generate the chord charts at no additional charge. If you hire someone to write out your chord charts, expect to pay $10 - $25 per song.

Photocopy the charts and bring enough copies to the session for each musician and engineer, as well as for yourself and any collaborators. This way you can all follow along. An example of a chord chart follows:

"That's Not Love"
(Jason Blume)

Intro:	C	A	B	B
	C	A	B	B
Verse:	C	A	B	B
	C	A	B	B
Pre-Chorus:	E♭	A♭	Fm	A♭/A
Chorus:	D	Bm7	Em7	C
	D	Bm7	Em7	G
	D	Bm7	Em7	C
	D	Bm7	G	F/G
Bridge:	D	E♭ (repeat four times)		

Repeat chorus and fade on choruses

In Nashville, chord charts are written using a method called "the Nashville number system." In this system, which is totally unique to Nashville, each chord is assigned a number, which is determined by its distance from the root chord. The advantage of this system is that it allows the musicians to transpose (change keys) with little effort. For instance, if the key of "C" seems too low for the singer, the charts still work perfectly in any other key. For example, in the key of "C":

C = 1
D = 2
E = 3
F = 4
G = 5
A = 6
B = 7

Sharps and flats are designated by a sharp or flat symbol preceding or following the number. For example:

C# = #1 (or 1#)
E♭ = ♭3 (or 3♭)

A minor key is designated by a dash (-) immediately following the number, or a lowercase letter "m." For example, in the key of "C":

C minor = 1- (or 1m)
F# minor = 4#- (or 4#m)

An example of a Nashville number chart follows:

"Hold On"
(Jason Blume)

Intro:	6m	4	5	5
	6m	4	5	5
Verse:	4	5	4/5	1
	6m	4	5	6m
	4	5	4/5	1
	1	4/b7	4	4
Chorus:	1	4	5	5
	1	4	b7	4
	6m	4	5	5
	b7	4	5	1

(Repeat verse and chorus)

Bridge:	1	4	1	b7
	1	1	5	4

Repeat chorus

There are many more symbols and intricacies involved in the Nashville number system. If you're interested in mastering this method, read *The Nashville Number System* by Chas Williams, which is available through NSAI.

Whether you need a conventional chord chart or one that uses the Nashville number system, if you are unable to generate it yourself, there are lots of professionals who can do that for you.

DECIDING ON AN ARRANGEMENT

A song's arrangement refers to the way the different sections of the song are "arranged" in relation to each other to build a complete song. For example, a song can be arranged as follows:

8-bar instrumental introduction
Verse 1
Chorus
4-bar instrumental turnaround
Verse 2
Chorus

8-bar instrumental solo
Chorus
Repeat chorus
Fade

The other crucial aspect of an arrangement is deciding which instruments will play which parts (i.e., will the lead solo be played by electric guitar or synthesizer or will the primary sound be keyboards or guitars?). You do not need to write out the specific notes that each musician will play. Your musicians create their own parts based on the input you provide them and your chord chart. That's partly why it's crucial to hire the best musicians your budget allows. The players bring not only their technical prowess, but also their ability to create parts that enhance your song and make it more "radio friendly."

The best musicians can make your song sound the way you'd always hoped, or even better. However, they need to know what you have in mind. If you want the guitar or the keyboards to take the "fills" (little instrumental phrases that fill in the bare spots where the vocalist is not singing) you've got to let the musicians know. They need to hear any specific instrumental melodic phrases you want them to play.

A great arrangement provides an imaginative setting for the song with tasteful use of the instruments at your disposal and a certain amount of simplicity. It should enhance the tune, rather than just state it.

Tom Scott (Grammy-winning arranger who has recorded with artists including Barbra Streisand, Paul McCartney, and Joni Mitchell) as quoted in *The Recording Industry Career Handbook*.

It doesn't take musical training or extensive technical knowledge to express how you envision your song—just plain English, some thought, and planning. It can also be tremendously helpful to let your musicians hear a tape of another song that has the feel or instrumentation that you imagine for your song.

If you have a specific signature lick in mind, include it on your work tape, or sing it *a cappella* for the musicians. You can compose these identifiable melodic phrases in advance, or you can ask the demo musicians to play a catchy lick during the introduction.

Exercise:

Creating a Song Arrangement

1. Choose a favorite song in a genre that you compose in. Be sure the song you select is not one that was written by the artist.

2. Get a recording of the song, study it, and answer as many of the following questions as you can:

♪ How many bars is the introduction?

♪ What instruments are playing during the intro, first verse, chorus, second verse, etc.?

♪ Does the arrangement seem to "build" or do all the instruments play right from the beginning?

♪ How many bars are there between the first chorus and the second verse (the turnaround)?

♪ Are new instruments brought in to add additional interest to the second verse?

♪ If there is an instrumental solo, how long is it and what instrument plays it?

♪ Does the song have an abrupt ending or a fade?

3. Create an arrangement for a song that you've written, by answering the questions listed above.

Karen Taylor-Good relates that while recording the demo of the Grammy-nominated song she co-wrote with Burton Collins, "How Can I Help You Say Goodbye," keyboard player Ed Tossing composed the musical interlude that became the signature lick. That extra hook was used, note for note, in versions of the song recorded by Patty Loveless, Al Jarreau, and Laura Branigan. One way or another, signature licks need to be included on your demo to give your song its best shot.

Here are the notes I brought to the studio regarding the arrangement for one particular song:

Start with an 8-bar intro

First 4 bars of intro—just acoustic guitar (finger-picking signature lick)

Second 4 bars of intro—bring in the full band
First verse—keep it sparse—mostly acoustic guitar with piano fills
Build into the chorus
Chorus—make it huge—have gritty electric guitars carry it
4-bar turnaround—just like the second half of the intro
Second verse—have acoustic guitar take the fills; add electric guitars
Second chorus—even bigger than the first
Fade on repeating choruses (use signature lick)

When the musicians ask you a question regarding the arrangement (i.e., "How do you feel about changing the G chord on the fourth bar of the chorus to a 'G sus'?"), if you don't understand, ask them to play it for you. Similarly, if you need to hear how it would sound to have the keyboard play the fills in the second verse, ask the musicians to play it for you.

DETERMINING THE PROPER KEY

The key refers to pitch—where you place your song on the musical scale. It determines how high or low the notes will go. The only way to know what key to record your demo in is to ask the vocalist. Singers don't have one particular key that they always sing in. It's determined on a song-by-song basis, depending on range and mood. Some songs sound best with the vocalist singing at the top of his or her vocal range. Other songs sound more pleasing using the singer's lower notes. Before your singer selects a key, you need to communicate whether you'd prefer the song to be belted out near the top of the singer's range, or sung softly, near the bottom of his or her vocal register.

Get a copy of your work tape to your singer at least a week prior to your recording session. Include all the pertinent information the singer needs to know regarding your session (i.e., the address and telephone number of the studio, your home telephone number, and the day and time of the recording session). This gives the vocalist ample time to learn the song and to choose the key that works best. If you are working with a singer who is not certain how to determine his or her key, have him or her learn your song and sing it for you where it's comfortable. Tell your musicians what the singer's first note is and they will be able to determine the key. If you don't play a musical instrument and don't know what the first note is that the vocalist is singing, record it. (Be sure you have good batteries in your tape recorder. Otherwise, when you play it back for the musicians, the pitch may be altered.)

You need to know the key prior to having the charts written, unless you are using the Nashville number system. It's a good idea to have the vocalist sing you a verse and a chorus of your song (even over the phone) in the key he or she has chosen to ensure it sounds like what you intend—before committing the music to tape.

HIRING THE BEST MUSICIANS

When I recorded my first demos in Nashville, I was living in Los Angeles, but was signed to a staff-writing deal in Nashville. The Nashville style of producing demos was totally foreign to me and I had no idea which musicians were the best. My publisher produced at least my first twenty Nashville demos, while showing me the ropes. (If you don't have a publisher to teach you how to produce demos, you might enlist the help of a more experienced songwriter, or an aspiring producer.) One thing I observed was that the musicians my publisher hired had a higher level of talent and professionalism than anyone I had previously worked with. I could hardly believe what they were capable of.

These demo players were the "A Team." The musicians were often booked a month or more in advance and played sessions like mine ten to fifteen times per week. They knew just what to do to make the songs they recorded sound like those on the radio. In a three-hour recording session, they transformed six songs they had never previously heard into what sounded like finished records. They added catchy instrumental licks and rhythms that took my songs to the next level.

Surprisingly, many of the top musicians will gladly play demo sessions on the days when they're not booked for "master sessions" (for record albums). After I had recorded at least a dozen demos with the musicians mentioned above, I was at a friend's home in Los Angeles and picked up a copy of the latest Garth Brooks album. I could hardly believe my eyes. Three of the players from my demo sessions were on Garth Brooks' album! Musicians who have played on my demos have recorded with a list of artists that reads like a "Who's Who" in the music industry: George Harrison, Bette Midler, Brooks and Dunn, Reba McEntire, Celine Dion, Patty Loveless, Monica, The Pointer Sisters, George Strait, All-4-One, Natalie Cole, Billy Ray Cyrus, and many more.

It may not be financially or geographically feasible for you to work with musicians of this caliber right away. Hiring the "best" means the best that you have access to at this point in time. No level of musicianship can change a poorly written song into a great one. But presuming that you've written a strong song, the creativity and expertise that professional musicians can contribute can make the difference between a demo that sounds "pretty good" and one that gets a "Yes!"

SELECTING THE RIGHT STUDIO

There are several factors to consider when choosing the studio that will best serve your needs: the number of tracks required; whether you're using a live band vs. synthesizers; the equipment available; and your budget.

The number of tracks you need immediately narrows your choice of studios. If you are recording a full band and multiple tracks of vocals, you probably want a studio with at least 16-track capability. A guitar/vocal or keyboard/vocal recording obviously requires fewer tracks.

Some studios are set up to accommodate recording many musicians at the same time. If you are working with a live band, you need a facility that has a room large enough to comfortably fit your musicians and their gear. Isolation booths keep the sounds of the acoustic instruments (i.e., acoustic guitar) and any instruments that are recorded by placing a microphone in front of a speaker (i.e., electric guitar) from "bleeding" into each other. You need a studio that has an isolation booth for each acoustic instrument that will be recorded at the same time (i.e., piano, acoustic guitar, fiddle).

Some studios consist of one small room designed to record synthesizers and vocals. If the musical tracks of your demo consist exclusively of electronic keyboard parts, this type of studio may best suit your needs.

Most studios are glad to provide prospective customers with a list of the equipment included in the price of the studio rental. Top-quality microphones and equipment that can achieve a variety of effects (i.e., reverb units, finalizers, compressors, etc.) play a big role in shaping the sound of your demo. You don't need to be able to operate or even understand the specific functions of these items. That's your recording engineer's job. But before deciding on a studio, check with your engineer to be sure that the equipment available is sufficient to produce the professional sound you require.

Budget limitations play a major role in selecting your studio. "You get what you pay for" definitely applies to recording studios. However, studio prices are often negotiable. A savvy studio manager will often offer a bargain rate rather than leave the studio empty. It pays to shop around. While you certainly want the best-sounding demo you can comfortably afford, your budget will probably dictate whether that means recording in a converted garage or in a posh setting with a hot tub.

The most important consideration is "How does the music sound?" Visit a studio in person before booking it. Ask to hear samples of demos that have been recorded there. If the studio price also includes a recording engineer, ask to hear demos that were recorded by the engineer you'll be working with.

Learning to Speak "Musician"

For those songwriters with limited knowledge of musical theory, trying to explain what you want your musicians to play can be a frustrating, difficult experience. Failure to accurately convey what you have in mind is even more aggravating. When producing a demo, if you can't find a way to express what you envision for your song, you won't get it.

It often feels as though the musicians are speaking in a secret language. The words sound familiar but they make no sense. (i.e., "On that fourth line of the second ending, when the 'E' over 'G' switches to the tonic, what about switching to the four over one split five?"). I used to feel intimidated and embarrassed by my ignorance. Now, I remind myself I have different skills and talents that are important and valid. In the many years that I've been producing demos I've learned quite a bit, but I may never be able to speak "musician" fluently. I don't have to—but I do need an interpreter.

You're a creative person. Use everything you have in your verbal arsenal to explain what you want—in plain English. Then ask one of your musicians to act as your interpreter. Confide to him or her that it's difficult for you to understand the technical jargon. Have your interpreter explain the things you're not clear about, and don't be afraid to ask the band to play you examples of what they're talking about. It takes a little longer in the studio, but you're far more likely to come out with a demo that represents your vision for your song—and you'll be learning in the process.

Choosing the Best Vocalist

No single element can make or break your demo as much as the singer. A singer who has problems with pitch or timing, or who is not up to the professional standard, distracts the listener from your song. On the other hand, an extraordinary vocalist can wring every drop of emotion from your words and music and play a big role in "selling" your song.

I'm a good singer. I've sung on television shows, been a lead singer in several bands, and have performed professionally in nightclubs. But I'm rarely the *best* vocalist I can find to "sell" my songs. When selecting a demo singer, I've learned to put my ego aside and act in the best interest of each song. When I demo a country song, I want a genuine country vocalist: someone who naturally adds the phrasing and embellishments that help my song sound like the real deal. Likewise, when choosing a singer for an R & B song, I want someone who lives and breathes that genre—not someone who is *trying* to sound as if he or she does.

Each song has its own particular needs. Choosing a demo singer is like casting a role in a film or a play. A great actor will not be suited for every role, and a great singer is not necessarily the right singer for every song you write. Mariah Carey is an amazing singer, but I wouldn't hire her to sing a country demo.

When you hear a great singer on someone else's demo, ask if you can have that singer's phone number. In Nashville, AFTRA (American Federation of Television and Radio Artists—the singers' union) holds periodic showcases where you can hear live performances by some of the best demo singers out there. If you are near a major music center, you can probably hear great singers performing in local clubs. You can also get recommendations from recording studios and demo services. Professional vocalists are glad to provide a tape that shows their range and various styles.

The vocalist is the most important (part of the demo) because they are selling the song.

Judy Stakee (Vice President of Creative Services, Warner Chappell Music Publishing)

Some of today's demo singers will become tomorrow's superstars. Among the artists who sang demos in Nashville while waiting for their big break are Garth Brooks, Alan Jackson, and Trisha Yearwood. This is the caliber of vocalist that is required to compete with the professionals. (I know someone who has framed the invoice he received from superstar Trisha Yearwood, requesting $35 payment for singing a demo!)

Many developing writers also have aspirations to be performing artists. It can be especially difficult for them to accept that they are not the best vocalist to sing a particular song. Nonetheless, it's no coincidence that when I began hiring professional demo singers to record my songs (instead of singing them myself) I began getting publishing offers. I've worked with many developing songwriters who are "good," but not great, singers. I've seen the hurt looks when I told them they needed to hire professionals to sing their demos. My suggestion to writers in this category is to hire the best singer you can find. After your professional singer has recorded his or her vocals, record your own version for your friends and family, and for your own enjoyment. But when it's time to pitch your song, use the version that gives your song its best shot.

Using vocalists with "star potential" can have additional benefits. Hit songwriter Wayne Tester told the following story:

> *I wrote "A Place For Us" with Jimmy Scott, who writes for Chrysalis music, and he knew the artist Kim Hill. He got Kim to come in and sing on the demo and she really liked it. She played it for the producer. He really liked it and they cut it. It was her first single on Starsong/EMI records and stayed at number one for two weeks on the Contemporary Christian charts.*

The price of hiring a professional demo singer varies in different areas. The going rate in Nashville currently averages $60 to $75 per song for country demos. R & B and pop vocalists can command double these amounts because demos in these categories often require additional background parts. Supply and demand also affects the price. Nashville is crawling with up-and-coming country singers, but top-notch pop and R & B singers are harder to find there. Similarly, a great country singer in Los Angeles can charge much more to sing a demo than he or she could in Nashville.

Demo singers command higher prices in Los Angeles and New York. The best studio vocalists earn $300 or more per song. While that may seem like a lot of money, a great singer's contribution to your demo is worth every penny. A pro vocalist also saves you time (and therefore money) in the studio. He or she will arrive prepared (having already learned your song), and will deliver a professional performance quickly.

Don't let your ego, or the cost of a professional singer, convince you to settle for second best. You can't afford *not* to hire the best vocalist available.

DECIDING WHETHER TO USE A MALE OR FEMALE VOCALIST

In many instances the decision as to whether your song is best served by a male vocalist or a female vocalist is clearly dictated by the song's lyric. Some songs contain lyrics that are obviously gender-specific. But other songs work equally well being sung by either a male or a female artist. In these instances, one option is to record two separate demos.

Recording the same song in two different keys, and hiring both a male and a female singer, is less expensive than producing demos of two separate songs. If you are using a live band, once the first version has been recorded it should only take your musicians another ten or fifteen minutes to duplicate their parts in another key. For a synthesizer programmer the process is often as simple as pressing the "transpose" button. Of course, you still incur the added expense of an additional singer, as well as the time to mix another version.

If your budget does not allow for both a male and a female version of your song, the conventional wisdom has always been to use a male vocalist. Female artists frequently record songs that have male vocalists on the demo, but men are far less likely to do the reverse. Several female rock stars are reputed to actually prefer demos with male vocals, but I've rarely heard of a male artist actively seeking out demos that have female vocalists. That's not to say that a male artist will never record a song that has been sung by a woman. Country star Collin Raye has recorded several songs that Karen Taylor-Good sang on the demos. But this is more the exception than the rule.

Generally, I use a male vocalist for those songs that could go either way. But for the songs that are my personal favorites, I usually invest the extra time and money to record a male and a female demo.

If all of this seems overwhelming, remember that it's a learning process. When I began songwriting I never imagined that I would ever be able to competently produce a demo session. But each time I recorded a demo, I learned a little bit more and was a little less stressed. Now I do it with great success on a regular basis.

Chapter 10
Mixing

*In a mixing situation you can take your song in so many
different directions. Do you want it to be really aggressive
sounding track-wise, or more laid back? What kind of
reverbs do you want to use? How hot is the vocal going to
be in the mix? Where are you going to place stuff like the
background vocals?*

*Before you mix you need to know which direction you want
to take, because it's like making a cake. You can have all
these ingredients but you need to know ahead of time
which type you're making—chocolate, vanilla, or three-
layer cake—or you can waste a lot of time. It's critical to
have the correct balance of all the ingredients.*

Lee Groitzsch (Recording Engineer/Studio Manager, Battery Studios)

In chapter 9 you learned about multi-track recording—recording each instrument and vocal on its own track. Using electronic equipment to improve the
quality of those sounds, finding the proper balance between them, and placing
those sounds (left, right, or center) within the track defines the art of "mixing."
Mixing is the job of your recording engineer, but ultimately, the songwriter producing his or her own demo session oversees the process and has the final say.

Mixes can be accomplished either manually (with the engineer sliding the
faders and turning the knobs by hand) or by using "automation." Automation
is generally found in more sophisticated studios. When it is used, the engineer
programs each "move" (change in level) into a computer and then the computer automatically executes those moves.

The advantage of using automation is that you are able to change the volume on any given track for any amount of time (i.e., you may want the piano
to be louder during one specific bar)—without altering the volume of the other

tracks. With automation, it's not necessary to re-mix your entire song to raise or lower the level of the sounds recorded on any given track. It's easy to adjust the volume of the vocals to make them louder or softer for different lines or words. This process is referred to as "riding" the vocal.

The recording engineer may spend an hour or more just adjusting the sounds of the various drums. Since I have no expertise in this area (and it's incredibly boring to listen to drum sounds) I hire the best engineers I can afford and let them do what they do best. When they have a "rough mix" ready, I listen and make suggestions. I may want the guitar solo to be a tiny bit louder, or I might want to raise or lower the level of several lines of the vocals.

Unless you are a skilled engineer, the recording console probably resembles the cockpit of an alien spacecraft—and is about as easy to operate. You don't need to know how to operate "the board," as it is frequently called. If something sounds too loud, or too soft, or the vocal sounds "muddy," or "tinny," ask the engineer to adjust the equalization "eq"—pronounced EE-CUE—levels. The eq refers to the high end (treble), low end (bass), and mid-range sound waves. Once again, it helps to use your verbal skills to describe what you want, or don't want, your demo to sound like.

It's helpful to listen to your mix on a stereo you're accustomed to (i.e., your car stereo or a boombox) during the mixing process. It can also help to listen to your mix while standing outside the studio control room, or down the hall. Be sure you can hear the vocals clearly.

If you're unsure whether you've captured the best mix for your song have your engineer run several "alternate mixes." For example, depending on the song, you may want to record a version with the lead vocal a bit louder, another with additional (or less) bass, and a third mix that places the guitars at a higher volume. Having done this, if you don't like one of the mixes when you listen to them away from the incredible studio sound system (where everything sounds great) you have several options.

TAPE AND RECORDING FORMATS

There are quite a few tape and recording formats you may encounter in the process of recording a demo tape. The formats discussed below are those most commonly used to record song and artist demos.

Cassette

When you play a song for a publisher or pitch it to a recording artist, label executive, or record producer, it is expected that your song will be presented on an audio cassette. Cassettes are manufactured in lengths varying from five minutes to fifty minutes per side. Using an hour-long cassette to pitch a three-minute song is wasteful and expensive. It also sends a signal to the listener that this tape has come from an amateur. Professional songwriters buy cassettes in various lengths in bulk. They can be purchased from wholesalers in most areas, or can be ordered via the mail. Tape wholesalers often advertise in songwriter publications.

After you've invested the time to craft your song to the very best of your ability, and the expense of recording a demo that captures the essence of your song, don't throw it all away by recording your song onto a so-called "bargain" cassette. All your hard work will be in vain if an inferior-quality cassette makes your demo sound as if it was recorded in a wind tunnel, if the tape has "drop-out" (sections of the tape that do not record), or, even worse, if it jams in the listener's tape recorder.

The "bias" of a cassette refers to frequencies the tape is capable of reproducing. It's not necessary for songwriters to understand the technical aspects of bias and frequency. But you should be aware that high-bias cassettes produce better sound. "Normal" bias should be used only to record the spoken word—not music. Your song deserves a high-bias, professional-quality cassette.

Reel-to-Reel

As the name implies, this format consists of two separate reels of tape—the "supply" reel and the "take-up" reel. Several of the multi-track formats use reel-to-reel tape in a variety of widths: 24-track analog recorders use 2-inch reel-to-reel tape; 16-track analog recorders use ½-inch, 1-inch, or 2-inch reel-to-reel tape, depending on the machine; 32-track digital recorders use 1-inch digital tape; and ¼-inch reel-to-reel tape is generally used only for 2-track or 4-track recording.

Most reel-to-reel tape recorders offer the option of recording at "low" or "high" speeds. (Recording speed is measured in inches per second, "ips.") Faster speeds result in better recording quality. But, the difference in sound quality between songs recorded at high speed versus low speed is so subtle that most listeners are unable to differentiate. Therefore, when recording a demo, many writers opt for using the slower speed, which uses less tape and results in a lower cost.

Until the late 1980s it was standard practice to mix multi-track recordings onto a ½-inch reel-to-reel format. This became the "master" recording, from which all other copies were generated. Reel-to-reel masters have since gone the way of 8-track tapes, vinyl record albums, and dinosaurs. The current industry standard requires mixing your multi-track recordings onto a DAT master.

DAT

An acronym for "digital audio tape," a DAT is about two-thirds the size of a regular audio cassette and contains digital recording tape. DATs are manufactured in varying lengths that can record from just a few minutes to up to two hours. The DAT has become the standard format for a master tape. When your demo is mixed, it is recorded onto a DAT. This becomes your "master" from which your cassette copies or CDs are recorded. When you play a song for a publisher it may be on a cassette or a DAT. However, if the publisher decides to publish your song he or she will need a DAT copy.

ADATS

"ADAT" is an acronym for Alesis Digital Audio Technology. Alesis is the name of the company that manufactures this 8-track digital recording format. The ADAT recording format is found in many home studios. One advantage of ADAT recording is that it is relatively inexpensive. Also, several of these 8-track machines can be linked up to each other to allow 16, 24, 32, 48, or more tracks of recording. The primary disadvantage of this format is that when two or more machines are linked together, there is sometimes a delay of several seconds before the recorders "sync up," or are ready to record. The recording machine itself and the high-resolution (S-VHS) tape used in this format are both referred to as "ADATs."

CDs

Compact discs, or CDs, are an additional type of digital recording format. Although it is not the industry standard, it is becoming more common for song demos, and especially artist demos, to be recorded onto CDs. Machines referred to as "CD burners" have become commercially available and provide songwriters with an inexpensive way to record their material onto CDs. The advantages of the CD format include the "clean" digital sound and the capability to reproduce copies to other digital sources without sacrificing the quality of the sound. The other benefit of the CD format is the ease with which you can locate any given song on a CD.

Hard Drive

Technology is now available that makes it possible to record directly onto the hard drive of a computer. When using this recording format, a computer serves as a multi-track recorder. The digitized musical information on each separate track is recorded directly into the computer. This information is stored onto a hard drive, as any other data might be.

The most common hard-drive recording technology in current use is called Pro Tools. Pro Tools is the most popular equipment for pitch correction. Using this system your engineer can tune a vocal or instrument that was recorded flat or sharp. Radar (Random Access Digital Audio Recording) is another popular system of hard-drive recording.

Hard-drive formats provide amazing capacity to manipulate recorded information. Using these formats it's easy for a competent engineer to move and alter any of the recorded data. During one recent recording session (using the Radar system) I loved the way my singer sang the first line of the first chorus, so I had my engineer copy it and insert it into every chorus. (This is often referred to as "flying" a line; i.e., "Would you fly the first line of the chorus into the second and third choruses?") There was a place within my song where the singer didn't clearly enunciate the "T" sound at the end of a word, so my engineer copied a "T" from another word and inserted it. On that same song, in the final measure the drums were a bit sloppy so my engineer copied that same drum pattern from a spot where it had been better executed.

The advantages of hard-drive formats are: Since no actual tape is used, any tape noise, or hiss, is eliminated; there's no time required to rewind or fast-forward—you can go instantly to any location within the song; there's an "undo" command if you make a mistake; it's easier to edit and manipulate data without losing any sound quality with this format; and you can splice without the risks inherent in putting razor to tape.

Analog vs. Digital

The analog recording process records the actual wave forms of the sounds onto magnetic particles on the tape. The digital recording process records sound waves by converting them to digital numbers (ones and zeros). During playback, the digital numbers are converted back to sound waves. This is all far too complicated for me to comprehend. I can barely program my VCR, so I leave the technical matters to my engineer. But you should be aware of some differences between analog and digital recording.

Analog recording is done onto reel-to-reel tape or audio cassettes. Digital recordings may be recorded onto DATs, CDs, digital 1-inch reel-to-reel tape (for 32-track digital machines), ADATs, or directly onto the hard drive of a computer.

Producers with very discerning ears sometimes prefer the sound that can be achieved via analog recording, as opposed to digital—or vice versa. Analog recording is reputed to have additional warmth. Digital recordings are said to be cleaner, more accurate sound reproductions. One of the big advantages of the digital format is its capability to record from one digital source to another digital source (i.e., DAT to DAT, or DAT to CD) without sacrificing the sound quality. The sound remains virtually the same, no matter how many generations removed you are from the original "master" DAT. But when copies are made from one analog source to another (i.e., cassette to cassette) each successive recording has less clarity and more unwanted tape "hiss" than the previous one.

LEARNING ABOUT TRACK MIXES

A "track mix" is a recording of the final mix of your song without the vocals. A "TV mix" includes all the music and the background vocals, but no lead vocal. Although the TV mix has other uses, it was so named because it allows a performer to sing live on television to pre-recorded music tracks that include the background vocals.

There are several reasons why it is crucial to always record a track mix and a TV mix, in addition to a complete mix. Let's say you decide to rewrite your lyric after your demo has been recorded. If you have a track mix on a DAT, all you need to do is "dump" (transfer) your track mix onto a multi-track recorder. Then, when you record your new vocal, your music tracks are already mixed. All the engineer needs to do is mix the vocals into the pre-mixed musical tracks. You save the considerable expense of having to start from scratch to mix your song again. When you record a track mix (or a TV mix) do not fade the track. Your engineer can initiate a fade at the spot that sounds best with your new vocal.

Having a track mix also allows you the flexibility to put a different vocalist on your song, without incurring the expense of an additional full mix. There are instances when artists may request a track mix so they can practice singing your song and determine whether it is something they want to record. Hit songwriter Wayne Tester related the following incredible story:

> *When Garth Brooks' producer heard "The Change" he put it on hold. Garth called and said, "I'm not sure if it's my kind of song." A few days went by and he called back and said, "Give me the demo track without the vocal on it so I can practice it." A week went by*

*and he called back and said "I want to put my vocal on the demo
track to see if it works for my voice." He called back and said he
wanted to cut it. It was a single and was used as a tribute for the
victims of the Oklahoma bombing.*

Always run a track mix.

Probably the most important skill to acquire as a demo producer is the ability to surround yourself with the most talented musicians, vocalists, and recording engineers you can afford. Like most of the other elements of songwriting, learning to produce demos that successfully communicate and "sell" your songs is a skill that takes patience and practice to develop. It's not realistic to expect the first several demos you produce to be perfect. It's a learning process and there will be successes and failures along the way. But as you learn new ways to express your vision for your songs, and find those professionals who can help you achieve it, you'll find that you can produce demos that make your songs sound as good as you'd imagined—and sometimes even better!

DEMO CHECKLIST

Photocopy this checklist and refer to it when planning for and evaluating each of your song demos.

Prior to Recording:

☐ Song has been critiqued and deemed ready

☐ A work tape has been recorded

☐ Chord charts have been prepared

☐ An arrangement has been created

☐ The proper key has been determined

☐ Signature licks have been written (or planned for)

☐ Blank tape has been purchased (or arranged for)

☐ A singer who is appropriate for this particular song has been selected

☐ Musicians, studio, and vocalist have been confirmed

After Recording—Evaluating Your Demo's Effectiveness:

☐ The quality of your musicians measures up to the professional standard

☐ The recording is clear (no discernible hiss or distortion)

☐ The vocalist's pitch is accurate

☐ The vocal is easy to hear and you can understand the words

☐ A track mix and TV mix have been recorded

Step V
Taking Care of Business

The most successful writers I've seen are the ones who really get out there. It's imperative to do the business.

Franne Golde (Hit songwriter with cuts by artists including Whitney Houston, Celine Dion, the Kinleys, and Diana Ross)

Chapter 11
Learning Where the Money Comes From

One of the things songwriters can do to help themselves is literally to sit down and go through the Songwriters Guild of America (song publishing) contract paragraph by paragraph, with a large yellow pad nearby. Any words or concepts they don't understand should be written down—even if they fill up ten pages. This list will give them all the questions they'll need to ask from industry people. I think it's unfortunate when songwriters spend too much time on the craft and neglect the business side and then get taken advantage of.

Aaron Meza (Western Regional Director, The Songwriters Guild of America)

Many developing songwriters resent having to be a businessperson. I've heard them lament, "I've written the song—now let somebody else take care of the business." But the reality is that this is the music *business*. The greatest song in the world will not become a hit if it's neither demoed nor brought to the attention of music business professionals. Although it's perfectly acceptable to write solely for your own pleasure, if your goal is to be successful in the music business you have to pay as much attention to the *business* as you do to the *music*.

When I was beginning to develop my songwriting skills, I attended more workshops and classes than I can count. My teachers tried to explain how songwriters got paid, but the source of that money somehow remained a mystery to me. It was only after I began receiving income from my songs that the pieces of the puzzle started to fit together.

Before continuing further, it'll be helpful to understand the difference between a music publishing company and a record label. A publishing company (also referred to as a music publisher or a song publisher) has many functions (see chapter 12). However, its primary function is to generate income from songwriters' songs. This income typically results from getting these songs recorded by recording artists, or included in television shows or films. The term "publisher" is often used interchangeably to refer to an individual who's employed by a publishing company to pitch songs and to the company itself.

A record label (or record company) is a company that's in the business of producing, distributing, and selling albums (i.e., CDs and cassettes). A record label signs recording artists (i.e., singers, bands, and instrumental performers). If these artists do not write their own songs, members of the record label's A & R (Artists and Repertoires) department will typically meet with publishers in the hopes of finding hit songs for their artists.

Songwriters' incomes come from a variety of sources. Songwriters earn money primarily from mechanical royalties, performance royalties, print royalties, synchronization licenses, and publishers' advances. If a songwriter is also a recording artist or producer, he or she will earn additional royalties, but those royalties are totally separate from monies generated by the songs themselves. This chapter will give you a basic understanding of how a song generates money. Hopefully, before long, your songs will be earning income—and then all this will make perfect "cents!"

MECHANICAL ROYALTIES

"Mechanical royalties" is the name given to revenues paid for the "mechanical reproduction" of musical compositions on sound recordings. It refers to royalties paid for the sale of a physical, tangible product containing music—audio cassettes, compact discs, record albums, and videocassettes all generate mechanical royalties. In plain English, mechanical royalties are the monies you are paid for the copies of your songs that are sold.

In the United States, the mechanical royalty rate is established by Congress and is called the "statutory rate." With one exception (the 3/4 rate, discussed later in this chapter) it is not negotiable and applies equally to all songwriters. Therefore, Michael Jackson, Diane Warren, Garth Brooks, and you all receive the same mechanical royalty for each album or single sold.

Payment is made per unit. A "unit" refers to one recording of a song on an audiocassette, CD, or record, whether it's an album or a single. Each song included on an album is considered one unit. If you are lucky enough to have written ten songs on an album, you will be paid for ten units for each album sold. Occasionally, more than one version of a song may be included on an album or a single (i.e., the radio mix and a dance mix, or urban mix). In these instances, the writer is paid for each version of the song, just as if it were a separate song.

For single releases, mechanical royalties (sometimes referred to as "mechanicals") are paid equally for the "A" side (the song that is sent to radio stations and marketed as the probable hit) and the "B" side (a song that the buyer is probably not familiar with). Therefore, the writer of the hit song and the writer of the unknown song receive the same amount of money for the sale of each single. This may not seem fair, but don't worry. As you'll learn later in this chapter, the writer of the hit will earn the bulk of his or her income from performance royalties.

The mechanical royalty rate for the United States has been negotiated to allow for increases in songwriters' incomes through January 1, 2006. The rate structure, which took effect January 1, 1998, is as follows:

January 1, 1998:	7.10 cents
January 1, 2000:	7.55 cents
January 1, 2002:	8.00 cents
January 1, 2004:	8.50 cents
January 1, 2006:	9.10 cents

These rates are applicable for compositions of up to five minutes in duration. Compositions exceeding five minutes are paid 1.3 cents per minute. Some quick math shows that, using the rate in effect January 1, 1998, a song included on an album (or a single) that sells 500,000 units generates $35,500 in mechanical royalties. Using this same rate, each song on a million-selling album earns $71,000. The mechanical royalty earned by one song included on an album that sells twenty million copies is $1,420,000! (An explanation of how this money is divided between writers and publishers appears in chapter 12.)

Mechanical royalties are paid from the record label to the publisher. The publisher distributes the writers' share of the income to the writers either quarterly or biannually. Payments for sales within the U.S. are made approximately six months after the sale of the product. However, it sometimes takes eighteen months or longer to receive mechanical royalties generated outside the U.S. Collecting the money is not always an easy job for music publishers. Therefore, the majority of publishers contract an outside firm (i.e., The Harry Fox Agency or Copyright Management Inc.) to handle the paperwork involved in the collection of their mechanical royalties (see appendix).

The Harry Fox Agency, Inc. (HFA), is the main organization for the administration of mechanical rights in the United States. HFA represents more than

19,000 music publishers, licensing the use of music on records, tapes, and CDs. They distribute more than $400,000,000 per year in royalties.

Although the mechanical royalty rate is set by Congress, there are instances in which a record label contacts a publishing company and requests that it (acting on a songwriter's behalf) accept only three-quarters of the regular (statutory) mechanical royalty rate. This is referred to as the "¾ rate," or "controlled composition clause," and most commonly occurs when the record label anticipates that the recording artist or record producer will be writing, or co-writing, his or her own songs. If you collaborate with a recording artist or producer, some of the record labels insist that the artist, producer, and his or her co-writers agree to accept a ¾ rate.

Other instances in which a record label might feel justified to pay a ¾ rate include the re-release of a product as part of a lower-priced "catalog" series, inclusion in a compilation, or inclusion in a box set that will be sold at a lower price. When these situations occur, the songwriter may be consulted by the publisher, but it is the publisher's decision as to whether to accept a reduced mechanical royalty rate.

DOMESTIC AND FOREIGN ROYALTIES

Those royalties generated from sales within the United States are referred to as "domestic royalties." As you have already learned, mechanical royalties in the U.S. (and also in Canada) are determined by legislative process. They are a fixed amount regardless of the selling price of the recording.

"Foreign royalties" are those that come from sales outside the United States. The mechanical royalty rate varies from country to country and is often considerably higher than in the U.S. In the vast majority of countries outside the U.S. and Canada, the mechanical royalty rate is arrived at by calculating a percentage of the selling price of the recording. Throughout Europe, the mechanical royalty rate is 9.306 percent of the wholesale selling price. In Latin America the mechanical royalty rate is 6.75 percent of the retail price. In Japan it is 5.6 percent of the retail selling price.

Foreign mechanical royalties are typically collected by "sub-publishers." A sub-publisher is a publishing company that acts on another publisher's behalf to represent their catalog and collect royalties in other countries ("territories"). Publishers may contract a different sub-publisher in each of the countries where their catalog is generating income, or they may choose to work with one major company that has offices throughout the world. For a percentage of the mechanical royalties they collect, sub-publishers eliminate the administrative responsibilities, some of the expense, and the hassle (i.e., language barriers) of collecting income from foreign countries.

PERFORMANCE ROYALTIES AND PERFORMING RIGHTS ORGANIZATIONS

"Performance royalties" are monies paid for performances of a song. However, the definition of "performance" in this instance encompasses far more than live concerts. Performances include radio airplay, television broadcasts, and the use of live or recorded music in a variety of establishments that use music in an effort to enhance their business. Music played on jukeboxes, on airplanes, in restaurants (with some exceptions, based on the size of the restaurant), bowling alleys, roller rinks, nightclubs, retail stores, at sporting events, and in many other establishments constitutes performances which generate performance royalties.

Songs fall under the category of intellectual (non-tangible) property. Under the U.S. Copyright Act, they cannot be performed for commercial profit without paying the copyright owner. Therefore, businesses and individuals that use songs for commercial profit are required to pay the writer and publisher of those songs. Before continuing with the discussion of performance royalties it will be helpful to have an understanding of performing rights organizations.

When a song becomes a major hit it is often broadcast on the radio more than ten thousand times per week. It's impossible for songwriters and publishers to keep track of all of the performances of their songs, and to collect royalties for those performances. Performing rights organizations have been established for those purposes. These organizations acquire the rights to collect performance royalties on behalf of the writers and publishers they represent. In the United States, the performing rights organizations (PROs) are ASCAP (American Society of Composers, Authors, & Publishers), BMI (Broadcast Music International), and SESAC (formerly known as Society of European Stage Authors and Composers).

Songwriters and publishers must join a performing rights organization in order to receive performance royalties. A songwriter may be a member of only one organization at any given time. However, a publisher must be a member of each organization that collects performance royalties for copyrights he or she controls. For instance, if a publisher represents a song written by an ASCAP-affiliated songwriter, the publisher must be ASCAP-affiliated. It's quite common for major publishers to be ASCAP-, BMI-, and SESAC-affiliated in order to accommodate songwriters who are members of each of those organizations.

It's perfectly acceptable and quite common for members of the three different performing rights organizations to write with one another. When that collaboration results in a recorded song, each organization distributes the share of the performance royalties earned by its respective affiliated writers and publishers. For songs receiving performances outside the United States, there are reciprocal agreements that allow the performing rights organizations to collect from their international counterparts and distribute those monies accordingly.

For a fee, ASCAP, BMI, and SESAC issue "blanket licenses" to radio stations, broadcast and cable television stations, and hundreds of thousands of other establishments. A blanket license grants the recipient the right to play any music that is licensed by the performing rights organization. The amount of money it costs an establishment to secure a blanket license is determined by a number of factors, including the amount of revenue earned by the establishment and its size. After operating expenses are deducted, ASCAP, BMI, and SESAC distribute the money collected as licensing fees to their affiliated writers and publishers.

Each of the performing rights organizations has its own system for keeping track of how many times a song has been played. ASCAP tape-records hundreds of hours of broadcasts on various television and radio stations. From this sample, statistical projections are made to estimate the total number of times a given song is being played. BMI chooses a scientifically representative cross section of radio each quarter, logging approximately 500,000 hours of commercial radio programming each year. The stations being sampled supply BMI with logs that list all music performed during the period being evaluated. From the information collected they estimate the total number of performances a song receives during any given quarter. SESAC, the smallest of the U.S. performing rights organizations, uses technologies that encode audio signals, allowing them to track every broadcast performance.

Performance royalties are not paid by performing rights organizations for dramatic usage of songs (i.e., musical theater, ballet, and opera). The rights to use songs in theatrical settings are called "grand rights" and for those uses payment is negotiated and paid directly to the copyright holder. The right to use music in non-theatrical venues (i.e., radio, nightclubs, and television) is called "small rights."

In the United States, songs that are included in movies do not receive performance royalties when the films are in theatrical release. A "synchronization license" (discussed later in this chapter), which grants the right to include music in a film or television show, is negotiated for that purpose. With this license, songwriters and publishers are paid directly by the film production company. However, after its theatrical run, if a movie is broadcast on network, local, or cable television, the music included in that film does earn performance royalties. Outside the U. S., performance royalties are paid for performances in movie theaters. Through reciprocal agreements with the foreign performing rights organizations, ASCAP, BMI, and SESAC collect and distribute those royalties.

Songs that are commercially released as singles receive the vast majority of radio airplay. A hit single typically earns its writer much more money from performance royalties than from mechanical royalties. The amount of money a hit song earns from performances varies considerably because different songs receive different amounts of airplay. For instance, a song that has a slow climb up the charts, taking twenty-two weeks to reach number one, accumulates much more airplay than a song that zooms to the top of the charts in just eight weeks. The figures that follow are estimates. A pop or country song that reaches number one on the charts typically earns in the range of $400,000 to $600,000 in performance royalties. (As you'll learn in the next chapter, this amount is divided between the song's co-writers and publishers).

The amount of radio airplay a song receives largely determines the amount of performance royalties it earns. If a song crosses over and becomes a hit on more than one chart (i.e., pop, country, and urban), it may get double or even triple the amount of airplay that a hit song typically receives. For a song to reach the top ten on the charts, it must receive the maximum amount of radio play ("heavy rotation") at almost every radio station whose format it fits. Since performance royalties are based primarily on the amount of radio airplay a song receives, the writer's income from performance royalties significantly increases each week that a song remains in the top ten. In exceptional instances, a song has remained in the number one position for several months, generating performance royalties in excess of $4,000,000! However, this occurrence is so rare, it may happen only once every ten years.

The writer's portion of the performance royalties earned by a song is paid by the performing rights organizations directly to the songwriter. The publisher's share is paid by the PROs to the publisher. These monies are paid quarterly, approximately six to nine months following the performances. Monies from foreign territories typically take an additional year to be distributed.

In addition to collecting and distributing performance royalties, the performing rights organizations offer workshops, seminars, and panel discussions in major music centers and throughout the country. They also have writing rooms available for their affiliated writers to use. Representatives may be willing to meet with you, evaluate your songs, and make career recommendations. Before deciding which performing rights organization is right for you meet with membership representatives at each of the organizations. (See the appendix for a listing of the performing rights organizations within the United States.)

PRINT SALES

"Print sales" refer to the sale of sheet music, which represents an additional source of revenue for songwriters. Of course, if few people have heard your song, there will be little demand for its sheet music. Therefore, only songs that are major hits generate significant sheet music sales. Songwriters can earn quite a bit of money from print sales—but usually, only if they've already made far more money from performance royalties. The kind of songs that are performed by bands at weddings, and by lounge singers, create the biggest demand for sheet music. However, choral and band arrangements of songs that are not well known can also earn significant income from the Christian and educational markets.

Sheet music may be sold individually, or in a book called a "folio." Folios are compilations of sheet music of various songs that have been grouped together because they have a common bond. A folio may contain songs that have all been recorded by the same artist on various albums, songs that were initially included on one album, or, in the case of a "mixed folio," songs that have been popularized by a variety of artists (i.e., *The Greatest Rock Hits of 1999*, which includes the sheet music for rock songs that were recorded by various rock stars). When a song is included in a folio, the income is pro-rated among the various songs.

Two companies, Warner Brothers Publications and Hal-Leonard Corporation, publish the vast majority of sheet music. These companies issue payment to song publishers, who in turn pay the songwriters. The amount a songwriter earns per unit of sheet music sold is negotiable and may be represented as either a percentage of the retail price or a flat fee. It is preferable to receive 50 percent of all royalties received by your publisher for print sales. In the event that you have a huge hit and your publisher then has the leverage to renegotiate and increase the fee he or she earns from the sheet music publisher, you reap the benefits rather than being locked into a set fee per unit sold. The amount of money a publisher agrees to pay the songwriter for print sales is an important point in the song publishing contract negotiation.

Publishers and songwriters may receive additional income from lyrics reprinted in books (like this one) or magazines. Permission and a license must be obtained from a song's publisher to reprint song lyrics. This type of income typically represents a tiny fraction of a songwriter's income.

SYNCHRONIZATION LICENSES

"Synchronization licenses," often referred to as "sync" licenses, are another source of income for songwriters. A sync license is required to "synchronize" music to visual images in an audiovisual work. A sync license grants the right to include music in a film or television show. The income it generates is in addition to any performance royalties earned as a result of network or cable broadcasts. Synchronization licenses are issued for cable or broadcast television, motion pictures, commercials, and videotapes. However, when a singer sings his or her latest hit on the *Tonight Show,* a sync license is not required because the song is neither part of the story nor being synchronized to an existing picture. However, the songwriter and publisher do receive performance royalties when the show is broadcast.

The first time I had the opportunity to grant a sync license it was for a song I co-wrote for the television show *Fame.* I did not have a publisher at the time, so I acted as my own publisher. I had been submitting songs to the show's music supervisor for months. Many times my songs almost made it to the final cut, but were ultimately rejected—usually in favor of a song that sounded nothing like what I had been requested to write! Finally, the music supervisor said, "Yes!" My song was to be sung by a minor character in the series. It was the first time he'd be featured in a solo number. I was ecstatic and became even more excited when I was invited to attend the taping of the show. Hearing the strings at the intro to my song almost made me cry for joy. Then the nightmare began.

The song had been pre-recorded and the character would be required to lip-sync during the filming. I later found out that during the recording session the actor couldn't sing my song very well. After numerous tries, the musical director had decided to instead record the music to my song and have the actor recite the lyrics—as a love poem. No one had told me this, so you can imagine my shock when my lyrics were spoken instead of sung. I rushed over to the musical director and said, "It had a melody," to which he responded, "Not when *he* sang it!" I consoled myself by saying that I'd still get paid, and even more importantly, that I was earning my first major television credit.

It was almost impossible for the actor to lip-sync perfectly to the spoken words. The director became so exasperated that he threatened to shoot the scene over the actor's shoulder, or worse—scrap the song altogether. Finally the actor got it right and my song (which was now a poem) was included in the show.

That sync license fee earned me and my two collaborators about $300 each. The Mercedes convertible would have to wait. But, since that license had only been granted for a five-year period, five years later I received another check to extend the licensing period for an additional five years. This time the licensing fee went up a bit. When that second license expired another five years later, I was asked to grant a license in perpetuity. This time, I was paid thousands of dollars. The license I granted did not include the right to include my song on video versions of the show that might be released in the future. If the production company wanted to acquire that right, they would have to pay additional thousands of dollars.

Over the years, the episode of *Fame* that included my song aired hundreds of times, domestically and internationally, generating thousands of dollars in income above and beyond the few hundred dollars I'd received for the synchronization license. When negotiating the fee for a synchronization license, it's important to take into account the additional performance royalties your song is likely to earn as a result of its inclusion in a particular television show or film.

The fee paid for a synchronization license typically varies from a few hundred dollars up to hundreds of thousands of dollars. The amount a production company will pay is determined by how the music is used in the film or TV show. For example, if your song is the "end credit theme" (the song played during the closing credits) of a major Hollywood film, it will generate a significantly larger sync fee than if twelve seconds of it can barely be heard coming out of a car radio in the film. If a song has previously been a major hit and its inclusion is crucial to the film in order to evoke a time period or a specific feeling, it can, of course, command a higher fee than an unknown song.

The amount of the sync fee is also determined by the specific rights being granted, as well as by the length of time covered by the agreement. For example, if you are licensing the right to include your song in all formats and all future uses (i.e., video release, video compilations, and CD/ROM), throughout the world, and in perpetuity, it's likely your publisher will be able to negotiate a higher fee than for a one-time usage.

If an advertiser believes that including a specific, well-known song in a commercial has the potential to generate millions of dollars in increased sales for his or her client, a synchronization license might generate hundreds of thousands of dollars for the songwriter and publisher. If an existing recording of a song is being used, a fee, in addition to the sync license paid to the writer and publisher, is negotiated with the owner of the master recording (typically, the record label).

The synchronization fees that result from placing songs in television shows and films can be a significant source of income for songwriters and publishers. They can also lead to additional royalties if a soundtrack album is produced, or if a film receives television airings or theatrical release in foreign territories. On top of that, it's really exciting to hear your song in a hit movie or TV series!

WORK FOR HIRE

When writing for film or television, a writer is sometimes hired to produce music that is considered a "work for hire." This means the production company is contracting the writer to compose specific music in exchange for a flat fee. In these instances, the songwriter acts essentially as an employee, retaining no rights to future royalties, unless otherwise specified.

While composing a work for hire may seem unfair to the songwriter, there are benefits that may outweigh the disadvantages. For instance, gaining access to scripts, as well as the chance to discuss what the music supervisor is looking for, gives the songwriter a far better shot at having his or her song included in the project. The writer may be paid a substantial fee as soon as the work is completed, instead of having to wait a year or more for royalties to be paid. Also, when a songwriter gets the opportunity to write for a specific television or film project, he or she gets an inside track.

Chapter 12

Understanding What Music Publishing Really Means

The writer's job is to write the songs. The publisher's job is to exploit those songs, turn those songs into money, and protect them when they need protecting.

John Van Meter (Director, Creative Services, Sony/ATV Tree Music Publishing)

Long before the invention of CDs, cassettes, and record players, if a music lover wanted to hear the latest hit song, he or she would go to the local music store and purchase the sheet music. That music would likely provide the basis for a sing-along in the parlor as the family gathered around the piano. Back then, having a song published literally meant generating sheet music for sale.

In the current market, securing the manufacture of sheet music is a very small part of a publisher's job. Today's music publishers' primary responsibilities are the "exploitation" of the copyrights they've acquired, and collecting the money those songs generate. ("Exploitation," in this instance, means to facilitate the uses that will generate the maximum income.) Publishers are also responsible for the acquisition of songs for their company's catalog. They may acquire songs one at a time or by signing staff-writers. Ideally, publishers help to develop the songwriters they work with as well.

For many beginning songwriters, getting a song published seems like the ultimate success. But in reality, it's only one more important step along the journey. As you learned in chapter 11, the bulk of a song's income comes from mechanical and performance royalties. In order for either of these types of royalties to be earned, your song must first be recorded and commercially released by an artist who generates sales and/or airplay. From the songwriter's point of view, securing those recordings is a publisher's most important function. Before continuing to explain a publisher's function it's important that you understand the nature of a publisher's income.

All income generated by a song is divided equally between the "writer's share" and the "publisher's share." For each dollar earned by a song, 50 cents represents 100 percent of the writer's share, and the remaining 50 cents equals 100 percent of the publisher's share. When songwriters say they have "published" a song, they're saying they've assigned the publishing rights (representing 50 percent of any income the song generates for that writer) to an individual or company whose function includes generating and collecting income from that copyright. If you have not published a particular song, you own the writer's *and* publisher's share of any income this song generates.

> *(Many people) believe that a published song is going to make them tons of money, and that all they have to do is write one published song and poof—they are millionaires! If only that were true. What counts now is being recorded and released. Even being recorded isn't enough, since a significant percentage of songs that are cut are never released for various reasons.*
>
> **Gloria Sklerov (Hit songwriter and two-time Emmy Award winner)**

The writer's share (50 percent of the song's income) is divided among all of the song's co-writers. If there are three co-writers, barring any other agreement between them, each owns one-third of the writer's share (one-sixth of the total) of any income the song generates. In addition, each writer also owns a percentage of the publisher's share, equal to the percentage owned as a writer, unless the writer signs an agreement assigning the publishing rights to another individual or publishing company. If twenty songwriters contribute to the same song, this song may have twenty publishers. In theory, just as there's no limit to how many writers may collaborate on any given song, there's no maximum number of publishers who can divide the publisher's portion of the pie.

How to Get a Publisher—and Why

As you just learned, publishing a song is analogous to giving away 50 percent of your income. For a big hit, that could amount to hundreds of thousands of dollars. Why would anyone want to do such a crazy thing? There are several good reasons, but probably the best reason to assign your publishing rights and income to a music publisher is because 50 percent of an enormous amount of money is better than 100 percent of nothing.

Successful publishers maintain a high level of credibility by representing excellent songs, and recognizing which songs might best suit a particular recording artist. They have the connections to get your songs heard by the industry professionals who have the power to get them recorded. A substantial part of a music publisher's job is developing the relationships with artists, managers, record label executives, and producers that lead to getting songs recorded.

Often, the most valuable thing a publisher does is provide constructive feedback and an atmosphere where a new writer can make contacts, as well as be exposed to the work of other professional writers. A good publisher will be able to see your strengths and arrange collaborations with other writers that will complement your talents and help you improve your craft.

Teri Muench-Diamond (President, Diamond Cuts/Diamond Mine Music, publisher of "I Can Love You Like That," "Let Me Let Go," and "The Day That She Left Tulsa")

At various times I've seen superstar recording artists (including Reba McEntire, Wynonna, and Bryan White) at my publisher's Music Row offices, looking for songs. I've been at the office when Garth Brooks telephoned for this same purpose. While no publisher has direct access to every recording artist, the best publishers have good business relationships with the A & R executives, artists' managers, and producers who look for hit songs for virtually every major artist. Effective publishers also make it their business to know which artists are looking for material at any given time, and what type of songs those artists are looking for.

Another important part of a publisher's job is setting up collaborations between the songwriters they represent and other writers and artists. These collaborations are often ones that the writer might never have been able to establish on his or her own. Many of my most successful songs are the result of co-writes initiated by my publisher. In fact, my life changed dramatically as a result of one of those opportunities.

One morning in June 1998 my publisher called and told me I had fifteen minutes to get into my car and head to Muscle Shoals, Alabama, if I wanted to co-write with Kevin Richardson (a member of the superstar group the Backstreet Boys) and Gary Baker ("I Swear"). This opportunity was possible because my publishing company (Zomba Music Publishing) owns Jive Records, the Backstreet Boys' record label. The chance to write with that artist, and the credibility and money the resulting Backstreet Boys' cut earned me, would never have happened without my association with my publisher.

Ideally, a publisher helps a writer to achieve his or her highest creative potential by offering constructive critiques of the writer's songs. Good publishers have their fingers on the pulse of the current market and can help their writers craft songs that have the best chance of being recorded. They can also guide the writers by pointing out the strengths and weaknesses in their songs, and encouraging rewrites.

When I signed my staff-writing deal in 1991, I was in an unusual, and enviable, position. After eleven and a half years of struggling, I found myself with a cut on the Oak Ridge Boys' *Unstoppable* album. My song, "Change My Mind" (co-written with A.J. Masters), was slated to be the single that would follow a top five single for the Oaks. All indications were that I was finally about to have a big hit. Thanks to my savvy attorney at the time (Adam Sandler), three years earlier I had retained the majority of my publishing rights to that song. Those rights became very valuable the moment the Oak Ridge Boys recorded it.

Because I was willing to assign my publishing rights to "Change My Mind" (*after* the Oak Ridge Boys recorded it), I had the leverage to sign a staff-writing deal with almost any publishing company in Nashville. It was a low-risk situation for any publisher. In exchange for payment, and the staff-writing deal I wanted more than anything in the world, whatever publishing company I signed with would acquire the publishing rights to a song that seemed certain to become a hit with an established recording act. The publisher wouldn't even have to secure the cut—it was already recorded, included on the album, and scheduled for release as a single.

Although I lived in Los Angeles, the Oak Ridge Boys cut gave me a level of credibility in Nashville that I lacked in LA, so I decided to pursue a staff-writing deal in Nashville. I met with at least a half dozen music publishers and narrowed down my choices to two companies. At most of those meetings, the publisher listened to my songs (the same songs no one was interested in prior to my getting the Oak Ridge Boys recording) and pronounced them "good"—just what my ego wanted to hear.

But when I met with Michael Hollandsworth at Zomba Music, he said that my songs would be stronger if I made some changes. He pointed out specific lines he wanted me to rewrite and suggested different angles to approach the title from. Although it hurt to hear that my songs weren't as good as I'd thought, I knew those critiques were exactly what I would need to compete in such a tough business. Another advantage to signing with Zomba was that it is the parent company of Jive Records, an enormously successful R & B and pop music label—and I had aspirations to write in those genres, as well as country.

Although another company offered me an advance of $5,000 more than Zomba to sign with them as a staff-writer, my gut told me that in the long run, the sometimes brutal critiques and the opportunity to be plugged directly into the R & B and pop market would be far more valuable than cash up front. I was right.

In addition to the creative benefits, there are financial incentives to working with a publisher. It's unlikely you'll receive an advance to publish a single song, unless that song has already been recorded. However, a publisher may pay to record a professionally produced demo of your song, or reimburse you for your demo costs. It is a good idea to take advantage of a publisher's demo producing expertise. (The financial and other benefits of a staff-writing deal are more extensive and are discussed in chapter 13.)

It very seldom works to call and say, "I'm new in town and I want to have a meeting." That's like us accepting an unsolicited tape—usually we don't. With the increased litigation possibilities I prefer someone who has been referred by someone I know, or from one of the performing rights societies. That's where I've found the majority of staff writers without track records that I've signed. Going through the songwriters' organizations and showcases to find other songwriters who have publishing deals is a good, creative way to make inroads and have more impact. Turn those contacts into introductions to publishers.

Michael Hollandsworth (Vice President/General Manager, Zomba Music Publishing)

An additional financial benefit of working with a publisher is that publishers absorb many of the expenses of doing business—for instance, the costs of long-distance phone calls, office supplies, making tape copies, envelopes, and postage. (Depending on your contract, some of these costs may be recoupable.) Many publishers, especially in Nashville, provide writing rooms where writers can work. In these rooms, the publisher may also furnish a guitar, keyboard, and recording equipment. Office equipment (i.e., fax machines and computers) and access to recording studios may be available, too.

You can see that there are many advantages to working with a music publisher. However, it's impossible to place a price tag on one of the most important benefits a publisher offers. The credibility that accompanies being associated with a reputable publishing company opens up doors (to record labels, producers, managers, and artists) which might otherwise remain permanently locked. When I introduced myself to A & R executives as the newly signed staffwriter at Zomba, I was able to get appointments to play my songs at every major record label. The importance of that built-in credibility should not be underestimated.

So, now you know why to get a publisher. But how do you get one?

When I first moved to Nashville, I was hired to teach songwriting at Watkins Institute, one of the nation's oldest establishments for education in the arts. In preparation for my classes, I called at least a dozen music publishers and asked for permission to include them on a list of publishers who were willing to review unsolicited songs. (The term "unsolicited" is commonly used to refer to material that is neither requested nor represented by a reputable music publisher, artist manager, or entertainment attorney.) In every instance the answer was a resounding "No." When I asked these publishers where they typically found new material and writers, I heard the same answer over and over again—referrals.

Referrals may come from a variety of sources, including other songwriters, performing rights organizations, and songwriters' organizations. However, your work needs to be strong to induce industry professionals to put their own credibility on the line by referring you to their associates.

One way to attract the attention of a publisher is by attending an event (i.e., a songwriter's expo or workshop) where publishers will be reviewing songs. (I found my first publisher at the Los Angeles Songwriter's Expo.) It'll take an exceptional song to grab their ear, but if a publisher critiques your song and loves it, you should be able to parlay that into a meeting, or an invitation to send additional material.

Here's a "guaranteed" formula for getting a foot in the door with any music publisher:

1. Co-write an incredible song with a songwriter who has already established a relationship with a publisher. (Note: I did not say a "pretty good" song.)

2. Have your collaborator present the song to the publisher he or she works with.

3. Call to introduce yourself as the co-writer of the song and thank the publisher for his or her praise and enthusiasm.

4. Request a meeting to discuss plans for the song, and to play several others.

If your portion of the publishing rights is available, the publisher will be anxious to acquire it, since he or she will be pitching your song anyway, on your collaborator's behalf. Obtaining your publishing rights will be a feather in his or her cap because it will double his or her company's share of any income your song generates—all for the same amount of work. Besides, if your song is exceptional, any publisher will be excited to hear additional songs you've written.

While "cold calling" is not typically the most effective way to find a publisher, occasionally it can work. Another way to find a publisher is by responding to ads in songwriter publications. Major companies don't actively pursue songwriters. However, several of my students have published songs and begun good working relationships with small publishing companies they found this way. *American Songwriter* magazine (see appendix) includes a comprehensive listing of music publishers (including many small, independent companies) in one of their issues each year. *The Songwriter's Market* is another excellent resource for writers seeking publishers.

Many songwriters explore the pros and cons of signing with small, independent publishing companies versus affiliating with larger publishers. Independent publishers operate "independently" from large music business conglomerates. They may be owned and operated by one individual, or may have significant financial backing and a staff of employees. Some independent publishing companies have a small stable of staff-writers, while others acquire songs individually. The "independents" are smaller companies and have fewer songs in their catalogs.

Major publishing companies either are subsidiaries of large corporations or are companies that have grown from independent status to attaining a significant market share. It's not unusual for a major publishing company to have anywhere from 30 to 100 staff-writers. If, as an unsigned writer, you are dealing with a company that has numerous staff-writers, and a catalog of thousands of songs, it's unlikely that this company will have a need for your song.

I remember a particularly frustrating meeting I had with a publisher at Jobete Music, a division of Motown. After listening to one of my songs, he said it was a "staff-writer song." When I asked what he meant, he explained that this song was of equal quality to those songs that any of his staff-writers were capable of turning in on any given day. If I was writing songs that were as good as his staff-writers' songs, why couldn't I get a publishing deal? At the time I didn't understand that for a major publisher with a large staff of exclusive writers to sign one of my songs, my song had to be different, or better than anything he had in his catalog. I also didn't take into account that while I could write a song as good as his staff-writers' any day, I couldn't yet write songs as good as the hits his staff-writers wrote on their exceptional days.

There are reasons why certain songs get cut. If you compare your songs to those on the radio and think, "My song is just as good as that, that has a bunch of clichés, it's not really that good," that is not going to help you as a writer. There are reasons why that song got cut—many political reasons behind the scenes. There's the producer and the producer's wife and the producer's staff-writers who are being paid to come up with songs, so the quality of songs on the radio isn't always the measure of what you've got to surpass. They can always come up with those "average" songs. You have to be better than that in order to get your songs cut.

    Steve Diamond (Hit songwriter/producer)

Large companies typically have greater financial resources and are able to offer an established writer more money for a staff-writing deal. They are often accused of acting as glorified banks for successful songwriters, meaning that they provide little more than money. But being signed to a major publishing company can have many benefits.

The advantages include having your songs pitched by top-notch songpluggers, the level of credibility that comes along with the company name, and the increased opportunities for co-writing with other successful artists and writers also signed to that firm. In addition, with a large staff of songpluggers, if one doesn't like a particular song you've written, other pluggers may love it. The biggest disadvantages of working at a large publishing company are the increased competition, the lack of individual attention, and the risk that your material may be overshadowed by songs written by more successful writers.

Most developing songwriters find it easier to place songs, at least initially, with smaller independent publishers. Independent companies are more likely to have a genuine need for your song to fill a particular slot in their smaller catalog than a company representing 100,000 songs. But there are other advantages to working with a smaller publisher as well.

Smaller companies can often provide additional attention to developing writers. They may be better able to nurture and devote more time to developing a fledgling writer's career by helping to produce demos, suggesting ways to improve the songs, and recommending collaborators. An independent company may also be "hungrier," more aggressive, and more determined to place your song. There are plenty of legitimate, small, independent publishing companies that have great success placing songs with recording artists, as well as in films and television. However, there are also many independent companies that, despite the best intentions, lack the resources and means to effectively promote songs.

Many beginning songwriters are so anxious to publish a song that they jump at any offer. It's important to remember that a song with potential to become a major hit is a tremendous resource. Before assigning publishing rights to any company, explore your options. If your song is special enough to attract the attention of one publisher, it's likely that others will also recognize its merits. Before signing any song-publishing contract (but especially one with a small, independent firm), take the time to develop relationships with key individuals at the company. Get feedback about the company's track record and trustworthiness from other industry professionals, and always have an entertainment industry attorney review your contract.

Whether you decide on a major publishing company or an independent publisher, don't be afraid to ask questions. It's perfectly acceptable to ask a prospective publisher, "Who do you hear recording this song?" (Also, be prepared with your own list of artists appropriate for the song.) If the publisher's answer is, "Garth Brooks," ask how he or she might get your song heard by Garth. Look for answers along the lines of: "I have a good relationship with Pat

Quigley at Capitol Records. I usually get a call back when I drop tapes off for Allen Reynolds (Garth's producer) at his studio, and I'll also see if I can schedule a lunch with Bob Doyle (Garth's manager)." If the response is vague or unprofessional (i.e., "Uh, I once met his bus driver's wife at the Piggly Wiggly store and she might just show up again some day") you haven't yet found the right publisher.

WORKING WITH YOUR PUBLISHER TO ACHIEVE YOUR GOALS

Let's assume you've written a wonderful song and it's been published by a music publisher who loves it. Now what do you do? If you assume your work is over and that it's the publisher's job to get your song recorded, it's likely you'll be very disappointed. Publishers have hundreds, if not thousands, of songs in their catalogs. The song that your publisher was so excited about when you turned it in may find itself on a shelf collecting dust several months later.

The proper relationship between a publisher and a writer is that the publisher works for the writer—not vice versa. It's a cooperative relationship. Ninety percent of the time, what is in the best interest of the writer is also in the best interest of the company. Maintain contact with your publisher. Try to be aware of the things the publisher is doing. It helps if the writer is involved in the music community, aware of what artists are recording and when. Also, writers can help pitch songs. But, the best thing a writer can do to help me get them cuts is to write great songs.

John Van Meter (Director, Creative Services, Sony/ATV Tree Music Publishing)

Approach the relationship with your publisher as a partnership. Your song won't generate any income for your publisher if it doesn't earn anything for you, so you're helping if your efforts result in getting your song recorded. Establish a game plan together. Use a pitch sheet (discussed in chapter 14) to identify an initial group of artists to target and be specific about what exactly each one of you will do. For instance, your publisher may say, "I'll set a meeting with the artist's producer and A & R person." You may respond with, "I'll drop off a cassette at the artist's manager's office." Then, follow up with your publisher two or three weeks later to discuss your progress, as well as any feedback either of you may have received.

"Out of sight—out of mind" definitely applies to your relationship with your publisher. It's important to visit your publisher often. I can't count how many times I've overheard a casual conversation at my publisher's office regarding an artist who was looking for songs. In many of those instances, I was able to suggest a song of mine that my publisher might not have thought of—and my song got pitched.

Although it's important to maintain regular contact with your publisher, remember that there's a fine line between persistence and pestering. Call every few weeks for an update. It's not inappropriate to ask if he or she has had opportunities to pitch your song, and if so, what the feedback was. Ask your publisher to send you a pitch sheet or casting list (a listing of artists who are currently looking for songs). Discuss possible pitches for your song. (Be realistic. No song is appropriate for every artist.) All of these actions will help your song avoid drifting to a back burner—if it's as strong as you and your publisher initially thought. But, if a publisher receives consistently poor feedback about a particular song it's likely he or she will not continue pitching it.

As you continue to work in the music business, your list of contacts expands. You may have opportunities to pitch your songs yourself. Talk about those possibilities with your publisher to be certain you're on the same track.

SELF-PUBLISHING

Unless you have entered into a publishing agreement, thereby assigning your publishing rights to someone else (i.e., a publishing company), you own the publishing rights, and the corresponding publishing income, to any song you have written or co-written. When you write a song by yourself, you own 100 percent of the writer's share, as well as 100 percent of the corresponding publisher's share of any income that song may generate. If you have one collaborator, you each own 50 percent of the writer's share and 50 percent of the publisher's share.

Therefore, if you've written a song (and haven't published it) you are a song publisher. Maintaining your publishing rights has two big advantages: You earn double the money and you have leverage in the event your song is recorded. Once you have a song to represent (either one of your own compositions or another writer's song whose publishing rights have been assigned to you) it's

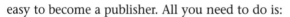

easy to become a publisher. All you need to do is:

♪ Choose a name for your company;

♪ Decide which performing rights organization to join;

♪ "Clear" the name you've selected (by checking with your performing rights organization to be sure no other company is already using it); and

♪ Print up some letterhead on your computer.

But owning the publishing rights and successfully exploiting the song are two very different things. Earlier in this chapter you learned the functions of an effective publisher. Before you decide to become your own publisher you need to honestly assess whether you have the necessary time, personality, and resources to properly exploit your song.

If your time is limited due to the responsibilities of working a "day job," then the work you do as your own publisher is taking valuable time away from your songwriting. To successfully publish your own songs, on an ongoing basis you need to:

♪ Investigate who is looking for songs.

♪ Develop business relationships.

♪ Make tape copies.

♪ Type cover letters, J-cards, and labels.

♪ Mail or deliver your packages.

♪ Follow up those pitches with phone calls.

♪ Handle administrative functions (i.e., applying for copyright registration, registering your songs with your performing rights organization, keeping track of royalties, etc.).

In addition to the time investment, publishing your own songs requires an outlay of money. Expenses incurred by song publishers include:

♪ The purchasing of tape duplicating equipment (probably a cassette dubbing deck, a DAT machine, and a machine capable of generating CDs)

♪ Equipment maintenance

♪ Office supplies (including mailing envelopes, letterhead, mailing labels, etc.)

♪ Blank tapes

♪ Postage

♪ Photocopying (lyric sheets and correspondence)

♪ Long distance telephone charges

♪ Demo production expenses

A computer and fax machine are also tremendously helpful, if not manda-tory. While many of these expenses may be tax-deductible (see your accountant for details), they still add up to a considerable amount.

Perhaps the most important factor to consider when deciding whether you should represent your own songs is your personality type. Song publishing (like songwriting) requires long-term persistence and the ability to withstand repeat-ed disappointment and rejection—without losing faith in your songs. Successful publishers have the ability to discern which songs are best suited for particular artists. They also have the tenacity and the ability to forge the rela-tionships necessary to get your songs considered by the professionals who call the shots. Publishers need to have excellent communication skills, both over the telephone and in meetings. If you're shy or nervous about making cold calls or "selling" yourself, self-publishing is probably not for you.

Throughout my career I've never had a publisher. I publish my own songs and I've had to shop my own songs. I find the fact that I'm able to pick up a telephone and call people certainly helps. You've got to have the goods first, but it also helps to have the ability to talk to people—to sell one's self and one's songs.

Billy Steinberg (Songwriter of hits including "True Colors," "Like A Virgin," "Eternal Flame," and cuts with artists including Whitney Houston and Tina Turner)

Many songwriters publish their own material as a temporary measure, while looking for a publisher to represent their songs. During the period when I did that, I was frequently making tape copies and typing letters and lyric sheets after midnight. I didn't have much success self-publishing, but that was due as much to the quality of the songs I was writing at that point in my career as anything else. Songwriters who love the business side of the music business and fit all of the criteria listed above may enjoy great success publishing their own material. But those who are self-publishing because they can't find a legitimate publisher to represent their material would put their time to better use by concentrating on honing their songwriting skills. Remember: 100 percent of nothing equals nothing.

USING SONGPLUGGERS

Since one of a music publisher's primary functions is to "plug" songs (pitch songs to recording artists and industry professionals who screen songs for artists), publishers are often referred to as "songpluggers," or "pluggers." But there are individuals who pitch songs for a fee—without necessarily acquiring ownership of the publishing rights—who are also referred to as "songpluggers."

A small but growing percentage of songwriters engage the services of a songplugger to augment the efforts of their publisher, or to act in lieu of a publisher. There's no standard payment in these situations. It's negotiated between the songwriter and plugger. Many songpluggers command a retainer of $200 to $500 per month for their services. In addition to these upfront payments, the agreement with the songwriter may also entitle the plugger to substantial bonuses in the event that he or she is responsible for securing a major recording of a song.

Bonus payments are typically determined by the highest chart position attained, and the number of units sold. Depending on the agreement between the writer and plugger, the payment for securing a number one hit may exceed $10,000. While this may sound like an enormous amount of money, keep in mind that it may amount to only 10 to 15 percent of the songwriter's income on that song. That's a relatively small price to pay considering that without the plugger's efforts, there might be no income generated at all.

Some songpluggers work exclusively on a bonus system. They get paid only upon securing a recording for the writer. Obviously, this is an ideal situation for the songwriter because if the plugger fails to get results, it costs the writer nothing. Agreements that do not require upfront payments typically provide higher bonuses, since the plugger is working solely on "commission." There are also songpluggers who receive a percentage of the publishing income if they successfully secure the recording and release of a song.

The best songpluggers are extremely selective about the writers whose catalogs they represent. They have close relationships with the decision-makers and set meetings to play songs for them. When they secure a meeting with a high-level industry professional, they know they must present exceptional songs in order to maintain their credibility and an open door. They usually place a strict limit on the number of writers they'll represent at any given time, so they are able to give attention to each writer's songs.

Beware of unscrupulous songpluggers who will, for a hefty fee, represent any writer's songs—regardless of the quality or commercial potential of those songs. These individuals rely on upfront payments to earn their living, since it's highly unlikely the songs they represent will ever be recorded. Pluggers who fall into this category can be more of a detriment than a help, since their reputations precede them. While they may indeed deliver or mail copies of your songs to industry professionals, it's doubtful they will be listened to. It's unlikely these individuals will be able to secure the important sit-down meetings to play songs. If they do, they certainly won't be invited back.

The rewards are high and the competition is fierce in the music business. There may be thousands of songs in a major publishing company's catalog, but when a publisher has a meeting to play songs for a recording artist or his or her representative, there may only be time to play a few songs. A good songplugger increases your opportunities to have your song played for industry pros.

My career was propelled to a whole new level as a result of the efforts of a Nashville songplugger named Liz Rose. Liz was responsible for securing the John Berry recording of "Change My Mind," my first top ten single. Many of the best songpluggers get offered positions at publishing companies. Liz has since become a successful song publisher.

Effective independent pluggers provide an important service for those writers with top-notch, competitive songs who need some extra help pitching them. But for those writers who have tried repeatedly, and have not been able to place their songs with a publisher, it's highly unlikely that an independent plugger will be able to secure legitimate recordings of those songs.

Chapter 13
Understanding Publishing Agreements

There is no such thing as a "standard" songwriting contract. PERIOD! My advice to any writer, but particularly the writer looking at his or her first publishing deal, is to find an attorney experienced in entertainment law and surrender the negotiation of your contract to that person. You are dealing with a document that will have an effect on your income and, if you are signing a staff-writing deal, it will govern the business relationship between you and your publisher for three to five years on average. Contracts are a serious professional matter and should be treated as such. And by the way, a legitimate publisher will encourage you to seek independent legal counsel and may refuse to sign you if you do not. If you want to be a pro—act like one.

C. Stephen Weaver, Esq. (Entertainment attorney)

A publishing agreement is a contract entered into to assign publishing rights from a songwriter to another individual or firm. Publishing agreements set out the terms that define the amount you will be paid for various uses of your song. They specify the territories (countries) covered and the length of time the agreement will remain in force. They also define the publisher's responsibilities to the songwriter (i.e., how and when royalties are to be distributed).

There are many other points covered in publishing agreements, including:

♪ The degree to which the songwriter will be consulted regarding any creative changes the publisher may want to implement

♪ The amount paid for print sales (and whether that amount will be expressed as a dollar figure or a percentage of the publisher's income)

♪ Monetary advances

♪ What costs shall be recoupable by the publisher—and what sources of income will be applied toward recoupment

♪ Whether the publisher pays for a demo

♪ Each party's responsibilities in the event of a copyright infringement suit or other legal problems

♪ When royalty statements are to be issued

♪ The writer's rights to audit the publisher's books

♪ Maximum percentage to be paid to sub-publisher

♪ How translations to foreign languages will be handled

Some publishing agreements exceed twenty pages in length and appear to be written in a foreign language that only vaguely resembles English. It's crucial to retain an entertainment attorney prior to signing any song publishing agreement. (Your cousin Seymour who's studying to be a divorce lawyer does not have the expertise required.) Depending on the amount of clout you have, and your attorney's expertise, many of the contract points are negotiable. Points that may seem insignificant when you enter into a contract can be monumental if your song becomes a huge hit.

While it's not realistic for you to expect to have an attorney's knowledge of every detail of your publishing agreement, a savvy songwriter will learn what the major contract points mean. When you review your contract make notes and ask questions prior to signing. The National Academy of Songwriters (see appendix) offers its members reduced fees for legal services by a panel of music industry professionals. *This Business of Music,* by Sidney Shemel and M. William Krasilovsky (Billboard Books), is an excellent resource for additional information about song publishing contracts and other technical aspects of the music business.

SINGLE SONG AGREEMENTS

If a publisher feels strongly enough about one of your songs to want to publish it, you will be asked to sign a single song agreement. As the name implies, a single song agreement is the contract a writer and publisher sign in order to publish one song. The terms laid out in this type of agreement apply exclusively to that one song.

There's no such thing as a "standard agreement," although some publishing agreements may have that phrase printed on top of the page. While a contract may be "standard" for a given publisher, many of the points may still be negotiable. The terms of the agreements between songwriters and publishers are limited only by the imaginations of the parties involved. A publisher's willingness to negotiate is determined by your track record and clout, your attorney's expertise, and, most importantly, by how badly the publisher wants to have that particular song.

The Songwriters Guild of America (SGA) has developed a song publishing agreement designed to represent the songwriter's best interests. While it's unlikely that a publisher will agree to every point in the SGA contract, a copy of it may be obtained from the Songwriters Guild and can be used as a model for the writer (see appendix).

REVERSION CLAUSES

A reversion clause is a crucial point in single song agreements and it's one you need to understand. It's the part of the contract that states that the publisher must achieve certain criteria within a set amount of time—or all rights to the song "revert" back to the songwriter. Typically, this clause requires the publisher to secure a commercially released recording, or inclusion of the song in a film or television show, within a specified amount of time.

It's in the publisher's best interests to ask for a long period before the song reverts back to the writer. Some publishers are hesitant to offer any reversion clause, or ask for a period of three or even five years before the reversion may be invoked. Of course, from the writer's point of view, if the publisher has not secured a commercially released recording, it's advantageous to have a shorter amount of time before the rights revert back.

One year, eighteen months, or two years should be sufficient time for a publisher to show what he or she is capable of accomplishing with a given song. Although the publisher may not secure a cut in that amount of time, if he or she is still excited about your song, is continuing to actively pitch it, and is getting some interest, it's likely the songwriter will choose not to invoke the reversion clause, or to extend the agreement for another year or more.

A reversion clause is your primary protection against any of the following possibilities:

♪ If your publisher is not successful in placing your song

♪ If your publisher leaves the company

♪ If your publisher loses interest or excitement in your song

♪ If the company goes out of business or its catalog is sold

During the process of writing this chapter I spoke with two developing songwriters visiting Nashville to record demos and meet with publishers. They attended a workshop I had taught several months earlier. As we discussed the progress of their careers, they expressed their frustration at having difficulty placing their songs with publishers. They said that one particular independent publisher, with a good reputation and track record, wanted to sign several of their songs—but the writers refused because the publisher insisted on retaining the songs for two years before the rights would revert back to the writers. They felt that was too long to tie up their songs.

I explained to these writers that while one year, or eighteen months, would be even better, two years is a reasonable amount of time to allow a publisher to work their songs. It's tough to get songs recorded in the current market. There are numerous examples of enormously successful songs that have taken years to be recorded. Most artists record approximately one album a year. If a publisher has the right to represent your song for only one year, there may not be sufficient time for an artist to record your song and have an album commercially released before your song reverts back to you. Songwriters need to be protected, but they also need to be fair to their publishers and not put up unnecessary roadblocks to success.

STAFF-WRITING DEALS

A staff-writing deal is an exclusive publishing deal. The writer is not an actual employee of the publishing company, but the publisher is assigned the exclusive right to publish everything the staff-writer writes during the term of the contract. Under most circumstances the publisher pays the writer an advance in exchange for that right. The money paid to the writer is typically recoupable from the writer's share of mechanical royalties generated by any of the songs written under the terms of the agreement. In the event that the songs written during the contract period do not generate sufficient income to allow the publisher to recoup the money advanced to the writer, the writer is not responsible for reimbursing that money.

Staff-writers are required to fulfill a quota—a specified number of songs per year. The number of songs required to meet this quota varies and is an important part of the contract negotiation. Typically, a songwriter is required to turn in ten to fifteen songs per year, provided the writer has written 100 percent of the song. If each of the songs is a 50/50 collaboration with either another staff writer or someone outside the company, the writer would be required to submit twenty to thirty songs per year to fulfill the same quota. These songs must be "acceptable" to the publisher. The definition of what constitutes an acceptable song is vague, however. This clause is almost always included to avoid a situation whereby a writer churns out ten songs in a week for the sole purpose of fulfilling the quota.

Hit songwriter A.J. Masters ("Change My Mind," "An Old Pair of Shoes," "Love Ain't Like That") has said, "My publisher wouldn't care if I only wrote one song per year—if it was 'Song of the Year.'" I suspect that would be true of most publishers. A songwriter who writes a handful of extraordinary songs per year will generate far more income for his or her publisher than the same writer would by turning in fifty mediocre, or even "pretty good," songs.

You may wonder why a publisher would want to incur the financial risk of signing staff-writers. There are several reasons. When a writer signs a staff-writing publishing agreement, he or she grants the publisher the right to publish all songs he or she creates during the length of time covered by the agreement. The contract typically encompasses a one-year period, followed by two or three additional one-year options. In the event the publisher exercises the additional options, the amount of the advances to be paid is negotiated when the contract is initially drafted. The decision as to whether to exercise those options belongs solely to the publisher.

A publisher wouldn't sign you to a staff-writing deal unless he or she believed very strongly in your potential to write hit songs and generate significant income. A publisher may be able to sign a developing writer (with no major track record) by paying a recoupable advance of as little as $12,000, $15,000, or $20,000 per year. The writer may be contractually locked in for two or three additional one-year option periods at only slightly higher money. If one, or more, of the writer's songs becomes a smash hit during that period, the publisher will have earned the right to exclusively publish everything written by a "hit" songwriter—for a fraction of what it would cost the publisher to sign an already established writer.

It's in a publisher's best interests to keep hit songwriters happy. So, in most instances, if you do write a hit, your publisher will be willing to increase the amount of your advances, even though he or she is not contractually bound to do so. Any monies you are given by your publisher are typically advances against your own future mechanical royalties. If you have royalty income in the pipeline, your publisher is not risking anything by advancing additional money to you. Sometimes a publisher is not willing to pick up an option with the amount previously negotiated, and a lower amount may be offered.

When I was signed to my staff-writing deal at Zomba, I brought a major cut (by the Oak Ridge Boys) to that deal, and seemed to be poised to have a hit single. Therefore, my attorney was able to negotiate a relatively high advance for the first year. He also stipulated that the amount of my advance would increase for each of the three subsequent option periods covered by the contract.

By the end of my first year as a staff-writer, I had received an invaluable education in becoming a professional songwriter. I had also written several strong songs that my publisher believed had a good chance of eventually being recorded. But my "sure thing" Oak Ridge Boys single had been a dismal disappointment, with only a few weeks at the bottom of the charts. There were no additional cuts, and I had generated very little income for my publishing company.

By the time my publisher called me into his office to discuss whether he would exercise his first option (giving me an additional year as a staff-writer) I was shaking. I'd been a nervous wreck for weeks. I felt like everything I had dreamed of, sacrificed, and worked so hard for was about to slip through my fingers. I was prepared to be devastated. Instead my publisher said that he believed in my ability, and wanted to continue working with me. But, he wasn't willing to pay the high advance that had been negotiated based on the assumption of a level of success that I hadn't achieved. Since a higher amount had been stipulated in my contract, I had the option to leave if he were not willing to pay that full amount.

I took the first of several pay cuts that year. I was living hand to mouth, and even took a part-time job, but I was living my dream. I doubt many other publishers would have been willing to stand by me year after year, as I continued to have "close calls," but no big hits. I'm grateful that my publisher believed in me enough to exercise those options for five years—until it finally paid off big for both of us.

The majority of successful songwriters are signed to staff-writing deals. During the development stages of a writer's career, the monetary advances may allow the writer to quit his or her "day job" and focus exclusively on songwriting. Unless a writer has a proven track record, or brings songs that are already generating income to the deal, it's unlikely he or she will get rich from the advance. Depending on where they are located and other factors (i.e., their clout, length of the contract, and their attorney's skill) beginning staff-writers are typically paid between $200 to $500 per week. Advances are often higher in Los Angeles and New York than they are in Nashville. Those advances may be paid weekly, monthly, or even annually.

Although it's not commonly done, I know of several instances in which a writer signed an exclusive publishing agreement without receiving any monetary advance. These writers decided they needed the benefits they receive as a staff-writer even more than the money.

The benefits of being a staff-writer typically include:

♪ Receiving an advance so you don't have to work a "day job"

♪ Having a staff of songpluggers to pitch your songs

♪ Access to feedback and creative input

♪ Having demo expenses paid

♪ The credibility that comes with being associated with a reputable publishing company

♪ Access to tape dubbing equipment

♪ A room to write in

♪ Possible access to a recording studio

♪ Access to information about who is looking for songs

♪ The added discipline of having a song "quota" to fulfill

♪ Opportunities to network and collaborate with other staff-writers at that company

♪ In the event you receive an advance, your publisher has a vested interest in your success (i.e., wants to recoup the investment)

However, there are also advantages to remaining an independent songwriter:

♪ In the event you secure a recording of your song you retain 100 percent of the income.

♪ When a publisher goes to the effort of signing a single song, you know that publisher is enthusiastic about the song.

♪ In the event you become very successful, you have more clout if you later decide to pursue an exclusive publishing deal, or assign the publishing rights to one of your songs that has already been recorded.

♪ You can place different songs with various publishers and see who is most effective in securing cuts.

♪ There's no risk of being signed exclusively to a publisher who loses interest in your songs, or doesn't meet your expectations.

♪ You have your publishing rights to offer as incentive in the event a producer or artist requests a portion of your publishing in exchange for recording your song.

♪ You do not have the pressure of a song "quota" to meet.

There are no hard and fast rules regarding how to secure a staff-writing deal. However, there are two scenarios that most commonly lead to deals:

1. The writer publishes a single song with a given publisher. They develop a good working relationship, and over a period of time, the writer consistently presents songs the publisher feels have strong commercial potential. The publisher signs several more of the writer's songs using single song agreements, and begins to get some "action," or interest in the songs. During this period, the publisher may set up collaborations and evaluate the writer's attitude and progress. Simultaneously, the writer assesses the publisher's ability to secure recordings, provide valuable creative input, and make proper business decisions. If both parties are satisfied with the relationship, it's likely (if the publisher has the budget and an opening for a staff-writer) that the writer will be offered an exclusive songwriting deal.

2. The writer "brings something to the table." The writer has either proven himself by writing songs that have been recorded, or is willing to grant the publishing rights to a song that is already generating income, or has money in the pipeline.

Signing a staff-writer is a major investment as well as a risk for a publisher. Quite often, a publisher does not recoup the advances paid to a writer during the time that writer is signed to the company. (Although songs written during a writer's contract period remain in the publisher's catalog and may generate income for the publisher after the writer has left.)

It's difficult, even for a major publisher, to secure recordings in this highly competitive market. Therefore, publishers are most likely to sign writers who not only write strong songs, but also demonstrate the ability to help generate their own cuts. Writers who are also record producers or recording artists provide built-in outlets for their own songs, as well as for other songs in a publisher's catalog. In addition, many publishers sign aspiring writer/artists and help them to secure record deals.

Particularly in the pop and R & B markets, where the vast majority of songs are written or co-written by the artist or the producer, it's much tougher for a songwriter who "only" writes to secure a staff-writing position. If you are neither a recording artist nor a record producer, you can increase your chances of becoming not only a staff-writer, but also a successful songwriter, by developing business and co-writing relationships with individuals who are pursuing those goals.

In addition to writing great songs, one of the keys to securing a staff-writing position is developing long-term relationships with publishers. This can be accomplished by collaborating with writers who are signed to publishing companies. It's unrealistic to expect to set a meeting with a publisher, play three good songs, and be offered a staff-writing position. Developing a staff-writer represents a major investment of time, energy, and money for a publisher. (In my case, it took over five years before my publisher began to see a profit from his investment.) It's extremely unlikely that a music publisher will make such a commitment to an "unproven" writer without taking time to allow the relationship to unfold.

CO-PUBLISHING DEALS

A co-publishing deal allows a songwriter to retain a portion of his or her publishing rights and income (often referred to as "the publishing"). By becoming one of the publishers of a song, a writer participates in the publisher's share of the revenues. Co-publishing deals may apply to a single song agreement or an exclusive (staff-writing) deal.

Publishers are understandably reluctant to relinquish a portion of their income and typically do so only when a writer has established a significant level of clout and credibility (i.e., major hit songs, co-writing with a major artist, or being signed to a deal as a recording artist). A co-publishing deal may assign any percentage of the publishing rights and income to the various parties. To make the following examples less confusing, assume the writer is the sole writer of a song.

If a writer and his or her publisher split the publishing 50/50, the writer retains 100 percent of the "writer's share" and 50 percent of the "publisher's share." For each dollar earned, the writer receives 50 cents (100 percent of the writer's share) and an additional 25 cents (50 percent of the 50 cents allocated to the publishers). If a writer owns 25 percent of his or her publishing, for each dollar generated by a given song the writer receives 50 cents (100 percent of the writer's share) and an additional 12.5 cents (one-quarter ownership of the 50 cents of publishing income).

Under the terms of a co-publishing agreement, the writer (as "publisher") may be responsible for a percentage of costs incurred by the publisher (i.e., demo costs, copyright fees, postage, etc.). Typically, this percentage corresponds to the percentage of the writer's share of ownership.

Retaining a portion of your publishing increases your income and has an added benefit. In the event your songs generate significant long-term revenue, you have the option of selling your own catalog (assigning your publishing rights to another publisher) at some point in the future, for a substantial sum. As in any publishing agreement, when negotiating a co-publishing deal, it's important to be represented by a competent entertainment attorney.

Chapter 14
Making Connections and Pitching Your Songs

The songwriter who sits and depends on a publisher,
publishing company, producer, or friend is in denial.

Franne Golde (Hit songwriter)

Successful songwriters, including those signed to exclusive publishing deals, frequently secure many of their own recordings. This doesn't mean that working with a publisher isn't valuable for those writers. A publisher may provide many other services that contribute directly or indirectly to a writer securing recordings of his or her songs, including setting up collaborations and providing introductions to music industry decision-makers.

It's a safe bet that since the first time a caveman grunted out a melody, there's never been a songwriter who felt his or her publisher was providing the attention his or her songs deserved. Publishers have hundreds, if not thousands, of good songs in their catalogs, so it's unlikely that every one of your songs is among your publisher's top priorities. The reality of the music business is such that songwriters need to take an active role in networking in the industry, developing connections, and pitching their own songs.

NETWORKING

Networking is the act of interacting and sharing information with others who share a common interest. We've all heard it said that success in the music business is based on who you know and what connections you have. There's a lot of truth to that statement. But, while very few songwriters are born with those connections, somehow, the successful ones manage to develop them. When I first came to Los Angeles (and later, Nashville) I didn't know anyone in the music industry. Now, among my friends are music publishers, record producers, record label executives, Grammy-winning songwriters, and successful recording artists.

The last time I attended a songwriting workshop as a student, I had an opportunity to have one of my songs critiqued. That song was "Change My Mind." It went on to become a top five single, and be included on five different albums. (It also plays on the doorbell of my house!) At that same workshop, the student sitting to my left was Jud Friedman. The song he brought in for evaluation was "I Don't Have The Heart" (co-written with Allan Rich), which went on to become a huge hit for R & B/pop artist James Ingram. Jud has since become a successful songwriter/producer and has had songs recorded by artists such as Whitney Houston and Barbra Streisand. Many years later, when I read that Jud had produced an album by Melissa Manchester, I wished I had been a little friendlier!

Developing songwriters should find a way to connect with the industry in some way to network and expand their horizons. Take advantage of seminars and showcases. Even if you are not performing, go to meet other writers and industry people. Relationships are essential to evolving in this industry, and those seeds need to be planted and nurtured over what are sometimes long periods of time. But, they do pay off. Everyone needs help and feedback.

Brendan Okrent (Senior Director of Repertory, ASCAP)

It's easier to establish relationships with people who are working toward success than with those who have already achieved it. Today's record label receptionist may well be tomorrow's A & R executive. The songwriter sitting next to you in a workshop may become a Grammy-winner five years from now. The vocalist who's singing your demo for $75 may be signed to a major record label tomorrow. That's the nature of the business.

Networking with those who are on their way up is important for success in any business, but it's crucial in the songwriting business. One of the best ways for developing writers to hone their skills, learn about the music business, and begin networking is through membership in a local songwriting organization. These organizations provide an opportunity for songwriters to share information and resources, provide and receive feedback and support, and, most importantly, connect to the songwriting community. Most of these organizations meet monthly and some periodically sponsor educational seminars featuring guest speakers who are successful music industry professionals.

Nashville Songwriters Association International has chapters throughout the U.S. and the world. According to Membership Director Evon McKay:

> *NSAI is the world's largest not-for-profit songwriters' trade associa-*
> *tion. We exist to protect the rights and the future of the profession of*
> *songwriting. For aspiring songwriters there's a great opportunity to*
> *learn more about their craft and improve it, and also to learn more*
> *about the business side of things. We have an opportunity for song-*
> *writers to network with industry professionals through over ninety*
> *regional workshops across the country. We have a Nashville work-*
> *shop every Thursday night. We have a song evaluation service where*
> *songwriters can get feedback from professionals who've had success*
> *in the business, a ready to pitch service, in-house bookstore, newslet-*
> *ter, publications, and more. Members can use the office facilities,*
> *phones, computer, dubbing deck, and writers' rooms in Nashville.*
> *There's also a counseling service to answer questions about the*
> *industry.*

NSAI also offers three-day educational retreats called "Song Camps," as well as the Tin Pan South Songwriters' Festival, and Spring Symposium (a two-day educational symposium). For information about contacting NSAI, or to find the local chapter nearest your home, see the appendix.

Songwriters Guild of America (SGA)/National Academy of Songwriters (NAS) provide services that include the review of contracts, collection of mechanical royalties (for a 5.75 percent fee), and review of royalty statements and publisher audits. Educational activities include Ask-A-Pro (an opportunity to ask questions of music industry professionals), song critiques, and hosting songwriter shows. They also sponsor educational workshops, the Los Angeles Songwriters Showcase (featuring song critiques and an opportunity to pitch songs to industry profes-sionals—also available through the mail for out-of-towners), song evaluation (by mail), a Collaborators Network (a bimonthly listing of members looking for col-laborators), and reduced fees for legal services. In addition, NAS sponsors the Songwriter's Expo, an annual event in the Los Angeles area featuring three days of classes, panels, and workshops on various aspects of songwriting and the music business. The Expo provides an excellent networking opportunity, as well as a chance to pitch your songs to publishers, record company executives, record producers, and music supervisors (see appendix).

The bottom line is that writing songs in the privacy of your own home—and keeping them there—won't accomplish your goals. Another way to expand your network of music industry contacts is through collaboration.

COLLABORATING

Collaboration is the act of co-writing a song with one or more writers. Some of the best-loved songs in popular music have been written by teams, including Lieber and Stoller ("Hound Dog," "Heartbreak Hotel"), Rodgers and Hammerstein ("The Sound Of Music," "South Pacific"), George and Ira Gershwin ("Porgy And Bess," "Anything Goes"), Burt Bachrach and Hal David ("Do You Know The Way To San Jose," "Walk On By"), Holland-Dozier-Holland, ("Heat Wave," "You Keep Me Hangin' On"), and, of course, Lennon and McCartney ("Yesterday," "I Want To Hold Your Hand").

Co-writing is a great way to step outside yourself to expand your creative horizons; to expand your craft, and gain some perspective. Co-writing is often like playing tennis . . . you want to find someone better than yourself so you can improve. Not all people make good matches, but like all personal relationships there should be at least a few people out there who will work well with you. Even if you eventually wind up writing by yourself, it can be an excellent experience and exercise. You may do things you might never have done by yourself.

Brendan Okrent (Senior Director of Repertory, ASCAP)

Some songwriters collaborate because they write only words or only music. However, many writers who are adept at writing both lyrics and melody choose to collaborate to take advantage of some of the additional benefits co-writing can offer. Naturally, the main reason to collaborate is to write a song that's different, and hopefully better, than one you would have written on your own. Here are some of the other reasons to collaborate:

♪ **"Writing Up":** The best way to push yourself and expand your songwriting skills is to co-write with someone who's a step ahead of you on the ladder. (Note: I said one step ahead on the ladder.

It's not realistic for an unpublished writer to expect to co-write with a Grammy-winning songwriter.)

♪ **Political Considerations**: Success in the music business can definitely be influenced by who you know. Your co-writer's publishing company may have access to an artist you want to write songs for, or may have successful producers and recording artists on staff. Or, you may want to establish relationships with the publishers themselves.

♪ **Writing with an Artist or Producer:** There's no better route to getting a song cut than co-writing it with an artist or producer. While this doesn't guarantee a cut, there will be no question that your song will be heard by the right people—and, all other things being equal, the artist or producer will have a vested interest in recording your song. Note: You still need to write a very strong song.

♪ **Increased Pitches:** By writing with another writer, you double your staff of songpluggers. You may both have publishers pitching your song, and hopefully, you'll both also be actively pitching your song.

♪ **Someone to Inspire You:** A good collaborator encourages you not to settle for mediocrity. You can push each other to do the best work you're capable of.

♪ **Expand Your Network:** Co-writing expands your network of connections and contacts. If your collaborator is a published writer you'll likely gain an open door at his or her publishing company. You may also be introduced to your co-writer's demo musicians and vocalists, as well as the studios he or she works in, and may meet some additional co-writers.

♪ **Promote Discipline:** Having writing appointments that are scheduled in advance causes many songwriters to write on days when they might not feel creative. Your responsibility to another writer may cause you to work a little bit harder at developing an idea, or work on yet another rewrite.

♪ **Emotional Support:** The art and business of songwriting can be wonderfully rewarding, but it can also be frustrating and disappointing. Co-writers can provide much-needed emotional support and encouragement.

The best collaborations are the result of a hard-to-define chemistry between co-writers. I've heard it said that it's not like putting two champion thoroughbreds together to produce a prize-winning racehorse. The personalities and skill levels of the writers affect the outcome. I've written mediocre songs with tremendously successful writers for whom I have great respect and admiration. I've also written some very good songs with writers who have not yet established proven track records.

If you're going to collaborate, write with writers who are as good or better than you so that you're always learning. I think a lot of writers who are shy and withdrawn have a harder time unless they write with someone. In a lot of teams one person is more aggressive and the other one is more laid back. It's a great dynamic when the one that's the aggressor is out there pumpin' and doing the biz.

Franne Golde (Hit songwriter)

Although I've written with more than a hundred different collaborators, my best songs have been written with only a handful of them. For a reason I may never understand, when I write with these particular co-writers, something more comes out of me because they're in the room—and they report the same phenomenon. To find that chemistry with a co-writer you may have to work with many different collaborators, and the chemistry may not be apparent the first time you work together.

The first time I wrote with a certain collaborator my publisher had set me up with I knew we had written a hit song—but it was like pulling teeth. We were on different wavelengths creatively, and it was a frustrating, stressful experience I had no desire to repeat. But, the resulting song was so strong that my publisher asked me to give it one more try. This collaboration has now developed into one of my favorites—and has produced some of my strongest songs.

When collaborating, it's important to define your business arrangements prior to beginning the creative process. Establish what the "split" will be (i.e., will each writer own 50 percent of the song?). It's unlikely that each writer will contribute exactly 50 percent, but typically that is the split between two collaborators. It's not productive to count who wrote which words and notes in order to determine the percentages of ownership. It may be one specific word or melodic phrase that's responsible for the song's success. In a long-term collaboration, inevitably there will be some songs that include more of one writer's contribution and others that have more input from the other writer in the team.

It's also important to establish how the publishing portions of the song will be divided. Unless otherwise specified, each writer owns the publishing portion of a song equal to his or her writer's share. (For instance, if there are two writers, each owns 50 percent of the writer's share and 50 percent of the publisher's share.) Clarify these arrangements before you begin working.

It's important to discuss how your co-written song will be demoed. One of the writers may assume there will be a full-band demo with a $500 budget, while the other may expect to sing and play on a homemade guitar/vocal demo. It's impossible to determine what kind of demo best serves a given song before you've written it. But you can discuss the issue by stating, for example, that if the song that results from this collaboration is an up-tempo or dance song, the demo will be approached in a specified manner.

What if you don't like the resulting song? When writing for the first time with a new collaborator, suggest that if you're not both happy with the song you co-write, you can each take back your respective contributions. For example, if one writer brought in an existing lyric or melody, he or she may choose to give that lyric or melody to a different co-writer. This way you eliminate the risk inherent in bringing a great lyric idea or melody you've been saving to the collaboration.

Collaboration can be a delicate process. It sometimes requires baring your soul and risking criticism. It's important in any successful collaboration for all of the writers to feel respected and safe. There needs to be a level of comfort that allows you to share whatever pops into your head without fear of being harshly criticized. By blurting out a line that you think is "stupid," you may spark something in your co-writer that leads to his or her coming up with the great line you've been looking for. I've had students ask me what to do when their collaborators are not open to rewriting, or have a totally different vision for a song. My suggestion is that they look for another collaborator.

Many successful collaborations take place with the co-writers in the same room, feeding off each other's creative energy. However, it's also possible to collaborate "long-distance." I co-wrote two songs with Grammy-winner Todd Cerney and had one of them recorded before ever meeting him. In those instances, I mailed finished lyrics to Todd, who set them to music. Co-writing via mail can be a viable option for songwriters who live in an area with limited access to many potential collaborators. Fax machines and e-mail make the process even more immediate, allowing almost instant feedback.

Hang out with people who are smarter, more creative, and more talented than you are and aspire to their level. I think that's what mentoring is all about and that's what the songwriting community is all about. You should hear and be exposed to as many people who are better than you are as you possibly can and hope that through osmosis it sinks in.

Robert K. Oermann (Music journalist)

How to Find a Collaborator

As in so many areas of the music business, networking is typically the key to finding that special co-writer who brings out the best in you. There are many ways to find writers whose work you respect, and with whom you feel at ease. However, your odds improve if you place yourself in a setting where there are many songwriters. If you don't live in or near a city with a thriving music scene, you may be able to spend your vacation attending a songwriter's event in a major music center. Music industry publications advertise these events. You can also find out about them from songwriter organizations.

Writers' nights, classes, and workshops where songs are critiqued present an opportunity to hear other writers' work. Approach writers whose songs appeal to you, and whose writing style and personality seem compatible with yours. As mentioned previously, "writing up" is important. Your skills will increase as you work with collaborators who share their knowledge and contacts.

When approaching a potential collaborator, remember that he or she also wants to "write up." You need to bring something to the table to make the other writer want to write with you. This may be a great title or idea, a draft of a strong lyric, a beautiful melody, great music business connections, or your attitude and enthusiasm. It's a good idea to exchange tapes of your songs, or samples of your lyrics, if you are primarily a lyricist, prior to committing to a co-writing session.

"I really respect your work. I have a great idea for a song. Would you be interested in discussing it and possibly collaborating?" is an ideal way to approach a potential co-writer. If your ideas are indeed exceptional, you may be able to attract writers who are further along in their careers. Some professional songwriters have a policy of never writing with unsigned writers. Some are just too busy, and others might not be looking to begin any new collaborations. Don't take these rejections personally. As in any relationship, you may have to approach many different writers before you find your perfect match.

For songwriters who are unable to find collaborators via networking, there are several other options. The National Academy of Songwriters (NAS) offers its members a "Collaborators Network," a bimonthly listing of NAS members looking for collaborators (see appendix). You might also run an advertisement seeking collaborators (or answer one) in a music industry publication. *Music Connection* magazine (see appendix) includes the world's largest listing of musicians' classified ads.

HOW AND WHEN TO COPYRIGHT YOUR SONGS

Before pitching your songs you need to protect them. However, you cannot copyright a title or an idea for a song—only actual melody and lyrics. If another writer hears your brilliant idea and writes another song that expresses your exact same idea, but with different words and music, it does not constitute copyright infringement.

When you write a song, you own it—whether you've registered your song with the copyright office or not. But in the event that its ownership is contested, a copyright is the best evidence of having created the song on the date specified.

Many major music publishers do not copyright the songs in their catalogs until they've been recorded and commercially released. However, some songwriters choose to copyright their material before playing their songs in public or distributing demo tapes. This is certainly the safest way to protect your songs, but it can get expensive if you're a prolific writer. The fee to copyright a song is $30. However, there are less expensive alternatives.

One option is to compile a collection of songs you've written or co-written, and copyright them together under one name. For instance: "The Best Songs of Janice Cook: Volume One." Your compilation may include as many unpublished songs as you can fit on one audio cassette. Formerly, to register a song with the Copyright Office, you had to send a leadsheet. Today, it's acceptable to submit a leadsheet, or a recorded version of your song on cassette or CD.

If you register a collection of songs under one name by submitting a cassette, state the title of each individual song prior to recording it. In the event that one of the songs in your collection is published, or recorded and commercially released, it will become necessary to copyright the song individually. (In the space provided for that purpose on the PA Form, specify that the song has previously been copyrighted as part of a collection of songs that were collectively registered under one name.)

An alternative to copyrighting your song is to send it to yourself via registered mail and keep the envelope sealed. The postmark will serve as evidence that you claimed ownership of the song on that particular date. This is sometimes referred to as the "poor man's copyright." There are also inexpensive, alternative song registration services, notably the National Academy of Songwriters Song Bank (see appendix). Although these methods are better than no protection, they are not as reliable as legitimate copyright registration.

The U.S. Copyright Office website (see appendix) provides extensive information including registration procedures and copyright laws. Copyright forms and instructions may be downloaded at no charge from the website.

Whether you decide to invest $30 for copyright registration, choose the "poor man's copyright," or use an alternative song registration service, it's safest to have some form of protection for your song before pitching it or playing it in public.

FINDING OUT WHO'S LOOKING FOR SONGS AND WHAT THEY'RE LOOKING FOR

Timing is crucial in pitching your songs successfully. You may have written the quintessential Whitney Houston song, but if Ms. Houston's album has just been finished, the best you can hope for is for her and her record label's executives to still be enthusiastic about your song a year from now. While there are instances of artists holding onto songs for a year or more prior to recording them, those examples are rare. It's far more common for artists to tire of songs after several months. Songs that have been pitched too early are frequently replaced during the recording process when an exciting, new song comes along.

Artists, and those who screen songs for them, typically begin actively looking for songs three or four months prior to recording. Producers and A & R executives tend to focus on finding hits for their "next" project. So, how can you know who's currently looking for songs?

One way to know which artists are looking for songs is by networking with other writers who are actively pitching their songs. At events held by songwriter organizations, guest speakers from publishing companies or record labels may provide valuable information. Another way to gather information regarding who is looking for songs (and what they're looking for) is by contacting the record labels directly. Some of the labels maintain "Hotlines," pre-recorded messages that tell the listener what type of songs the A & R (Artists and Repertoires) department is looking for. The A & R department at a record label is responsible for song selection for those artists signed to the label, as well as signing new artists to the label.

It's important to do your research. Prior to calling the record label, find out the name of an A & R executive at the label and ask to speak with his or her assistant. The easiest ways to get that information are by reading trade magazines and pitch sheets. (More about pitch sheets later in this chapter).

In chapter 12, you learned that if you are not affiliated with a publishing company, you are essentially acting as your own publisher. Labels tend to give more credibility to publishers than songwriters. So, when you call, introduce yourself as Jane Jones, with "John Doe Music Publishing" (of course, insert the actual name you've chosen for your company) and be very professional and confident.

There's no need to be intimidated by the person on the other end of the phone. You're simply doing your job and besides, he or she does not hold the key to the success or failure of your entire career. Let the A & R assistant know that you represent a small catalog of songs you feel strongly about and ask who on their roster is currently looking for songs. When you get that information, ask what direction each of those artists is going in, and if they're looking for something specific (i.e., up-tempo songs versus ballads). The answer you'll most often hear is, "We're looking for hits." But occasionally you may be told, "We need a positive love ballad with a mature lyric," or something just as specific and helpful.

Sometimes you may encounter an assistant with an attitude. I once had one tell me, "If you were a legitimate publisher, you'd already know who's looking for songs." There was nothing I knew to say or do to break through that particular wall, so I went around it and pursued the information from other sources. More often, you'll get the information you need.

If the thought of being a salesman and making cold calls makes you nervous, try rehearsing what you'll say. Role-play with another songwriter and take turns being the caller and the A & R assistant (or publisher). This is the music business, after all, and you have to conduct business, in addition to writing hit songs, if you want to achieve success.

Music industry publications (*Billboard's Talent and Touring Directory, The Billboard Sourcebook,* and the *Los Angeles Music Industry Directory*), as well as trade magazines (i.e., *Billboard, Music Connection, American Songwriter Magazine,* and *Music Row*) provide a wealth of information (see appendix). By reading the music charts, you can learn who the producer, publishers, and writers of any given song are. Music industry magazines often include interviews and articles about recording artists, producers, and music industry executives. There can often be valuable information in these articles regarding the recording projects these individuals are working on.

USING PITCH SHEETS EFFECTIVELY

Pitch sheets (also referred to as "tip sheets" or "casting lists") are publications (see appendix) that list artists who are looking for songs. They also typically describe the type of songs these artists are seeking, and the name and address of the individual reviewing songs for the project. By subscribing to a tip sheet, essentially you are paying to have someone else do some of your investigative legwork. The publisher of the pitch sheet has his or her staff contact record labels, producers, and artists' managers on a regular basis to determine the songs they need. This information is passed along to subscribers.

Some of the tip sheets include interviews with industry professionals, articles, and information about songwriting contests, as well. *New on the Charts,* one of the most popular pitch sheets, also includes a listing of current pop, country, and urban hits listed in the *Billboard* and *Gavin* charts. In addition, it provides the names, addresses, and telephone and fax numbers of the publishers, producers, record labels, managers, and booking agents for every song and artist on the charts. See the appendix for a listing of the most popular pitch sheets.

Taxi is a pitch sheet with a twist. Twice per month, members receive listings of music publishers, record labels, artists' managers, and film and television music supervisors who are looking for songs and/or recording artists. Many top producers and record labels do not want to be deluged with songs from amateurs. *Taxi* addresses this issue by pre-screening the material and sending only the best. Submissions are sent directly to *Taxi* where they are reviewed by a staff of industry professionals, including former A & R executives. The best and most appropriate tapes are forwarded to the publishers, record labels, and others who requested material. There is a membership fee of $299.95 for the first year, and $199 for subsequent years. There is also a $5.00 fee for each song submitted for each project. If your song is not forwarded, a critique is provided. This is a legitimate firm that provides an important service for writers who have excellent songs, but limited industry connections. The downside is that a significant percentage of *Taxi's* members pay a lot of money to find that their songs are not good enough to be forwarded to the industry professionals in *Taxi's* listings. See the appendix for information about how to contact *Taxi.*

When I was Production Coordinator for record producer Steve Gibson, one of my responsibilities was screening songs for the artists Steve produced. Those artists included Aaron Tippin, Engelbert Humperdinck, and Randy Travis. When tip sheets available to the general public listed that we were looking for songs, I received some of the worst tapes imaginable—unintelligible, *a cappella* versions of songs that were not even in the ballpark of the industry standard.

Being a songwriter, I'm far more sensitive to the plight of the developing songwriter than most individuals who screen tapes. I wanted to give unpublished writers a chance and kept hoping to find that undiscovered gem. But after spending far too many hours reviewing substandard songs, when I would receive queries from certain pitch sheets asking who we were looking for songs for, I learned to say, "No one." My time was better spent listening to songs submitted by publishers and writers with track records. Many producers and record labels choose not to list their projects in pitch sheets that are available to the general public. That's why it's not smart to rely solely on them for your information.

Some of these publications are available only to publishers and professional writers, or require an audition tape. In addition to information regarding major labels and producers who choose to be included, pitch sheets are often a valuable source of information regarding artists who are looking for material to release on small, independent record labels. While those recordings typically do not generate significant income, they may help connect you to artists and producers on their way up the ladder. Some of the pitch sheets (particularly *SongLink International*) include tips, as well as articles relating to the international as well as U.S. markets. That information can be expensive and difficult to find on your own.

Most music publishers use commercially available pitch sheets, and in addition, often compile their own. When you meet with a publisher with whom you have a good relationship, ask if he or she will provide you with a copy of a casting list (pitch sheet) on a monthly basis, so you can make pitch suggestions, and augment his or her efforts with your own.

It's always best to call first before sending your tape to anyone listed on a pitch sheet. Although most of the publications do a good job, there are instances when the information listed is not accurate. Artists' recording plans may change, or projects may already be finished by the time you receive your pitch sheet. It's also a good idea to confirm that the recipient is willing to review your tape, and to confirm the spelling of his or her name, as well as the address. Use this call as an opportunity to present yourself professionally and confidently. It can be as simple as:

"Hello. This is Jason Blume calling from JB Songs. I wanted to confirm that you're still looking for songs for Celine Dion's album." Presuming you get an affirmative answer, you might add: "I'm an independent publisher and have a song I feel strongly about for the project. I wanted to let you know to expect the package within the next few days." Confirm the address and the spelling of the recipient's name—and get your tape copy ready!

PITCHING YOUR SONGS TO THE RIGHT PEOPLE

Presuming you've got a fantastic demo of a potential hit song, to whom should you pitch it? The first step in successfully placing your song is deciding which artists the song is appropriate for. That's called "casting" and it's a talent in itself. When matching a song to an artist some of the factors to consider include:

- ♪ The vocal range required.
- ♪ The lyrical content—is it appropriate for the artist's image? (For instance, Tina Turner is known for her tough "survivor" persona and would be unlikely to record a song with a lyric that presented her as weak, vulnerable, or a victim).
- ♪ The musical style—is it consistent with other songs this artist has had success with?
- ♪ Does the artist ever record "outside" songs? (There's not much point in pitching songs to bands or singer/songwriters who write all their own songs).

Many developing writers make the mistake of thinking their new song is so wonderful, any artist would surely want to record it. They indiscriminately spend their time and money sending out fifty or more copies of their demo with little regard for whether the song is right for the artists they are targeting. No matter how well written any song is, the same song is probably not appropriate for pop-rockers Aerosmith, R & B divas En Vogue, and Christian/pop star Amy Grant. Even within the same genre there are songs that are a good fit for certain artists, but not for others. It can help to seek out casting suggestions from other songwriters.

A common pitfall is pitching a song to a given artist because it's similar to another song that artist has previously recorded. The last thing Bette Midler would record is a song with the same message as "From A Distance." She's already been there and done that. While it's true that certain artists have consistent success with specific types of songs (for example, Celine Dion is best known for her soaring, rangy ballads), artists do not want to repeat themselves.

Once you've decided which artists your song is genuinely appropriate for, how do you get it to them? The best answer is, "Any and every way you can." I once had an instance where I was convinced I had the perfect song for country star Lorrie Morgan. My publisher and my co-writer's publisher each sent copies of the song to various members of the A & R staff at RCA, Morgan's record label. The publishers also sent the same song to her producer (at the time, Richard Landis). To cover my bases I sent a copy of the song to Morgan's manager, as well. I had previously worked at RCA, and had recently had a song recorded by the Oak Ridge Boys (who were signed to RCA at that time), so I felt comfortable sending a tape to the label president. He responded with a note saying he thought the song would be a hit for Morgan and he had forwarded it to her producer. Apparently, others concurred because when I met with Morgan's producer, he had six copies of my song sitting on his desk! The song went "on hold" but Ms. Morgan didn't feel as strongly about it as everyone else did, and it didn't survive the final cut.

When I am looking for a song for a particular artist, there are factors I take into consideration. In addition to looking for a great song or a "hit" song, I have to take the artist's needs into consideration. This may include range, lyrical content, or even the artist's personality. There are a lot of variables.

Frank Liddell (Director of Artists & Repertoires, MCA/Decca Records)

As this story illustrates, when pitching songs there are many routes to take and it's best to pursue more than one of them. Here are the most direct avenues to pursue to get your song listened to and considered for recording projects.

A & R Staff

One of the major functions of the A & R (Artists and Repertoires) department at a record label is to oversee song selection for artists' albums. The A & R executives and their assistants are deluged with tapes—and most of those tapes come from publishers and professional songwriters with track records. Therefore, many of the record labels have a "No Unsolicited Tape" policy. "Unsolicited" refers to any material sent without being requested, or songs from sources other than legitimate music publishers, artists' managers, or entertainment attorneys.

Few things are more frustrating than having your tape returned, stamped "Unsolicited Material: Return to Sender." Prior to sending any tape, call to ascertain the company's submission policy (as well as to confirm that they are looking for songs for the project you're targeting). You may need to obtain a permission code. A permission code may be a word, a phrase, or a number. Including this code on the outside of your package tells the recipient that you've secured permission to submit your material.

I'm not looking for a song my artist can make into a hit. I'm looking for the song that will take the artist to the next level in his or her career.

Debbie Zavitson (Senior Director, Artists & Repertoires, Giant Records)

Addressing a tape "Attn: A & R Department" is the kiss of death. Take the time to research whose attention your tape should go to. Various A & R executives at the same label may be responsible for different acts. Ask the A & R assistant to whom you should direct your tape for a particular artist.

The A & R Registry is a listing of the A & R staffs at major and independent record labels in the U.S., Canada, and the U.K. It does your research for you, providing the names and titles of the entire A & R staff, their assistants' names, direct phone and fax numbers, e-mail addresses, and company websites. This information is updated every two months and a one-year subscription (six issues) costs $325 (see appendix).

An A & R executive represents the first level in a series of hoops your song has to jump through. In the event that an A & R person feels strongly about your song, he or she will play it for the artist and the producer. Members of the A & R staff can be important allies and generate excitement about your song, but they rarely are able to secure a recording of your song unless the artist and record producer share their enthusiasm.

Producers/Production Coordinators

One of the record producer's most important responsibilities is finding hit songs for his or her artist to record. Circumventing the A & R department by getting your song directly to the producer eliminates one hurdle. But it is often difficult to locate record producers and to get them to listen to your songs, particularly if you don't have a proven track record.

If you have well-established relationships with publishers and A & R executives, they may be willing to provide you with a producer's address and telephone number. Otherwise, you might have to do some investigating to locate a producer's address, but it's usually possible.

If you're unable to find a producer's address and phone number, here's a hot tip: Many producers are also songwriters. If the producer you're looking for is a songwriter, the publishing information will be listed on recordings he or she produced, as well as on the charts. It's likely that the producer picks up correspondence and tapes at the publishing companies he or she is signed to. Some producers maintain offices at their publishing companies, or regularly work out of certain recording studios which are likely to be listed as part of an album's credits. There's no guarantee that they will listen to unsolicited material from an unknown source, but by sending it to a producer's publishing company or recording studio, it will likely get directly into the producer's hands.

Artists

Getting your song directly to an artist is the best route to take whenever possible. Typically, an artist with considerable success has the clout to insist on recording certain songs he or she loves. In these instances, getting your song to that individual eliminates the necessity of having it approved by a committee of record label executives and the record producer, any one of whom may nix it along the way.

Grammy-nominated songwriter Karen Taylor-Good said that after having written a hit single for country star Collin Raye, she had an opportunity to send a tape containing her songs directly to him. At the end of this tape, she included a very special song that she had written with Lisa Aschmann. That song, "The Eleventh Commandment," addresses the issue of child abuse in an exceptionally powerful manner. Karen said she included the song because she wanted to share it with the artist and thought he would appreciate it—never dreaming he would record it.

By anyone's standards "The Eleventh Commandment" is not a "country" song, nor is it geared to country radio. It's extremely unlikely this song would have survived a series of screenings. Yet, Collin Raye fell in love with the song and convinced his record label to create a very special spot for it on one of his albums. Very few songwriters have personal access to many recording artists, but there are ways to get to artists—if you are creative.

A local band was opening a show for country star Sammy Kershaw. I had somebody in the band give him a tape with a song of mine—and he cut it!

Wade Kirby (Hit songwriter)

I once met a songwriter at a party who told me a great story. He had written a song that he was convinced would be a hit for Jimmy Buffett and took a copy of it with him to one of Buffett's concerts. He struck up a conversation with the sound engineer and told him that when his band played this song at local clubs he'd been told repeatedly it was a perfect Jimmy Buffett song. The engineer agreed to listen to the cassette. Severals months later, the songwriter (who was previously unpublished and unrecorded) received a phone call congratulating him on his Jimmy Buffett cut!

There's also a legendary story about a writer who slipped Garth Brooks a tape under a toilet stall, and another about a determined songplugger who gave Faith Hill a tape at a shopping mall. The song, "Love Ain't Like That," became a hit single for Faith and was included on a multi-platinum-selling album. Randy Travis' "An Old Pair of Shoes" was delivered to the country star by his bus driver. While it's not always possible to get your song directly to an artist, when you are able to accomplish that, it's often the most direct route to getting your song recorded.

Artists' Managers

It may not be easy to get your song directly to an artist, but it's not difficult to get songs to artists' managers. Some managers screen songs and decide which songs to play to their artists. Others simply forward all songs and correspondence they receive to the artists they represent.

I once dropped off a song for Randy Travis' manager and soon afterwards received a call notifying me that the song had gone "on hold." When I inquired as to who had placed the song on hold, I was told Randy Travis had been at the office and popped the tape into a stereo. He liked the song and asked his record label to request the hold. It didn't wind up being included on his album, but I knew I had done my job by getting it listened to.

There are several ways to find out the name of an artist's manager. The manager is almost always listed as part of the album credits. There are also publications that list artists, as well as addresses, phone, and fax numbers for their managers, booking agencies, publicists, and record labels. Billboard's *Talent and Touring Directory* is updated annually and includes this information (see appendix).

Some managers do not accept tapes, preferring songs to go to the A & R department at the record label. Others may only accept tapes from publishers and professional songwriters. It's advisable to call first to confirm submission policies, as well as the address.

The art of pitching songs can be as creative as writing them. When you believe you've got that one extraordinary song that's ideal for a specific artist (and you are receiving objective professional feedback confirming your belief) make every effort to be sure your song gets listened to by someone with the power to say "Yes."

Frequently, you don't receive any acknowledgment that your tape has been received or reviewed unless the recipient is excited about your song. Companies that receive box loads of tapes don't usually take the enormous amount of time required to return those tapes, or to write rejection letters. So, there's no way to know what percentage of the tapes you send are ever actually listened to. If you feel very strongly about a specific pitch, cover all your bases. Send copies of your song to each member of the A & R staff, the artist's producer, manager, publicist, hairstylist, video director, makeup artist, and anyone else you can think of. The "right" person to pitch to is all of them.

DEVELOPING YOUR PITCH PRESENTATION

I can't over-emphasize the importance of making a good first impression with your songs and presentation. Be sure to receive strong, positive feedback from objective professionals (i.e., songwriting teachers and professional critiquing services) before allowing your song to represent you to publishers, A & R executives, artists, producers, or other music business contacts.

It's always preferable to get a sit-down meeting, as opposed to dropping a tape off. However, it's very difficult to get meetings with high-level industry professionals unless you have an established track record. It's much easier for them to listen to tapes in their car or alone at home—without having to take the time to provide feedback.

When you are able to meet face to face you'll be better able to begin developing a working relationship. You may also get specific feedback that will help you craft stronger songs. In addition, you might get a better sense of the type of songs the person you're meeting with responds to. You may have to settle for dropping off your tapes initially, but when an industry pro feels strongly about your songs, he or she will be more likely to schedule a meeting with you.

A songwriter doesn't need pictures or bios. That's not important. Any publisher who's worth his salt will be signing you because of the songs, not because of what high school you went to or your slick package. Try to make the presentation as professional as possible. Try to get in and get out without taking too much time. Do follow-up calls, but not excessively. Too many calls can do more harm than good. If you don't get called back after two or three times, take the hint because a lot of people have trouble telling writers "no." The standard line is "It's really good, but it's not what we're looking for at this time." I'd rather say, "You need to change this or that."

Michael Hollandsworth (Vice President/General Manager, Zomba Music Publishing)

Pitching to Publishers

Music publishers and other industry professionals review only complete songs—words and music. It's never appropriate to send a lyric (or a melody) to a publisher or an artist unless you have specifically been requested to do so. If you write only words or only music you need to find a collaborator.

Ideally, you will have received a referral prior to contacting a given publisher. If that is not the case, call to request permission to submit your songs before sending them. When sending songs to a publisher, do not target a specific artist. If a publisher feels strongly enough about your songs to make a commitment to represent them, he or she will presumably pitch them to a variety of artists. Therefore, when sending your song to a publisher it's not appropriate to specify you are sending it for a particular artist. However, it's not wrong to make a suggestion (i.e., "I think this song would be great for Barbra Streisand") in your cover letter.

When pitching your songs to a publisher, it is only appropriate to include a biography if your songs have been recorded and released. It's not appropriate to include a photo unless you are also pursuing a recording deal as an artist. If this is the case, include a professional 8-x-10-inch photo.

Let's discuss the components of the submission package.

The Cover Letter

Your cover letter represents you in your absence and tells the recipient a great deal about you. Be sure it's up to the same professional standards as your songs. When designing your letterhead, choose a logo that's eye-catching, yet business-like. Stationery adorned with fancy musical notes screams "AMATEUR." Present yourself as a professional. Save the bulk of your creativity for your songs and your pitching.

When composing your cover letter, keep it brief and to the point. Do not include extraneous information (i.e., how many songs you've written, where you work, or information about your personal life). Your cover letter, mailing label, cassette label, and J-card (explained later in this chapter) must be typed, and error-free.

It is not appropriate to include leadsheets. No publisher will take the time to learn your song and plunk it out at a piano. (In fact, chances are that no one at the publishing company will even be able to read your leadsheet.)

Never apologize for your song or demo. Nor should you explain what the song really means. A songwriting teacher once told me, "If your song requires an explanation, you'll have to write out thousands, if not millions of notes to attach to each copy sold." Also, do not describe your song. If the listener can't tell that it's a love ballad or an up-tempo song when he or she hears it, you're in big trouble anyway.

If you have major songwriting credits or other information pertinent to your song (i.e., "My songs have been recorded by artists including Dolly Parton and Prince," or "The enclosed song was awarded first place in the Billboard Songwriting Competition") include that information to establish your credibility. But a publisher will not be impressed by information like, "I once sang a song I wrote that got fourth place in my high school talent pageant."

On page 215 is an example of a well-crafted cover letter to a publisher.

Cassette

Your song must be professionally recorded and presented on a high-quality cassette. You may only need a guitar or a keyboard and a vocal, but the recording must match the industry standards, as discussed in chapter 9.

WILL B. AHITRITER
1234 Wannabee Lane, Hometown, PA 56789
(123) 456-7890

Date

Publisher's Name
Company Name
Address
City, State, Zip Code

Dear (Publisher's first name):

As we discussed, I was referred to your company by my collaborator, Juana Hitsoon. As promised, I've enclosed two songs I've written.

I feel strongly about these songs and appreciate your reviewing them. I look forward to speaking with you when you've had a chance to listen.

Sincerely,

Will B. Ahitriter

Encl.

Above: Sample cover letter

Your cassette should have nothing recorded on it but your professionally recorded song(s). It is never appropriate to speak on the cassette, or to announce the title of your songs (except when sending your tape to the U.S. Copyright Office). On your cassette label, type the title of the song, your name, address, and telephone number. If you have a fax number it may also be included. If you're sending more than one song, all of the songs should be included on the same cassette, unless you've been specifically instructed otherwise. Remember, as you learned in chapter 10, always use a high-quality, high-bias cassette of appropriate length to represent you and your songs.

J-Card

A "J-card" is the cardboard insert which is included in a cassette box and serves as a cover for the cassette. It is so-named because it is shaped like the letter "J." When sending a tape to a publisher, on your J-Card, type your song titles, as well as your name, address, and telephone number. Some writers also choose to include the songwriters' names. This is an acceptable option and can be especially effective if the writers have already established a level of credibility in the music industry. No additional information (i.e., lead vocals and all harmonies performed by Suzy Loungesinger) should be included on your J-Card.

If your tape is being pitched to an A & R executive or a record producer for a specific artist, in addition to your name, address, and phone number, include the name of the person the tape is being sent to, as well as the artist it's intended for. For example:

TO: JAMIE JONES
FROM: JASON BLUME

FOR: SARAH McLACHLAN

Lyric Sheet

Include a lyric sheet for each song on your cassette. Type your lyric sheet as in the example that follows on page 217. Note that the only information included on the lyric sheet is the song title, the lyric itself, the writers' names, a contact address, telephone number, the copyright mark, and the year of copyright registration. In the event that the song is published, also include the publishing information and writers' performing rights affiliation (i.e., ASCAP, BMI, SESAC).

CHANGE MY MIND

JASON BLUME
A.J. MASTERS

I don't want to lose you
But even a fool could see
Every day your love is slipping
A little bit further away from me

So I'll be the one to say goodbye
Cause your heart's already gone
I'll pack my bags and take the midnight train
Unless you say I'm wrong

> Chorus:
> CHANGE MY MIND
> Say you couldn't live without me
> Say you're crazy about me
> With a look - With a touch
> CHANGE MY MIND
> I'm looking in your eyes
> For the love we left behind
> It's not too late to
> CHANGE MY MIND

Something's come between us
But it's not another lover
One night we just stopped
Trying to please each other

But if it's really over
Why can't I walk away
Tell me I'm making a big mistake
Beg me to stay
> (Repeat Chorus)

Give me half a reason
To give it one more try
We could leave this leaving behind
> (Repeat Chorus)

Zomba Enterprises Inc. (ASCAP)
Bull's Creek Music (BMI)
© 1991
Contact: (Name)
(Address, Phone, & Fax)

Above: Sample lyric sheet

When you're listening to hundreds of tapes like I do, when somebody sends you a tape they forgot to rewind, it drives me nuts. My mind is in a forward motion and I've got to sit there and wait for the thing to rewind. Little elements like this don't seem like much, but in the big picture they are.

Tommy LiPuma (Chairman, The GRP Recording Company; co-producer, Natalie Cole's *Unforgettable* LP; producer of Anita Baker, George Benson, and Al Jarreau)

Pitching to A & R, Producers, Artists, and Managers

Publishers look for great songs. A & R executives, record producers, artists, and their managers look for great songs that are suited to their particular recording projects. When pitching to any of these professionals, be specific regarding which artist you are asking them to consider your song for. For example: "I've enclosed a song I feel strongly about for Amy Grant." Otherwise, the guidelines are essentially the same as those described in the previous section. But remember that while a publisher may be willing to listen to a rough, or sparsely produced demo, you typically need a fully produced demo for these pitches.

We get eight songs on a cassette for Lorrie Morgan and they're all rock and roll songs, or just out of whack. That's so far off that people aren't stopping to think.

Thom Schuyler (Hit songwriter; formerly Senior Artists & Repertoires Vice President, RCA Records)

Do your homework. When you target a specific artist, do your best to be objective about whether your song is truly a good match for this artist. The overwhelming majority of the songs that you pitch will not be recorded on the projects you pitch them for. That's reality. Therefore, a primary goal from the pitch should be to maintain credibility and an open door. You won't accomplish this if you send a demo of a song that's not up to industry standards, or is completely inappropriate for this particular artist.

When I worked in the A & R department at RCA Records we once received a very "special" delivery. A young man dressed in nothing but a gold G-string brought my boss a five-foot-tall teddy bear, along with a note telling her to expect a tape delivery. This songwriter/artist definitely got our attention. When the tape arrived several weeks later we listened immediately. Unfortunately, the music wasn't nearly as exciting as the delivery.

I admit that early in my career I was guilty of drop-offs that were more memorable than my songs. Once, after overhearing a producer at a songwriting workshop say that he loved cookies, I delivered a tape to the studio where he was producing an album for legendary singer Johnny Mathis. The cassette was in a bag of chocolate chip cookies. Unfortunately, in retrospect it's clear that the cookies were fresher and tastier than my songs.

If your songs are exceptional, and you take care of business, you probably won't need a lot of hoopla to attract attention. If your songs are not exceptional, a creative marketing campaign may get them listened to quicker—but it won't get them recorded.

Many A & R executives, record producers, and artists' managers will not accept material unless it comes from a reputable publisher, entertainment attorney, professional songwriter or is specifically requested. Consequently, it's always important to check their submission policy before sending your tape. Presuming you secure permission to send your tape, your package should essentially be the same as if you were sending it to a music publisher. A sample cover letter follows on page 220. Note that when contacting record labels, producers, managers, and artists, you may want to use your publishing company letterhead to gain added credibility. If you are acting as your own publisher, also include your publishing company's name and address on your J-card and cassette label.

KNOWING HOW MANY SONGS TO INCLUDE

Unless instructed otherwise, send no more than three songs at a time. Less is definitely more. You'll have greater success sending one incredible song than five mediocre ones. No industry professional wants to take the time to weed through a dozen songs. It's the writer's job to determine which songs are his or her strongest, or the most appropriate for a specific project, and send only these.

When I screened songs for artists I always listened first to those cassettes containing one song. There were two reasons for this choice: If the writer sent only one song, he or she must think it's very special and just right for the pro-

J'SONGS MUSIC
1234 Wannabee Lane, Hometown, PA 56789
(123) 456-7890

Date

A & R Executive/Producer/Manager's Name and Title
Company Name
Address
City, State, Zip Code

Dear (first name):

As discussed with your assistant, I've enclosed a song I feel
very strongly about for Bonnie Raitt's upcoming album. I
appreciate your listening and look forward to speaking with
you when you've had a chance to review the song.

Sincerely,

Will B. Ahitriter

Encl.

Above: Sample cover letter for A&R, producers, artists, and managers

ject; and I could get through more tapes by listening only to those with one song. (When I had a huge box of tapes to review, it felt good to see that number dwindle.)

Limiting the number of songs on your tape can be difficult. Early in my career I thought all my songs were terrific (they weren't!) and I was afraid to leave one off—what if it was the one that would have been a hit? As I wrote more songs I realized that they can't all be the "best." Now, I send one or two songs at a time—and always put the strongest song first on the tape.

When you send songs, it's quality—not quantity. How many great songs are there? Not a lot. The best thing is to play your best shot. How about one? Or two? Sometimes I'll call a publisher or a writer and say I'm recording "so and so" and they send six or eight things. It's like they're sort of asking you to edit through them.

Tommy LiPuma (Chairman, The GRP Recording Co.; co-producer, Natalie Cole's *Unforgettable* LP; producer of Anita Baker, George Benson, and Al Jarreau)

UNDERSTANDING HOLDS

A hold is an agreement whereby a writer or publisher agrees to reserve, or "hold," a given song for an artist. This agreement is typically between a writer or publisher and an A & R person, producer, artist manager, or recording artist. By granting a hold, the publisher and writer promise that they will not allow anyone else to record this song prior to its commercial release by the artist they've granted the hold for.

This is usually a verbal agreement, although on rare occasions an artist, producer, or record label will request that it be stated in writing. A hold is requested when a person reviewing songs feels there's a strong possibility of your song being recorded for a specific project. A hold allows the individual who requests it time to play your song for the other decision-makers involved in the recording process. If they concur, your song may remain on hold until the artist records his or her album.

My first hold came when the Oak Ridge Boys heard "Change My Mind" during a listening session in 1990. They held the song for several months until they were scheduled to record, and then recorded and released it on their _Unstoppable_ album. At the time I had no idea how lucky I'd been, or how unusual it was to have a hold develop into a cut.

The next time I had a song go on hold there was no happy ending, but I learned a painful, important lesson. I was so certain my song would be recorded that I began house-hunting based on all the money I would earn! My song was on hold for more than six months, remaining a contender each time the list was narrowed down—and I was devastated when it did not make the final cut. Since those early days I've learned to view a hold as a slim chance that my song will be included on this specific project, and more importantly, as validation that others think my song is as strong as I'd hoped.

I now typically get approximately thirty to forty holds per year. But my expectations have come in line with the reality that only a small percentage of songs that go on hold for a given album actually get recorded and released on that album. After its initial recording by the Oak Ridge Boys, "Change My Mind" was on hold twelve times for artists including Natalie Cole, Clay Walker, and Reba McEntire before becoming a hit single by John Berry. I have a song that's been on hold seventeen times. (It's actually been recorded three times— and has never been released!) I trust that if that many professionals have felt so strongly about this song it'll find a good home some day. When the same song goes on hold repeatedly, it's usually a good indication that it may eventually be recorded—but "it's not final till it's vinyl!"

Holds are more common in Nashville than in New York and Los Angeles, because country artists generally record using live musicians and, therefore, typically record their albums all at once (during a given week) or in two or three installments, several songs at a time. A country artist may not be scheduled to record for six months or more from the time he or she expresses interest in recording your song. If you want your song considered for a specific album you have no choice but to grant the hold, and keep your fingers crossed that the artist doesn't tire of your song, or find another one he or she likes better. Many pop and urban artists record songs one at a time, using synthesizers and drum programmers (as opposed to a full band of live musicians). Therefore, although a pop or R & B artist may be scheduled to record an album at a given time, such artists are better able to record an individual song at any time.

Many songwriters resent the hold process. To honor a hold you may have to refrain from pitching your songs for several months (or even longer). You may miss the opportunity to have your song reviewed and recorded by other artists in the interim—only to find that your song has been "bumped" at the last minute. The person requesting the hold has all the power in this situation. He or she may hold your song for a year or more without generating a cut. There is no penalty or inducement for industry professionals to limit the number of songs they hold, or the length of time they hold them. The only leverage songwriters or publishers have is to refuse to grant a hold to a given individual in the future if they have been burned too many times.

So, why honor a hold? The music business is a small one and it's built upon trust and relationships. Artists need great songs to sustain their careers and may be very excited about having found one that they believe will be a big hit for them. If you grant a hold and then revoke it because another opportunity to have your song recorded comes along, that artist, record label, manager, or producer may be very angry and might not be willing to work with you again.

Some writers and publishers adopt an attitude of "whoever cuts the song first, gets it." There are many stories of writers and publishers who have not honored holds with varying results. In some instances they've burned bridges. Other times, they've had sufficient clout to call the shots.

There always seems to be discussion among writers, publishers, and songwriter organizations about changing the way holds work. One suggestion proposed is to pay the writer and publisher in exchange for granting a hold beyond a reasonable amount of time. For instance, after holding a song for thirty days, if the artist, A & R person, producer, or manager wants to retain the hold, the record label must pay a fee each month that the song remains on hold.

This would certainly encourage those who place songs on hold to be selective about which songs they tie up. Also, once a song was placed on hold, the person requesting the hold would have an incentive to play the song and get an answer quickly from the other key players in the decision-making process. This would also encourage songwriters and publishers to honor holds. While there's been lots of talk, there's still no standard policy regarding holds and there are still many instances of songs being held for six months or more—without the artist even hearing the song. One of the reasons the system remains unchanged is that if a multi-million-selling artist asked for a hold—but was unwilling to pay for it—few writers or publishers would refuse. Granting and honoring holds is a decision you and your publisher have to make on a situation-by-situation basis.

Many developing writers get excited when an A & R person, producer, or other industry professional asks to "hold on to" a copy of a song. That individual is saying he or she likes your song enough to want to listen again before making a decision as to whether it might suit a particular project. This is not to be confused with having a song on hold. When a song is "on hold" it constitutes an exclusive agreement not to let any other artist record that song for a limited amount of time.

One reason that holds are important for the writer and publisher is the "compulsory license." This is the license that must be obtained from a song's publisher before the song may be recorded and commercially released. The copyright owner (the publisher)—or the songwriter, if the publishing rights have not been assigned to a publisher—has the right to decide to whom a compulsory license will be granted, only the first time a song is recorded. Once a song has been commercially released, anyone may record it, provided they obtain a license and pay the mechanical rate mandated by Congress (the statutory rate) or a lower rate negotiated with the copyright owner. Therefore, by choosing to grant a hold (or not) to a given artist, a publisher maintains control over who releases the first recording of a given song.

Technically, a hold is meaningless if a song has previously been released. Although your publisher may agree to refrain from actively pursuing other recordings while a given artist waits to record your song, your publisher cannot legally prevent any artist from recording your song subsequent to its first commercial release.

A songwriter who has not had songs published or recorded might wonder, "Why wouldn't you want an artist to record your song?" The reason is because if the first release is by a new artist, or by an artist with a track record of selling very few records, you run the risk of your song being exposed to the public, earning very little, and not being recorded again by a more successful artist. This has happened to me on several occasions. There's no harm done if your song is recorded but never receives significant airplay or chart exposure. But, if a song is released as a single (especially if there is a corresponding video to increase its visibility) and performs poorly on the charts, it'll probably lose its potential to be recorded by another artist for several years.

ENTERING CONTESTS

Songwriting and lyric-writing competitions offer an alternative way for songwriters to have their material reviewed by industry professionals. The rules and regulations to enter these competitions vary. Some contests are open to all songwriters, regardless of professional status, while others are specifically for individuals who do not earn the bulk of their income from song royalties. The fee to enter songwriting competitions is typically from $10 to $30 per song.

Songs may be entered in various categories (i.e., pop, country, R & B, gospel, etc.). Additional fees are typically required to enter the same song in more than one category. Prizes may include a publishing contract, an opportunity to have your song recorded, a live performance opportunity at a major music festival, cash, and merchandise.

There are essentially two types of songwriting contests. In the first type the song itself is judged, based solely on a recorded demo tape. The other type of contest requires a live performance by the songwriter. In the latter type of competition the winners tend to be professional performers. They're chosen as much for their vocal ability as for the quality of their songs.

One thing's for sure—if you don't send out your songs, nothing will happen. Don't wait for the record label to come to you.

Ira Greenfield, Esq. (Assistant Director, USA Songwriting Competition)

I learned a great deal about songwriting competitions when my song "Wrap-Around Memory" (co-written with Bryan Cumming) was selected as a finalist to represent the United States in the Castlebar, Ireland, International Song Festival (now defunct). At the point I entered this contest, I had published two or three songs, but had never had any of my material recorded. I figured I had almost no chance of winning, but something told me to go through the effort of procuring an Irish bank draft and sending off my tape.

I could hardly believe it when the telegram arrived notifying me that my song had been selected as a finalist. I received an all-expense-paid trip to Ireland and an opportunity to compete for the $10,000 grand prize. At the competition I appeared on a live television broadcast where I performed my song in front of the panel of judges—and a television audience estimated at 30 million. (I am not a seasoned performer and had never been on television. To say that I learned the meaning of sheer terror would be an understatement!)

Those who competed against me were either professional singers (who also wrote songs) or songwriters who hired top-notch singers to perform their songs for them. While the contest was supposed to judge the quality of the songs themselves, there was no way for the judges (who were celebrities—not music industry professionals) to separate the merit of the songs from the performances. Needless to say, I did not win the $10,000. However, I had a great vacation, an incredible learning experience, and an opportunity to network with songwriters and industry professionals from different countries.

Some of the largest competitions receive 30,000 or more entries. Most of these contests have a multi-tiered screening process to narrow down the contestants. The final judging is typically done by major music industry professionals. Therefore, if your song progresses to the final stages of the judging, it will be listened to by individuals who may be music publishers, record producers, artists' managers, or recording artists themselves. An added benefit of entering songwriting contests is that even if your song doesn't win, judges have the opportunity to contact you if they are interested in your song. (See the appendix for a listing of major songwriting competitions.)

Avoiding the Scams

While the majority of music publishers are legitimate, there are unscrupulous individuals and companies that prey upon unsuspecting songwriters. These scam artists are frequently referred to as "song sharks." When you register a song through the U.S. Copyright Office, your name and address become part of the public record and are available to anyone who requests it. Your name may also be sold as part of a mailing list if you subscribe to songwriter-oriented publications. Through these channels unethical companies find aspiring songwriters to victimize. Some of these companies also advertise in songwriter publications.

Typically the scam works like this: You receive an official-looking letter from a "Publishing Company" stating that they are seeking new songs (or lyrics) for publication and for recording by major artists. They offer to review your songs or lyrics at no cost to you. After your songs or lyrics have been submitted, regardless of the quality of the material, you receive a notification congratulating you and notifying you that your material has been selected to be published. All you need to do is to send a specified amount of money to cover "administrative costs" (or fees to record a professional demo) and your song (or lyric) will be published. Many hopeful songwriters are ecstatic and flattered that their song has been "chosen." They don't realize that the only criterion for "publication" is the songwriter's willingness to shell out exorbitant fees.

Another element of the scam may involve including your song on an album that will be sent to major record labels, as well as to an impressive list of other companies which may include radio stations, artists, producers, and artists' managers. The writer is promised a royalty for every album sold. The only thing the writer needs to do is to reimburse "recording and administrative fees," which may range from several hundred dollars up to thousands of dollars. The song sharks technically live up to their contractual obligation by indeed recording your song and sending it out to the places they've promised to send it to. When these albums arrive at the record labels, radio stations, and their other destinations, they are recognized for the scams that they are, and are either thrown away unopened or laughed at. The only people who ever purchase these albums are the songwriters whose songs have been included on them.

A co-writer of mine played guitar on a recording session for one of these albums and he gave me the inside story. Forty songs were recorded in one day. (For a legitimate album, three songs per day would be an accomplishment.) The musicians and vocalist rehearsed each song one time and then recorded it. Regardless of the quality of the recording or the inevitable mistakes, the song was "finished" after one take and then included on this dreadful album of songs written by unsuspecting amateurs.

Aspiring recording artists are also vulnerable to these unethical individuals and companies. I've heard stories of artists and writers being bilked out of more than $10,000 to have poorly produced demos recorded that should not have cost more than a few hundred dollars.

Remember that the music business is highly competitive and that it's even difficult for seasoned professionals to get their songs recorded. Any individual or company that solicits unpublished writers, offering them a publishing deal or a recording contract, is looking to make money from those writers. It's highly flattering to hear that your song has been selected to be published or recorded, but the reality is that legitimate publishing companies and record labels are deluged with tapes from professional songwriters and recording artists. They have no need to advertise or seek out amateur writers.

To protect yourself:

♪ Never pay to have a song published. Legitimate publishers do not require payment to publish a song.

♪ Never pay to have someone compose music to your lyric. If you do, your lyric will likely get paired with a melody that has been cranked out in five minutes by an individual with no professional songwriting credits. Legitimate co-writers work with you because of your talent not your bank account. Their payment is a percentage of any royalties your co-written song may generate.

♪ It's perfectly legitimate (and necessary) to pay to produce demos of your songs in order to pitch them to publishers. However, the fees you pay should be in line with the amounts listed in chapter 8.

♪ In the event that a fee is required to produce a demo of your song, a legitimate publisher will typically absorb the costs, although these fees may be totally or partially recoupable in the event that your song generates royalties in the future.

♪ Do not pay to have your material reviewed unless you are to receive detailed, constructive critiques from a professional songwriting teacher with major credentials.

♪ Ask about the company's credentials (i.e., what songs have they successfully placed with recording artists?).

♪ If you have any question about a company's legitimacy check them out through songwriter organizations and the Better Business Bureau.

They don't call this show art—they call it show business. It is a business but at the same time you don't want to lose sight of your craftsmanship and your art. There are too many writers today who are paying way too much attention to what is commercial and what is on the radio and too little to listening to their inner soul, to their inner heart. You have to find a way to bring both of those in to your writing to be a great writer.

I have nothing against a commercial, hooky, "instant hit" song, but I think it's really, really important to write from a perspective of innocence of the business. Trying to balance the two is the all-time challenge.

Robert K. Oermann (Music journalist)

BUSINESS CHECKLIST

Photocopy this checklist and keep a copy of it where you write. Refer to this list on a regular basis to evaluate how well you're taking care of the business side of the music business.

If you are seeking a publisher, are you:

☐ Networking

☐ Seeking referrals

☐ Reading music business publications

☐ Attending music business events

☐ A member of songwriters' organizations

☐ "Writing up"

☐ Phoning before sending tapes

☐ Following up pitches with phone calls

☐ Sending typewritten, concise cover letters (on professional-looking letterhead)

☐ Including typewritten lyric sheets

☐ Limiting the number of songs per pitch to a maximum of three

☐ Having an entertainment attorney review contracts before signing

If you have songs signed with a publisher, are you:

☐ Maintaining regular contact

☐ Suggesting pitches for your songs

☐ Actively pitching your own songs

☐ Aware of which artists are currently looking for songs (either from pitch sheets or your own research)

☐ Seeking collaborations with other talented writers, aspiring writer/artists, and writer/producers

Step VI
Developing Persistence

During my early songwriting period, I fortunately had a delusional idea that I was ready to make it big. Little did I know the years of disappointments and rejections I would have to endure before my first break. Had I known, I don't know that I would have had the perseverance to keep writing song after song.

Billy Steinberg (Hit songwriter)

Each of the six steps outlined in this book is necessary for songwriting success. But if I had to choose which one is the most important, I'd say that it's the sixth step, "Developing Persistence." There are hundreds of individual skills that add up to successful songwriting. On the surface, some of these skills appear to be simple and seem as though they ought to be mastered easily. Others can be acquired quickly. However, many of the skills required to transform your ideas and inspiration into songs with the power to touch millions of hearts typically take years of practice. It takes even longer before they're incorporated into your songs with little conscious effort.

An enormous amount of perseverance is required to weather the inevitable frustrations and rejections. Without it, you may not continue your pursuit long enough to master the tools of successful songwriting. I've worked with several co-writers who were far more talented than me, but who gave up pursuing their dreams of writing hit songs before achieving commercial success. These songwriters had all of the musical talent they needed, but lacked belief in themselves and the determination to stubbornly pursue their goals in a business that offers no guarantees. Choosing a more secure profession was a valid choice for these writers.

The music business isn't right for everyone, nor can it accommodate every person who wants to be a part of it. The cold, hard reality is that only the best will have success in this competitive field. But, even if you choose not to pursue songwriting as a profession, it can still bring tremendous joy and satisfaction as a hobby.

By learning the rules and acquiring the tools and techniques set out in this book you can shave years off your journey. However, it's still important to develop persistence because it's likely that the road to success will be a long one.

Chapter 15
Hanging In until the Big Break

I was a waiter for two-and-a-half years at The Source, a health food restaurant. I lived down the block and I chose it because it was convenient. Little did I know that it was a major music business hangout. I still remember the booth number (B-2) of Syreeta Wright ("With You I'm Born Again"), who was married to Stevie Wonder. I told her, "I'm a songwriter" and I thought "How could she possibly believe me with this apron around my waist? What kind of songwriter could she think I am?"

I sent her some songs and nothing ever happened, but I continued to see her in the restaurant. Then several years later, when Smokey Robinson had his "One Heartbeat" album, he did a duet with Syreeta Wright—and it was my song. They invited me down to the recording session. I was so thrilled and so excited, and when I was introduced to Syreeta, I asked her, "Do you remember me?" She said, "You look so familiar, but I can't place the face with the place." When I said, "I was your waiter at The Source," she let out a scream and gave me the biggest hug. She autographed my lyric sheet and wrote, "Dear Allan, music will prevail."

Allan Rich (Hit songwriter with cuts by artists including Whitney Houston, 'N Sync, Barbra Streisand, Patti LaBelle, Barry Manilow, and Gladys Knight)

There's a famous music business joke: "Oh, you're a songwriter. What restaurant?" Rod Stewart dug graves, Billy Ray Cyrus sold cars, Randy Travis washed dishes at Nashville's legendary Bluebird Cafe, Roberta Flack was a teacher, Garth Brooks sold boots at an outlet mall, and Faith Hill worked at McDonald's before achieving international acclaim. Most songwriters have to earn a living by doing something other than writing songs while honing their craft.

There's no doubt that it's tough to have a full-time job, maintain relationships, take care of all the responsibilities of life, and still have the time and energy left to write songs. But somehow, some way, virtually every songwriter currently enjoying success has managed to do it. It's not practical to borrow money from friends, put your everyday living expenses on your MasterCard, or deplete your retirement savings account to survive until you become an overnight success, because it's likely that it will take much longer than you're anticipating. Having realistic expectations can help you maintain a healthy perspective and avoid suffering a breakdown while waiting for your big break.

DEVELOPING REALISTIC EXPECTATIONS

From the time I said, "I'm going to be a successful songwriter," until I signed a staff-writing deal and earned a meager living writing songs, eleven-and-a-half years had elapsed. From this milestone until I began earning what I considered a "good" living, it was another five years. By 1997, I certainly wasn't a millionaire, but after more than sixteen years of struggling to make ends meet, I felt rich—finally earning enough money as a songwriter to buy a beautiful house and have a "cushion" in the bank. I got some lucky breaks along the way and made some great connections as a result of having a music industry day job—yet it still took me more than sixteen years to earn a good living doing what I love.

It took five years to get "I Swear" cut. In that time it was passed on by everybody, including the biggest stars in the business. Some of them deny it, but others still remember it.

Gary Baker (Hit songwriter)

Setting goals and developing a positive attitude are important, but when I hear beginning songwriters tell me that they're going to have a hit song on the charts in a year or two, all I can do is smile and tell them I hope that will be the case. The odds of this happening are approximately the same as getting hit by lightning—twice in the same day!

One of the biggest mistakes I see beginning songwriters make is that they believe that just because they write a song, something will happen with that particular song. What they don't understand is that in the early stages of writing, each song is really a stepping stone to the next, a learning process that gets you one step closer to the song which might have a chance of being successful. I remember my first songwriting class at U.C.L.A. (which I taught 15 years later). Our instructor would remind us to throw away our first hundred songs.

The only way to look at this picture and make sense of it is to see "flowers." Consider every song you send out as a seed cast in the wind. It must find a fertile spot where the sun will shine and the rain will fall. Many songs must be cast in the wind to increase the chances of finding that fertile spot for the flower to grow. Most get blown into oblivion. Discouraging? Yes, but it is reality. If your heart and soul tell you that you must be a songwriter, you will eventually grow "flowers" providing you have the courage to face rejection and the perseverance to accept the fact that nothing will happen to most of your songs. But when something does happen—there is no greater feeling— especially if the record turns out well.

Gloria Sklerov (Hit songwriter and two-time Emmy Award winner whose songs have been recorded by artists including Frank Sinatra, Anne Murray, Cher, and Kenny Rogers)

Learning to write effective songs is a developmental learning process. It's like a baby learning to walk—many individual skills have to be mastered. His muscles need to mature; he needs to acquire balance; and he must practice the various components that lead up to taking those first wobbly steps. Some of these can't be rushed—they simply take time to develop. It's a similar process with songwriters.

The exercises in this book will help, but unless you're exceptionally lucky, the road to successful songwriting is a long one, filled with twists and turns, disappointments and frustration. Hopefully, knowing this will help you to be patient with yourself during the learning process. I spent many unhappy years feeling like a failure, instead of seeing that I was on a long journey toward success. It often takes many years for writers to achieve commercial success—even after they've written great songs. There are hundreds of stories about extraordinarily successful songs that took many years to be recorded and become hits.

"Change My Mind" was pitched for three-and-a-half years and turned down more than a hundred times before being recorded by the Oak Ridge Boys. During that period, a major publisher, whose opinion I respected, told me to change the title. Another publisher told me that he didn't like the song—even after the Oak Ridge Boys had recorded it. It took five more years, a dozen "holds" that each fell through, and several recordings by various artists before John Berry's version established me as an "overnight success." Stories like this are far more common than stories about songs being recorded quickly.

MAKING THE TIME FOR YOURSELF AND YOUR CREATIVITY

As discussed earlier in this chapter, it's not easy to work a full-time job, attend to all of the responsibilities that go hand in hand with living in this world—and still have the time and energy to be creative. It's hard to write when the baby's crying, the kids want supper, the bill collectors are calling, or you're exhausted after a ten-hour workday. But it is possible—*if* you make it a priority.

At one point along my journey, I worked at a miserable "temp" job in the City Hall in Culver City, California, to pay my rent. My boss was the devil's sister, and with the jacket and tie dress code, rigid rules, and time clock, this job was the opposite of everything creative, joyful, and free that I wanted in my life. During one of the fifteen-minute breaks that I lived for, I went for a walk and from a place of the deepest frustration searched for answers. How could I possibly write the songs I was meant to write if I'm trapped behind a desk, being forced to be someone so different from the person I am inside? How could I ever escape this prison when I was so beaten down and exhausted at the end of the day that all I wanted to do was "veg out" in front of the TV?

At that moment it hit me. It *was* too late for me at the end of the day to create from the most genuine part of me. But there was a solution. It occurred to me that I could wake up thirty minutes or even an hour earlier each morning. Before squeezing my soul into a suit and tie, I could lie in bed with my notebook and tape recorder, and write from my heart. I could give myself the gift of thirty minutes of creative time that was just for me—before anyone or anything else got to stake its claims. Before the stress and pressures and bumper-to-bumper traffic, the overdue bills, the "Yes, Sirs," and the frustration and exhaustion had a chance to set in, I could write—just like I knew I was meant to.

If you really believe in a song, stick with it, even if it isn't one of your "newer, more exciting" songs. If it is truly great, it will eventually find a home.

Mike Sistad (Director of Artists & Repertoires, Arista Nashville)

It worked. I found that I could do some of my best work early in the morning. This method worked for me, but it may not be your solution. At other times, it's been effective for me to take a twenty- or thirty-minute nap after a long day of work. I frequently wake up refreshed, revitalized, and ready to write.

Some writers find it helpful to schedule a set time and place for their writing. A coffeehouse or the public library can be places to focus on your creative work without interruptions and distractions. Try setting a specific work time in your calendar and honoring that as you would any other appointment—because honoring your creativity and your writing *is* as important as any other appointment or obligation.

While it does not address songwriting specifically, *The Artist's Way* by Julia Cameron, a workbook with a spiritual slant, has been helpful to many of my students. Designed to help creative individuals in all genres to discover and recover their creative selves, it includes exercises to help you find time for creative pursuits and to break through to deeper levels of creativity.

When I hear writers complain that they "can't find the time" to write, I suggest they explore where they might have "lost it." How many hours slip by in front of the television? How many additional songs might you have written if you could recapture the hours spent in Internet chat rooms, browsing through catalogs, or playing video games? It's up to us whether we spend our hours productively—or complaining about not having the time to be creative.

Chapter 16

Getting Past No

---

*Be tenacious and persevere. Find the back door when the
front door is shut.*

Judy Phelps (Writer/Publisher Relations, BMI)

There are countless songs that have been initially rejected by artists who later
recorded them and had enormous hits. For example, R & B/pop superstar Chaka
Khan had to be convinced to record "I Feel For You," one of her biggest hits,
and Lee Ann Womack initially did not want to record "The Fool," which established her as a country star.

Hit songwriter Allan Rich told me an inspiring story about the fate of one of
his songs:

> I had a relationship with Patti LaBelle because I'd had two songs on
> her million-selling Winner In You *album, and then I had a song on
> her next album. I sent her some songs and I got a response back that
> she was holding three or four of them and that she really loved them.
> Many months had gone by and I never heard anything. I just
> assumed it was happening because she had said that she loved the
> songs and she was cutting them.
>
> I was in London, sitting at a table with songwriters and music busi-
> ness people, and someone just happened to say, "Did you know that
> Patti LaBelle's album is finished?" She'd held four of my best songs
> for nine or ten months without cutting any of them. When I got back
> to Los Angeles I thought, "She's a big star, but I just can't let this
> slide." So, I wrote her a very warm letter saying how disappointed I
> was that she'd held all my songs, promised me she was going to
> record them, and that I had to hear on the street that the album was
> finished. I said, "We have a long-standing relationship, someone
> should have at least called me," but I said it all very lovingly.
>
> To my shock, the phone rings one day and when I pick it up she said,

"Hi, Baby, it's Patti LaBelle." She said, "Baby, I got your note. I would never do anything to hurt you. We just hired all these top producers and Prince did a song and we went so far over budget that we can't record any more songs. I feel really sorry. I love the songs but we're over-budget."

Well I had written one of the songs specifically for her with Allan Scott. The title was something she had said at one of her concerts. I knew the song was meant for her and I just couldn't let it drop. I hung up the phone and all of a sudden a brainstorm came to me. Our demos were record-quality demos and they were cut in a key that was if not her very best key, very close to it. I called Allan and I said, "I know this sounds like an I Love Lucy episode, but what if I call Patti LaBelle back, tell her that you and I will fly in for one day, and pay the expenses to record her vocal on the two songs of the four that I really thought were the ones she should be doing? All she'd have to do is come to the studio and sing the vocals." That's how sure I felt that these were her songs.

My co-writer said I was out of my mind, but I felt it was a shot we had to take. I called Patti and she thought it was a great idea. It cost us a couple of thousand dollars versus what she was paying which was thirty or forty thousand dollars to people like Prince and the other top producers. It was like David and Goliath. One of our songs, "I'm Scared Of You," knocked a Prince song off the album. It was such a satisfying feeling—and we got credited as Producers.

More so than ever now, it takes a detective to succeed in this business, since there are so few slots for songwriters. It's even more important to somehow find a way into a camp or a project, because so many of the cuts are "in-house."

There are times when your song may be rejected because it's not as good as those written by your competition, or because it's not appropriate for a particular project. But individuals who screen hundreds of songs sometimes make mistakes. Virtually every music industry pro (who's honest) has stories about one or more hit songs that he or she has rejected. It's possible that "no" just means that you have to be creative and find alternate ways to get your song through the doors. The A & R person for a certain artist might not like your song, but the producer and artist may love it—if they get the chance to hear it. If you believe strongly in a song for a particular project, keep pitching until it's been heard by the artist and producer.

Similarly, being told "We don't accept unsolicited material" may signify a door that's genuinely locked and bolted shut—or it may mean that a different approach might be required to open that door. For example, you may want to seek a referral to this company, send a fax or an e-mail explaining how strongly you feel about this one song, or try approaching a different individual at this same company. If the professional feedback you've received about your song is that it's exceptional, don't let "no" stop you. You just may not have found the right door.

OVERCOMING THE OBSTACLES

If the craft and business of writing great songs were easy, everyone would be having hit records. There are many obstacles that stand in the way between the

---

Exercise:

Overcoming the Obstacles to Success

1. List your strengths as a songwriter, specifically focusing on the craft of writing as opposed to your strengths as a businessperson. (For example, "I write great titles and ideas, and hooky chorus melodies. I incorporate lots of detailed images and action into my lyrics. I fully understand successful song structures.")

2. List those areas in which you need to improve your songwriting skills. (For example, "I tend to write lyrics that are more poetic than conversational. My verse melodies don't seem very fresh. I rarely rewrite my melodies. There's not much repetition in my songs.")

3. List your strengths as a businessperson, as they relate to your songwriting. (For example, "I have no fear of approaching music publishers. I've developed a professional pitch presentation. I'm actively networking through membership in a songwriters' organization. I'm producing demos that are up to the professional standard.")

4. List the songwriting business practices you need to improve. (For example, "I've been writing songs but not letting anyone hear them. I haven't recorded any demos. I don't know any other songwriters. I have never had one of my songs professionally critiqued.")

developing songwriter and success. However, sometimes the biggest hurdles are those we put up ourselves. They're also often the hardest to see.

The thought of acquiring all of the skills necessary to become a successful songwriter can seem overwhelming. You not only need to learn about song structures, effective lyric writing, and melody techniques; you also need to produce demos, find a publisher, learn about the music business, network, and pitch your songs. But the good news is that you don't need to do all of these things today.

Make a list of your strengths as a songwriter. Be sure to include not only your lyric and melody writing skills, but also qualities like persistence, willingness to work hard, and ability to conduct your songwriting business in a professional manner. It's equally important to list those areas that need work. When you can see your strengths and weaknesses written down in black and white it's easier to isolate specific areas to concentrate on.

It can help to refer back to the list of your strengths and weaknesses and tar-

---

5. Devise a game plan that allows you to focus on those areas that need work.

    I will devote _____ hours per week to my songwriting.

    During that time I will concentrate on developing the following skills:

    _____

    _____

    _____

    _____

    _____

    _____

6. Devise a game plan that allows you to focus on those areas of the songwriting business that you need to work on.

    I will devote _____ hours per week to the business of songwriting.

    During that time I will concentrate on developing the following skills:

    _____

    _____

    _____

    _____

    _____

    _____

get one or two specific areas to work on, one at a time. For instance, looking over your list, you may realize that you'd benefit most from spending an additional thirty minutes per day for the next month improving your melody writing skills. Or you may resolve to seek out additional collaborators. Whatever you decide to concentrate your efforts on, remember that it's unrealistic to expect yourself to master all of the skills of successful songwriting immediately.

It's also important to make a game plan that reflects realistic short-term and long-term goals. It's self-defeating to say, "I'll have a number one song on the radio in three months." This isn't going to happen even if you wrote an extraordinary song yesterday. It takes longer than three months for a song to be recorded, be commercially released, and climb the charts. But it can be very helpful to say, "I'll write thirty minutes, five days per week for the next three months, concentrating specifically on writing lyrics that are conversational, have universal appeal, and come from my heart." Or, "I'll spend a minimum of one hour per week for the next two months pursuing contacts that have the potential to lead to developing a relationship with a publisher."

Life as an aspiring songwriter resembles being in a 12-Step program. You constantly have to take a personal inventory of your strengths and weaknesses with hundreds of questions that demand a tremendous amount of honesty. Are you a good lyricist? What kinds of songs do you write— or shy away from writing? What aspects of the business make you uncomfortable? Then, after you start answering those questions and facing the hard realities of the hurdles ahead, the next challenge is to do the necessary work while maintaining your optimism and keeping your dreams alive.

Phil Goldberg (Member Services Director, Nashville Songwriters Association International)

It's typically easier to make these plans than it is to stick to them, though. Find support to help you maintain your commitment to your songwriting. Some of my students make a daily commitment to a co-writer, and then call to report that they've fulfilled their commitment for that day.

Look for those obstacles you've built up for yourself, such as failing to develop specific skills, not pursuing your songwriting in a businesslike manner, not giving yourself sufficient time for your creativity, or negative thinking—and break through them one at a time.

At the beginning stages of your development as a songwriter it is best to focus on honing your skills and your craft. However, if you've been writing songs at least a year, and have completed at least twenty songs, you also need to begin pursuing the business side.

COPING WITH REJECTION

One of the key skills required for success in the songwriting business is resiliency in the face of inevitable rejection and disappointment. The ability to turn the pain of rejection into even stronger determination to succeed is what separates the writers who give up from those who realize their dreams.

We don't like their sound, and guitar music is on the way out.

Decca Records rejecting the Beatles, 1962.

Sometimes, the fact that a publisher chooses not to sign your song, or an artist decides not to record it, is not a reflection on the quality of the song itself. The publisher may have similar songs in his or her catalog or may have recently made a commitment to another writer who writes in the same style that you write in. The artist may love your song but feel that it's not right for him or her, or that it's not consistent with the other songs already recorded for this particular album.

Encouragement kept me in the game. Rejection challenged me, made me dig deeper, and probably made me a better writer in the long run. Maybe my big break was not getting too much too soon.

George Teren (Hit songwriter)

There are at least a thousand different reasons why your song may be rejected. If the responses you get imply that you've written a strong song which doesn't fit the needs of this particular company or artist, you may simply have not found the right home for your song yet. But, if you consistently receive feedback that your song is not up to professional standards, or has some specific problems, go back to the drawing board.

It's been estimated that income is generated by only 5 percent of the songs written by professional songwriters. That means that 95 percent of the songs written by professionals never achieve commercial success. It's ironic that in order to be successful, songwriters are frequently called upon to be vulnerable and to bare their souls through their music and lyrics, while simultaneously maintaining a tough exterior, capable of withstanding disappointment that can sometimes be devastating. It helps to develop a healthy sense of detachment from your songs. Remind yourself that your value as a human being is not determined solely by the level of commercial success you achieve as a songwriter.

I can think of three instances of songs I produced that became hits that had been turned down by many people. "Steal Away" (Robbie Dupree), "Break My Stride" (Matthew Wilder), and "Just To See Her" (Smokey Robinson) were all rejected as not being "hit" sounding songs by a number of individuals within the industry, but they all went on to be top five songs.

Rick Chudacoff (Hit record producer/songwriter)

Rejection is a normal part of the business. In a *SongLink International* magazine interview, superstar producer and record label and publishing company executive Quincy Jones spoke about artists he *didn't* sign:

Whitney Houston: "When she was 16, Ashford & Simpson told me about her and I couldn't do anything because I was in the middle of the Michael Jackson mania."

Luther Vandross: "He was on my record and you could hear his talent a mile away, but again, I was too busy to do more with him."

Bobby McFerrin: "He was also sent to me when I was busy working with Michael."

In each of these instances, artists who went on to Grammy-winning successes were "rejected." Although they received what must have been a devastating rejection, obviously it didn't mean they weren't talented. Nor did it mean they would not achieve their successes at a different point in time, or at a different company.

Coping with rejection is very different from not feeling the pain of rejection. Of course it hurts to be told that a publisher has decided not to represent your song, or that it won't be included on an album. It's devastating to learn that the company you've been negotiating with for months has decided to sign someone else as a staff-writer, or that the best song you've ever written has been recorded by a major artist—and is a dismal failure commercially. If you had no emotional response to these disappointments you'd probably lack the sensitivity required to write. But disappointment and rejection are part of the package that is the songwriting business.

Some writers fall prey to substance abuse, or engage in self-defeating behaviors that temporarily numb the fear and pain of rejection. Healthy ways to cope and to grow stronger from rejection include:

♪ **Learning from each experience.** Ask yourself if there are good reasons why your song has been rejected. Is there a lesson to be learned—something you might want to change in this song, or in future songs you write, or in the way you conduct business? Stay open to constructive criticism.

♪ **Increasing your determination**. Some of the most successful people in any field are those who use failure as a motivator to work even harder to achieve their goals. An attitude of "I'll show them how good my songs can be. No matter how long it takes, I'll write one that's so powerful they won't be able to resist it," is far more productive than, "I guess this proves I'm no good at this. The competition's just too tough. I'll never be successful."

♪ **Maintaining realistic expectations.** You may need to reassess your expectations. It's possible that your sights are set too high for your current stage of development as a writer. If you've only been writing a year or two, in your spare time, it's unrealistic to expect your songs to be as good as those written by top professional writers who may have been honing their craft for ten years or more.

♪ **Never giving up (as long as you're enjoying the process).**

Remember that the fact that you've not yet attained certain manifestations of success does not preclude the possibility of your achieving those goals in the future.

FINDING VALIDATION FROM WITHIN

Write whatever you want to write. I believe that if a writer has talent, and hones in and nurtures that talent, he or she will have his or her day in the sun. The great writers of this century are all originals. I bet if you take a look at the most respected writers of the last forty years, you will find that the vast majority of their work was not "commercial" until after it was successful.

Frank Liddell (Director of Artists & Repertoires, MCA/Decca Records)

Success can be defined in many different ways. For some individuals, songwriting success may be synonymous with number one records, Grammy awards, and a big bank account. Others may define success as the ability to get joy from their writing, to write songs that touch people's hearts, or to effectively communicate their emotions through words and music. Those who find satisfaction in the writing process itself are far more likely to enjoy their journey.

I live for my music. I live for the songs I write. That's my responsibility. I have control over how great that song is going to be. No one else is going to be responsible for that except me.

Diane Warren (Four-time ASCAP Writer of the Year whose hits include "Unbreak My Heart," "Because You Loved Me," "How Do I Live," and "I Don't Want To Miss A Thing," as quoted in *CloseUp* magazine)

There are countless stories about songwriters whose talents were not recognized for many years. Both Roger Miller and Kris Kristofferson had given up and left Nashville before the seeds they'd sown finally bore fruit. It's said that "Dang Me" was on the charts for three weeks before Miller, who had moved to California, found out about it. Kristofferson, a Rhodes Scholar who worked as a janitor and barely made ends meet in Nashville, had traded poverty for a solid living as a helicopter pilot for offshore oil digging operators when Janis Joplin had a smash hit with one of his old songs, "Me & Bobby McGee."

Kristofferson had written some of his biggest hits, classic songs including "For The Good Times" and "Help Me Make It Through The Night," before ever being acknowledged as a successful songwriter. Prior to their commercial successes, were these incredible writers "failures"? If you define success as writing extraordinary songs, both of these writer/performers were tremendously successful long before their talents were recognized.

In the music business there are hundreds of factors that contribute to a songwriter's success (or lack thereof). Most of these are completely out of the writer's hands. For instance, you have no control over how well an artist sings your song. And after your song has been recorded, circumstances such as the political climate at the artist's record label at the time of your song's release, the amount of the promotion budget allotted to your song, and whether the artist who has recorded your song is a priority at his or her record label are all factors that are out of your hands. Although they play a tremendous role in defining your commercial success as a songwriter—they have no bearing on the quality of your song.

Allowing your self-esteem to be determined by factors over which you have no control is a recipe for unhappiness. It's far more productive to concentrate on what you *can* control. For example, you can determine the amount of time you devote to developing your songwriting skills, the quality of your work, the care you give to producing your demos, your willingness to rewrite, and the amount of time you spend networking and pursuing the business aspects of your songwriting career.

Successful songwriter Wade Kirby tells a wild story about how one of his songs came to be recorded by Country superstar John Michael Montgomery. The Atlantic Records A & R staff were in the process of making the final determination regarding which songs would be included on Montgomery's next album. When a certain song was played, someone expressed his approval by saying, "That's the ticket." Hearing this phrase reminded another A & R person of the title of one of Wade's songs that was sitting on his desk. He played it for the committee and "You're The Ticket" was included on this hit album—a seemingly random act that had an enormous impact on the songwriter's life.

When I asked the writer how he copes with the unpredictable nature of the business, he answered that he thinks of it like spinning the wheel of fortune. If you're consistently writing excellent (not just "good") songs, it's likely that a certain percentage of times, the wheel will land on you and you'll get your shot. All you can do is write to the very best of your ability—and be ready when opportunity knocks.

I don't obsess about what the songs are doing on the charts, because that is not the way to judge yourself. If you attach your self-worth to that crap you will be in a rubber room. What makes me feel good is writing the songs and landing the songs. I went so long without getting anywhere that I came to the point where I decided to just write for me.

Craig Wiseman (Hit songwriter with over 100 cuts and 30 charted singles)

Sometimes, when we're deep in the disappointment, it's hard to remember that lacking a crystal ball, we may not know what's best for us. Prior to signing my staff-writing deal there was nothing in the world I wanted more than to earn my living as a songwriter. After more than ten years of honing my skills and learning about the songwriting business it finally seemed as if my most cherished dream was about to come true. The head of a small publishing company expressed interest in signing me to a staff-writing deal. We had several meetings and seemed to be in agreement on the major deal points. This publisher loved the songs that were my personal favorites—the ones that other publishing companies didn't get as excited about. We were clearly on the same wavelength and I knew this was the company I had always been meant to sign to.

I can't begin to express the devastation I felt when this publisher decided that the budget couldn't accommodate an additional staff-writer. As I drove home from the meeting, I heard Garth Brooks singing "Unanswered Prayers" on my car radio. The message of that song (written by Brooks and Kent Blazy), which thanks God for prayers that didn't come true, gave me hope and strength to continue pursuing my goals. Many years went by before I could plainly see that if I had signed to that particular publishing company, I would most likely have never achieved the success I've attained. I couldn't possibly have acknowledged it at the time, but I needed another year or two to develop my songwriting skills.

Write from the heart and be persistent. The way that I got "Lifestyles Of The Not So Rich And Famous" cut was I approached my co-writer Byron Hill in the hallway at MCA Music and said, "Byron I've got this great idea for a song, what do you think?" He said, "Let's cancel everything and write that song tomorrow morning." We wrote the song and did a guitar/vocal work tape of it and pitched it to Tracy Byrd's producer. He passed on the song. We played it at a showcase a couple of months later and Larry Willoughby of the A & R Dept. at MCA Records took a copy. A couple of months went by and we got a call from Tony Brown, President of MCA Records, who said, "I want to get this song cut on this artist and we want it to be the first single." So, the producer who originally passed on it went back in and cut the song on Tracy Byrd. It was the first single and it went to number four on the country chart. It goes to show—never, ever give up.

Wayne Tester (Hit songwriter)

If I had become a staff-writer at that time, it's probable that I wouldn't have gotten any songs recorded and would have lost my publishing deal within a year or two. I don't know if another deal would have been forthcoming. Instead, I was lucky enough to sign a year later with a company that had the belief in my abilities, as well as the financial resources necessary to nurture and develop my talents for five years before I began generating income for them. Finding a company to stick with you that long is a very rare situation.

Many songwriters and creative artists (myself included) find it difficult to separate their self-worth from their commercial successes. Remind yourself that:

♪ You've chosen a very difficult, competitive field.

♪ It may take years for your talent to be recognized, and there's a chance you may never achieve commercial success—regardless of the quality of your work.

♪ Being told that your song is not right for a given project or publisher is not the same as being told that *you* are not good enough.

♪ You can get great satisfaction from writing a wonderful song—even if it doesn't achieve commercial success.

DEALING WITH THE BIG CRITIC INSIDE YOUR HEAD

Most songwriters have been asked questions like, "When are you going to give up this crazy dream and get a real job?" from concerned parents, spouses, or friends. When my father asked me that question, I got angry, feeling that it implied a lack of belief in my talent. My answer was, "I'm going to give it one hundred years—and if I'm not successful by then, I'll go back to school!" Eventually, I came to understand that it was only natural that he was concerned for my happiness. It was hard for him to understand the desire that drove me to continue pursuing my dream in the face of rejection, disappointment, and financial hardship. It's not that my father didn't believe in my talent. He wanted to protect me from struggle and disappointment.

Writers with great attitudes and positive dispositions who crave feedback, and who can take constructive criticism, are usually the ones who make it.

Mark Mason (Director of Writer/Publisher Relations, BMI)

What I sometimes perceived as criticism and a lack of support was painful, but there is frequently no harsher critic than the one within us. "I'll never be good enough." "What makes me think my songs are better than everyone else's?" "There are millions of great songs—why would I think I could ever beat out the competition?" Few of us would tolerate this kind of negative thinking and criticism from others, and yet we so often say things like that to ourselves. Granted, it's hard to maintain a positive attitude without receiving some encouragement—and in the early stages of learning your craft it's likely that your songs will not measure up to professional standards. Instead of criticizing yourself for what you haven't yet achieved, be proud of yourself for pursuing your goal and for striving to improve your craft. That's an accomplishment in itself.

Look for the milestones and acknowledge them. They may be small at first. For example, maybe you've completed your first song by yourself, recorded a work tape, rewritten a lyric, scheduled an appointment with a publisher, or joined a songwriters' organization. Each is one more step in the right direction.

Don't wait for your songs to be perfect. This is a common pitfall that can

---

Exercise:

Ten Magic Minutes

Set a timer for ten minutes.

♪ During these ten minutes write whatever you feel like writing. It doesn't have to be a song. It doesn't have to rhyme. And, it doesn't have to be "good" or geared toward commercial success. You might jot down random thoughts, stream of consciousness, images, ideas, or potential titles—or you might simply write about your frustration, your joy, your fears, dreams, or anything else that's on your mind.

♪ The only rule is that there be no criticism. Tell your internal critic to stay outside the room until your ten minutes are up. As long as you write for ten minutes with no self-criticism or censoring, you have completed this exercise perfectly.

♪ As soon as your timer tells you that ten minutes have elapsed, stop writing. Having the writing period be a specific amount of time helps to remove the anxiety inherent in facing a blank page. If you choose to continue writing, you may do so. However, it's not required, as you have already completed this exercise perfectly.

♪ Repeat this exercise on a daily basis and you may be amazed. Some of my strongest (and most commercially accessible) songs have been started during these safe, "no-critics-allowed" ten-minute writing sessions. Sometimes we just need to feel safe in order to be creative. Other times, we need to clear out some of the baggage and the voices in our heads to allow the best writing we're capable of to emerge.

stop your progress. Your songs don't have to be perfect in order to record an inexpensive demo, seek out a collaborator, or let people hear them. Each of these actions can be a stepping stone to bring your songs to the next level. When that nasty internal critic says you're not good enough, remind yourself that:

- ♪ You're in the midst of a learning process.
- ♪ Successful songwriting appears deceptively simple, but it takes time and practice.
- ♪ It's unrealistic to expect your early songs to be competitive with those written by professionals.
- ♪ While it may be true that your latest song lacks Grammy-winning potential, that doesn't mean that you're not talented. Nor does it mean that you won't write an incredible song in the future.
- ♪ Every song you write can't be your best.
- ♪ Songwriting is a very difficult business and rejection is to be expected.

Few things can immobilize a songwriter more effectively than his or her internal critic. It's impossible to do your best writing with a voice inside you telling you that each line you write isn't good enough, or whispering over your shoulder that you'll never be successful. Being overly critical is one of the most common sources of writer's block. The exercise on page 251 can be a powerful remedy both for writer's block and for silencing the critic inside your head.

Write, Write, Write constantly . . . especially when you're an amateur. There is nothing like practice. There is also nothing like studying and learning. If you play (an instrument), learn the classics—study them, sing them. How did the writer move you? You can't rewrite that song, but there is a lesson to be learned. The radio to me is school and the writing is the student doing his or her lessons. Learn the rules and if you're lucky and smart you can break the rules. The dumb thing would be breaking the rules—and not knowing the rules. That means you're an amateur. Professionals break the rules on purpose.

Harlan Howard (Legendary Nashville songwriter)

PERSISTENCE CHECKLIST

Photocopy this list. Keep it where you normally write and answer the following questions on a monthly basis. They'll give you an idea of what areas you still need to work on in order to develop persistence.

☐ Are you making time for your creativity?

☐ Have you listed your strengths and weaknesses as a song-writer and a businessperson?

☐ Are you targeting specific areas to work on?

☐ Are you finding support for your commitment to songwriting?

☐ Have you devised a game plan? Are you sticking to it?

☐ Are you accepting rejection as a normal part of the songwriting business?

☐ Are you working on developing healthy responses to rejection?

☐ Are your expectations realistic?

☐ Are you finding satisfaction from the writing process itself?

☐ Do you separate your self-worth from your commercial success?

☐ Are you remembering to acknowledge your accomplishments?

Exercise:

Final Assignment

It takes time to assimilate some of the ideas presented in this book. They may represent a whole new way of approaching songwriting. Give yourself the gift of writing ten new songs that incorporate the tools you've learned from reading this book. Don't criticize or judge these songs—they're all part of your journey toward success. Be gentle with yourself. Writing songs that successfully communicate is not as easy as it seems, but you can acquire the necessary skills with patience and practice.

It is my observation that successful songwriters incorporate what I call "The Three L's of Songwriting Success" into their careers:

♪   LEARN all you can about:

1. The music **business**—it is the music business (not just "music")

2. The **craft** of writing—know, understand, and master the tools and techniques of songwriting to help you best express your creativity.

3. **Yourself**—you and your observations are the true source for creative expression.

♪ LISTEN:

1. To the wisdom and advice of others so you can learn. Be willing to grow.

2. To and also observe the world around you. Remember whom you are writing about and for.

3. To your own intuition. Trust yourself.

♪ LOVE what you are doing as you are doing it, not just when it's done. In other words, love the "process" more than the "prize."

Donna Michael (Director of Regional Workshops and Educational Programs, N.S.A.I.; composer; and songwriter)

Afterword

Reach down in your soul and write a truly great song. Make sure you've gone over it and it doesn't have any weak spots musically or lyrically. Then, if you keep every four leaf clover you find, always keep change in your pocket in case you pass a fountain, keep your eye out for shooting stars, and watch out for mirrors and ladders—that song has a chance.

Wade Kirby (Hit songwriter)

I strongly believe that somewhere deep inside, we each know what it is that we need to do to get past our own personal blocks. I've had several pivotal moments in my career journey, when I asked God/my heart/the universe/my higher power, and anything else I thought might help to show me my next step. Each time, an answer came to me that eventually did lead me to the next level. Answer the following questions and revisit them the first of each month:

♪ What is it I need to do to get to the next level?

♪ What's stopping me from achieving what I want?

♪ Why aren't I writing at the level I know I'm capable of?

♪ What do I need to do to achieve the success I deserve?

In some instances, you might identify specific skills that you need to practice. Maybe you'll want to structure additional time for your craft, or record a demo (even though you're afraid it won't be good enough). You might decide to take guitar lessons, give yourself permission to write a dozen songs that aren't commercial hits, say "no" to some social invitations so that you can stay home and write, or take a class. Maybe you'll decide you need to find a collaborator, go to a meeting of a local songwriters' organization, rewrite a melody one more time, plan a trip to Nashville, New York, or LA, or buy a hand-held tape recorder or a new notebook.

Listen to whatever it is your heart tells you. Instead of focusing on all the obstacles in your way, try looking for the solutions. You just might find them.

*Songwriters are a rare breed of humans who exhibit
incredible patience, spirit, energy, and faith. What they
bring to us enriches our lives in every corner of the world. It
is a noble and worthy profession. On top of any advice I
might give comes my thanks to all songwriters for the gifts
they give to each and every one of us.*

Brendan Okrent (Senior Director of Repertory, ASCAP)

Every writer who reads this book will not necessarily watch his or her songs climb to the top of the charts. Some will. But, every writer who works hard to learn the craft, while seeking and staying open to constructive criticism, will continue to grow and improve his or her skills. Finding pleasure in the writing process and feeling the sense of accomplishment that comes with knowing that you've communicated your idea in a way that can touch other hearts is success. Enjoy the journey.

To receive information about having your songs professionally critiqued (through the mail), recordings by Jason Blume, or scheduling a songwriting seminar in your area contact:

Moondream Music Group
9 Music Square South, PMB #352
Nashville, TN 37203-3203

Or visit my website at: http://www.jasonblume.com

Do not send tapes. You'll receive a flyer explaining proper submission procedure.

Appendix

SONGWRITER ORGANIZATIONS

NASHVILLE SONGWRITERS ASSOCIATION INTERNATIONAL (NSAI)

To find your local NSAI chapter contact:

NSAI, 1701 West End Avenue, 3rd Floor, Nashville, TN 37203 (800) 321-6008 (in Nashville: 615-256-3354) Fax: 615-256-0034; e-mail: nsai@songs.org; website: www.songs.org/nsai

SONGWRITERS GUILD OF AMERICA/NATIONAL ACADEMY OF SONGWRITERS (SGA/NAS)

website: www.songwriters.org.

New Jersey office: 1500 Harbor Boulevard, Weehawken, NJ 07087 (201) 867-7603; fax: (201) 867-7535; e-mail: klstrnad@aol.com

New York office: 1560 Broadway, Suite #1306, New York, NY 10036 (212) 768-7902; fax: (201) 768-9048; e-mail: SongNews@aol.com

Los Angeles office: 6430 Sunset Boulevard, Suite #705, Hollywood, CA 90028 (323) 462-1108; fax: (323) 462-5430; e-mail: LASGA@aol.com

Nashville office: 1222 16th Avenue South, Suite #26, Nashville, TN 37212 (615) 329-1782; fax: (615) 329-2623; e-mail: SGANash@aol.com

Following is a listing of additional songwriter organizations throughout the U.S. and Canada. To have your organization listed in revised editions, please send the address to: Moondream Music, 9 Music Square South, PMB #352, Nashville, TN 37203.

NORTH CENTRAL

American Composers Forum, 332 Minnesota Street, #E-145, St. Paul, MN 55101

Arts Midwest, 528 Hennepin Avenue, Suite 310, Minneapolis, MN 55403

Chicago Music Coalition, P.O. Box 41069, Chicago, IL 60641

Columbus Songwriters, 3312 Petzinger Road, Columbus, OH 43227

Country Music Showcase International, P.O. Box 368, Carlisle, IA 50047

Detroit Songwriters Association, 28935 Flanders Drive, Warren, MI 48093

Great Plains Songwriters, 706 Massachusetts, #208, Lawrence, KS 66044

Indianapolis Songwriters Association, P.O. Box 44724, Indianapolis, IN 46244

Metro Detroit Songwriters Association, P.O. Box 26044, Fraser, MI 48026

Midwestern Songwriters Association, 238 Eldon Avenue, Columbus, OH 43204

Minnesota Association of Songwriters, P.O. Box 581816, Minneapolis, MN 55458

Minnesota Composers Forum, 332 Minnesota Street, #E145, St. Paul, MN 55101

Missouri Society of Songwriters & Musicians, HCR 1 Box 157E, Eminence, MO 65466

Missouri Songwriters Association, 693 Green Forest Drive, Fenton, MO 63026

Missouri Songwriters Association, 3711 Andora Pl., St. Louis, MO 63125

Ozark Noteworthy Songwriters Association, 2303 S. Luster, Springfield, MO 65804

Songwriters and Poets Critique, 1616 Hawthorne Pk., Columbus, OH 43203

United Songwriters, 6429 Leavenworth Road, Kansas City, KS 66104

Whitewater Valley Songwriters, 480 N. Park Hill Drive, Liberty, IN 47353

Wichita Songwriters, 2450 Sommerset, Wichita, KS 67204

Wisconsin Songwriters, P.O. Box 874, Neenah, WI 54957

NORTHEAST

American Composers Alliance, 170 W. 74th Street, New York, NY 10023

Boston Songwriters Workshop, 14 Skelton Road, Burlington, MA 01803

Connecticut Songwriters Association, P.O. Box 1292, Glastonbury, CT 06033

Creative Music Foundation, P.O. Box 671, Woodstock, NY 12498

Folk Alliance, 1001 Connecticut Avenue, N.W., #501, Washington, D.C. 20036

Island Songwriters Showcase, P.O. Box 460, East Northport, NY 11731-0430

League of Women Composers, Box 670 Southshore Road, Three Mile Bay, NY 13693

Massachusetts Country Music Association, P.O. Box 2066, Abington, MA 02351

Massachusetts Songwriters Association, P.O. Box 211, Westfield, MA 01086

New England Songwriters Association, P.O. Box 207, Jamaica, VT 05343

New Jersey and Pennsylvania Songwriter Association, 226 E. Lawnside Avenue, Westmont, NJ 08108

Philadelphia Area Songwriters Association, 910 Pleasant Avenue, Wyndmoor, PA 19038

Philadelphia Songwriters Association, P.O. Box 1299, Brookhaven, PA 19015

Pittsburgh Songwriters Association, 523 Scenery Drive, Elizabeth, PA 15037

Rhode Island Songwriters, 159 Elmgrove Avenue, Providence, RI 02906-4230

Songcraft Seminars, 441 E. 20th Street, New York, NY 10010

Songwriter and Lyricist Club, P.O. Box 023304, Brooklyn, NY 11202

Songwriters Advocate, 47 Maplehurst Road, Rochester, NY 14617

Songwriters Collective, 301 Ampere Parkway, Bloomfield, NJ 07003

Songwriters of Washington, 4200 Wisconsin, NW #106-137, Washington, D.C. 20016

Songwriters Seminars/Workshops, 928 Broadway, #602, New York, NY 10010

The Black Rock Coalition, P.O. Box 1054, Cooper Station, New York, NY 10276

Songwriters Workshop, P.O. Box 238, Babylon, NY 11702

Vermont Songwriters, R.D. 2, Box 277, Underhill, VT 05489

Writers Guild East, 555 W. 57th Street, New York, NY 10019

NORTHWEST

Alaska Performing Songwriters Group, P.O. Box 240205, Anchorage, AK 99524

Alaska Songwriters Association, P.O. Box 33552, Juneau, AK 99803

Central Oregon Songwriters, 67055 Fryear Road, Bend, OR 97701

Central Oregon Songwriters Association, 68978 Graham Ct., Sisters, OR 97759-3107

Olympic Peninsula Songwriters Association, 110 E. 3rd , Suite 0209, Port Angeles, WA 98362

Pacific N.W. Songwriters, P.O. Box 98564, Seattle, WA 98198

Portland Songwriters Association, 1920 N. Vancouver, Portland, OR 97227

Seattle Songwriters Association, 770 Crestwood Ct., Port Orchard, WA 98366

Victory Music, P.O. Box 7515, Bonney Lake, WA 98390

SOUTH CENTRAL

Arkansas Songwriters Association, 6817 Gingerbread Lane, Little Rock, AR 72204

Arkansas Songwriters Association, 404 Kay Street, N. Little Rock, AR 72117

Arkansas/Oklahoma Songwriters, P.O. Box 1370, Van Buren, AR 72956

Austin Songwriters Group, P.O. Box 2578, Austin, TX 78768

Dallas Songwriters Association, 3630 Harry Hines, Box 20, Dallas, TX 75219

Ft. Bend Songwriters, P.O. Box 1273, Richmond, TX 77406

Ft. Worth Songwriters Association, 4833 Mobile Drive, Ft. Worth, TX 76137

International Alliance for Women in Music, ACU Box 8274, Abilene, TX 79699

Kerrville Music Foundation, P.O. Box 1466, Kerrville, TX 78029

Louisiana Songwriters, P.O. Box 80425, Baton Rouge, LA 70898

Network of Lyricists & Songwriters, P.O. Box 1342, Friendswood, TX 77548

Oklahoma Songwriters, P.O. Box 4121, Edmond, OK 73083

Oklahoma Songwriters and Composers, 6420 S.E. 15th Street, Midwest City, OK 73110

Oklahoma Songwriters Association, P.O. Box 57043, Oklahoma City, OK 73157

Red River Songwriters Association, P.O. Box 412, Ft. Towson, OK 74735

River Valley Songwriters Association, Route 1, Box 51A, Dover, AR 72837

San Antonio Songwriters, P.O. Box 413, Adkins, TX 78101

Southern Songwriters Guild, P.O. Box 6817, Shreveport, LA 71136

Texas Songwriters Association, Route 1, Box 160AA, Pickton, TX 75471

Texas Songwriters Association, 2700 Meadowlark, Tyler, TX 75701

Texas Songwriters, P.O. Box 1285, Chandler, TX 75758

Texas Songwriters, 1502 E. Houston, Marshall, TX 75670

Tulsa Songwriters Association, P.O. Box 254, Tulsa, OK 74101

SOUTHEAST

Alabama Songwriters Guild, P.O. Box 272, Garden City, AL 35070

Atlanta Creative Music, 1580 Avon Avenue, S.W., Atlanta, GA 30311

Birmingham Songwriters, P.O. Box 590011, Birmingham, AL 35259

Black Songwriters Association, 1758 Emerald Avenue, S.W., Atlanta, GA 30310

Blues Foundation, Handy's Home, 352 Beale Street, Memphis, TN 38103

Carolina Association of Songwriters, P.O. Box 4972, Rock Hill, SC 29732

Casement Songwriters Workshop, 859 Riveroak Drive E., Ormand Beach, FL 32174

Central Carolina Songwriters Association, 1144 Amber Acres Lane, Knightdale, NC 27545

Charlottesville Area Songwriters Association, P.O. Box 4825, Charlottesville, VA 22905

Georgia Music Industry Association, (404) 266-2666

Heartland Songwriter Association of Kentucky, 109 N. Mulberry Street, Elizabethtown, KY 42701

International Songwriters Guild, 5108 Louvre Avenue, Orlando, FL 32812

Knoxville Songwriters, P.O. Box 603, Knoxville, TN 37901

International Bluegrass Music Association, 207 E. Second Street, Owensboro, KY 42303

International Bluegrass Music, Route 1, Box 710, Pittsboro, NC 27312

Louisville Area Songwriters, P.O. Box 148, Peewee Valley, KY 40056-0148

Memphis Songwriters Association, 1494 Prescott Street, Memphis, TN 38111

Mid-South Songwriters Association, 5402 Brantford Road, Memphis, TN 38120-2440

Montgomery Songwriters, P.O. Box 11014, Montgomery, AL 36111

Muscle Shoals Songwriters Association, 1632 A Shenandoah Road, Florence, AL 35630

Music City Song Crafters, P.O. Box 120145 Acklen Station, Nashville, TN 37212

Nashville Pop Songwriters Association, 9 Music Square South, #169, Nashville, TN 37203

N.E. Georgia Songwriters Association, 2480 Webb Girth Road, Gainesville, GA 30507

Songwriters Association (Kentucky), 3884 Highway 81 North, Calhoun, KY 42327

Songwriters of Jacksonville, P.O. Box 10394, Jacksonville Beach, FL 32207

Songwriters Workshop of Nashville, 614 Forest Park Drive, Brentwood, TN 37027

South Carolina Songwriters, P.O. Box 16596, Greenville, SC 29606

S.W. Virginia Songwriters, P.O. Box 698, Salem, VA 24153

Tennessee Songwriters Association, P.O. Box 2664, Hendersonville, TN 37077

The Folk Alliance, P.O. Box 5010, Chapel Hill, NC 27514

Tri-County Coalition, P.O. Box 9459, Hickory, NC 28603

Virginia Composers, P.O. Box 2438, Petersburg, VA 23804

Virginia Organization Of Composers and Lyricists, P.O. Box 34606, Richmond, VA 23234

SOUTHWEST

Academy of Country Music, 6255 Sunset Boulevard, Hollywood, CA 90028

Arizona Songwriters Association, P.O. Box 678, Phoenix, AZ 85001

Golden State Country Music Organization, 3505 Sonoma Boulevard, Suite 20-348, Vallejo, CA 94590

Hawaii Songwriters Association, P.O. Box 88129, Honolulu, HI 96830

L.A. Songwriters Showcase, P.O. Box 93759, Hollywood, CA 90093

Las Vegas Songwriters Association, P.O. Box 42683, Las Vegas, NV 89116

Los Angeles Songwriters Society, 1209 N. Orange Grove, W. Hollywood, CA 90046

Northern California Songwriters Association, 1724 Laurel Street #120, San Carlos, CA 94070

San Diego Songwriters, 3368 Governor Drive, Suite F-326, San Diego, CA 92122

San Diego Songwriters Guild, 13828 Tobiasson Road, Doway, CA 92064

Santa Barbara Songwriters, P.O. Box 2238, Santa Barbara, CA 93120

Society of Composers and Lyricists (SCL), (310) 281-2812

Southern Arizona Entertainers, P.O. Box 55010, Tucson, AZ 85703

Southern Colorado Songwriters, 2023 Vinewood Lane, Pueblo, CO 81005

Utah Songwriters Association, P.O. Box 571325, Salt Lake City, UT 84157

CANADA

SOCAN (Society of Composers, Authors and Music Publishers of Canada), e-mail: socan@socan.ca
Main Office: 41 Valleybrook Drive, Don Mills, Ontario M3B 2S6, (800) 55-SOCAN or (416) 445-8700
SOCAN Edmonton: 1145 Weber Centre, 5555 Calgary Trail, Edmonton, Alberta T6H SP9 (800) 51-SOCAN or (403) 439-9049
Quebec Office: 600 Boulevard De Maisonneuve West, Suite 500, Montreal, Quebec H3A 3J2, (800) 79-SOCAN or (514) 844-8377
Dartmouth Office: 45 Alderney Drive, Suite 802, Queen Square, Dartmouth, Nova Scotia B2Y 2N6, (800) 70-SOCAN or (902) 464-7000
West Coast Division: 1201 W. Pender Street, #400, Vancouver, British Columbia V6E 2V2 (800) 93-SOCAN or (604) 669-5569

Canadian Amateur Musicians, 1751 Richardson #8224, Montreal, Quebec H3K 1G6

Canadian Academy of Recording Arts & Sciences, 124 Merton Street 3rd Floor,

Toronto, Ontario

Canada Council, 350 Albert Street, P.O. Box 1047, Ottawa, Ontario K1P 5V8

Pacific Music Industry Association, 400-177 W. 7th Avenue, Vancouver, BC V5Y 1L8

Pacific Songwriter Association (PSA), Box 15433, 349 W. Georgia Street, Vancouver, BC V6B 5B2

Songwriters Association of Nova Scotia, P.O. Box 1543, Halifax CRO, Halifax, Nova Scotia B3J2Y3

Toronto Musicians Association, 101 Thorncliffe Park Drive, Toronto, Ontario M4H 1M2

Canadian Music website: www.canmusic.com

MECHANICAL ROYALTY COLLECTION AGENCIES

The Harry Fox Agency, Inc., 711 Third Avenue, New York, NY 10017 (212) 370-5330, website: http://www.nmpa.org

Copyright Management, Inc., 1102 17th Avenue South, Nashville, TN 37212 (615) 327-1517

PUBLICATIONS OF INTEREST TO SONGWRITERS

Acoustic Musician, P.O. Box 1349, 1065 River Road, New Market, VA 22844, (540) 740-4005

American Songwriter, 1009 17th Avenue South, Nashville, TN 37212, (615) 321-6096 or (800) 739-8712, **website:** www.songnet.com/asongmag/

A & R Registry (see *The Music Business Registry*)

Billboard, 1515 Broadway, New York, NY 10036, (212) 764-7300, **website:** www.billboard.com

Billboard's Talent and Touring Directory, 1515 Broadway, New York, NY 10036, (212) 764-7300, **website:** www.billboard.com

Bluegrass Unlimited, P.O. Box 111, Broad Run, VA 20137, (800) BLU-GRAS, **website:** www.bluegrassmusic.com

Blues Revue, Route 1, Box 75, Salem, WV 26426, (304) 782-1971, **website:** www.bluesrevue.com

CCM (Contemporary Christian Music), P.O. Box 706, Mt. Morris, IL 62054, (800) 333-9643

Country America, 1716 Locust Street, Des Moines, IA 50309 (800) 374-8739

Country Music, One Turkey Hill Road South, Westport, CT 06880

Dirty Linen (Folk & World Music) P.O. Box 66600, Baltimore, MD 21239, (410) 583-7973, **website:** www.dirtylinen.com

Gavin, 209 10th Avenue South, Nashville, TN 37203, (615) 255-5010, **website:** www.gavin.com

Independent Songwriter Web-Magazine, **website:** www.independentsongwriter.com

JazzTimes, 8737 Colesville Road, 5th Floor, Silver Spring, MD 20910, (301) 588-4114, **e-mail:** jtimes@aol.com

Los Angeles Music Industry Directory, (805) 299-2405, **website:** www. musiciansphonebook.com

Music Business Registry:

 A & R Registry

 Music Publisher Registry

 Music Business Attorney, Legal & Business Affairs Registry

 Film & Television Music Guide

7510 Sunset Boulevard, Suite 1041, Los Angeles, CA 90046, (800) 377-7411 or (818) 769-2722, fax (800) 228-9411 or (818) 769-0990, **email:** mbr@pacificnet.net

Music Connection, 4731 Laurel Canyon Boulevard, N. Hollywood, CA 91607, (818) 705-0101, **website:** www.musicconnection.com

Music Row, P.O. Box 158542, Nashville, TN 37215 (615) 321-3617, **website:** www.musicrow.com

Musician's Guide to Touring and Promotion, Billboard, 1515 Broadway, New York, NY 10036, (212) 764-7300, **website**: www.billboard.com

NAS Songwriters Musepaper, 6255 Sunset Boulevard, Suite 1023, Hollywood, CA 90028, (323) 463-7178, **website**: www.nassong.org

Nashville Red Book, 1207 Fesslers Lane, Nashville, TN 37210, (615) 256-5456

Performing Songwriter, 6620 McCall Drive, Longmont, CO 80503, (800) 883-7664

R & R (Radio & Records), 10100 Santa Monica Boulevard, 5th Floor, Los Angeles, CA 90067, (310) 788-1625, **website**: www.rronline.com

Recording Industry Sourcebook, c/o Intertec Publishing, P.O. Box 12901, Overland Park, KS 66282, (800) 543-7771

XXL (Hip-Hop), 1115 Broadway, New York, NY 10010, (212) 807-7100, **e-mail**: xxxl@harris-pub.com

ONLINE RESOURCES

Billboard on Line, www.billboard.com

Cool Songwriting and Songwriting Links, http://pw2.netcom.com/~coolsong /coolsonglinks.html

Get Signed.com, www.getsigned.com

Glade's Songwriter Page, www.zapcom.net/~glade/

Harmony Central, www.harmony-central.com

Indie-Music.com, www.indie-music.com

Jeff Mallett's Songwriter Site, www.lyricist.com

Just Plain Folks, www.jpfolks.com

Li'l Hanks Guide for Songwriters, www.halsguide.com

Lyrical Line, www.lyricalline.com

The Muse's Muse, www.musesmuse.com

Music Network USA, www.mnusa.com

The Musician's Friend, www.sqaull.freeserve.co.uk

Official Website of Canadian Music, www.canmusic.com

Seth Jackson Songwriting & Music Business Page, www.mindspring.com/~hitmeister

Songwriters Q & A, www.songwritersq-a.com

ONLINE RESOURCES FOR WRITERS OF CHILDREN'S SONGS

Canadian Children's Songwriters Network (not restricted to Canadian residents), www.geocities.com/enchantedforest /cottage/5207/ccsn.html

Children's Music Web, www.childrensmusic.org

KIDiddles, www.kididdles.com

RESOURCES FOR WRITERS OF CHRISTIAN SONGS

Gospel Music Association (GMA), 1205 Division Street, Nashville, TN 37203 (615) 242-0303, **website**: gospelmusic.org/

Christian Artists & Songwriters, 200 Countryside Drive, Franklin, TN 37069

Christian Songwriters Group, website: www.christiansongwriters.com

Christian Music Place, website: www.placetobe.org/cmp/central.htm

Midwest Christian Songwriters Association, Dept. 2130, 1715 Marty, Kansas City, KS 66103

North Florida Christian Music Writers Association, P.O. Box 61113, Jacksonville, FL 32236

CHRISTIAN MUSIC FESTIVALS

Christian Artists (Music Festival and Competition), 1911 Eleventh Street, Suite 103, Boulder, CO 80302, (303) 247-9901, **website**: http://www.Christian-artists.com

The Alive Christian Music Festival, Canal Fulton, OH, (330) 854-0011, **website**: http://www.place2be.org/cmp/alive/

Cornerstone Festival, 920 W. Wilson Avenue, Chicago, IL 60640, (773) 989-2087, **website:** http://cornerstone.jesusfreak.com/

Creation Festival, website: www.gospelcom.net/creation/

Xcess Christian (Rock) Music Festival, **website:** www.xcess.org/

RESOURCES FOR WRITERS OF LATIN MUSIC

Billboard's International Latin Music Buyer's Guide, BPI Communications, Directory Central-Listings, P.O. Box 24970, Nashville, TN 37202, **e-mail:** direcen@bpicom.com

ASCAP Miami, 844 Alton Road, Suite 1, Miami Beach, FL 33139, (305) 673-3446

ASCAP Puerto Rico, 510 Royal Bank Center, 255 Ponce de Léon Avenue, Hato Rey, Puerto Rico 00917, (787) 281-0782

BMI Miami, 5201 Blue Lagoon Drive, Suite 310, Miami, FL 33126, (305) 266-3636

BMI Puerto Rico, East Wing, Suite 8262, Royal Bank Center, 255 Ponce de Leon Avenue, Hato Rey, Puerto Rico 00917, (787) 754-6490

SESAC Latina, 421 W. 54th Street, 4th Floor, New York, NY 10019, (212) 586-3450

PERFORMING RIGHTS ORGANIZATIONS

ASCAP, website: www.ascap.com
New York: One Lincoln Plaza, New York, NY 10023, (212) 621-6000
Los Angeles: 7920 Sunset Boulevard, 3rd Floor, Los Angeles, CA 90046, (213) 883-1000
Nashville: 2 Music Square West, Nashville, TN 37203, (615) 742-5000
Atlanta: 541-400 10th Street NW, Atlanta, GA 30318, (404) 753-4679
Chicago: 1608 West Belmont Avenue, Suite 200, Chicago, IL 60657, (773) 472-1157

Miami: 844 Alton Road, Suite 1, Miami Beach, FL 33139, (305) 673-3446
Puerto Rico: 510 Royal Bank Center 255 Ponce de Léon Avenue, Hato Rey, Puerto Rico 00917, (787) 281-0782
London: 8 Cork Street, London WIX ITB England, (011-44-171) 439-0909

BMI:
New York: 320 W. 57th Street, New York, NY 10019, (212) 586-2000
Los Angeles: 8730 Sunset Boulevard, Los Angeles, CA 90069, (310) 659-9109
Nashville: 10 Music Square East, Nashville, TN 37203, (615) 401-2000
Miami: 5201 Blue Lagoon Drive, Suite 310, Miami, FL 33126, (305) 266-3636
Atlanta: 3636 Habersham Road, Suite 1103, Atlanta, GA 30305, (404) 816-5655
BMI Puerto Rico: East Wing, Suite 8262, Royal Bank Center, 255 Ponce de Leon Avenue, Hato Rey, Puerto Rico 00917, (787) 754-6490
London: 84 Harley House, Marylebone Road, London, NW1 5HN England, (011-44-171) 486-2036, **website:** www.bmi.com

SESAC:
New York: 421 W. 54th Street, 4th Floor, New York, NY 10019, (212) 586-3450
Nashville: 55 Music Square East, Nashville, TN 37203, (615) 320-0055. **website:** www.sesac.com

COPYRIGHT INFORMATION

U.S. Copyright Office:
website: lcweb.loc.gov/copyright/
To request Copyright Form PA call the Federal Information Office at (800) 366-2998.
To ask questions about the copyright registration process, call the Copyright Office at (202) 707-3000.

PITCH (OR TIP) SHEETS

Note that the prices listed were accurate when this book was printed and are subject to change.

American Songwriters Network, (617) 576-8836, $140.00/year (geared to professional writers and publishers, however unpublished writers are also welcome)

New on the Charts, (914) 632-3349, $225/year (for professional songwriters and publishers)

RowFax, (615) 321-3617, $291/year delivered via fax, or $255/yr via e-mail (exclusively Nashville tips for pros and publishers, includes subscription to *Music Row* Magazine)

SongLink International, (213) 368-6741, $350/year if delivered by mail; $395/year via fax (available to pros, publishers, and to unpublished writers on an audition basis)

Songplugger, (818) 761-5859, $167/year (for professional songwriters and publishers only)

Taxi, (800) 458-2111 (outside the U.S. and Canada: 800-888-2111), **website**: www.taxi.com

The Leads Sheet, Allegheny Music Works, 306 Cypress Avenue, Dept. SW, Johnstown, PA 15902, $30/year

Tunesmith, (818) 761-5859, $63/year (geared to unpublished writers)

SONGWRITING COMPETITIONS

American Songwriter Magazine Lyric Contest, American Songwriter Magazine, 1009 17th Avenue S., Nashville, TN 37212, (800) 739-8712, e-mail: asongmag@aol.com

Cavan International Song Contest, Drumelis, Cavan, Ireland

Chris Austin Songwriting Contest, P.O. Box 121855, Nashville, TN 37212, **website:**www.merlefest.org/ songwritingcontest.htm

John Lennon Songwriting Contest, **website:** www.info@jlsc.com

Kerrville New Folk Songwriting Competition, website: www. kerrville-music.com/index.html

Mid-Atlantic Song Contest, (301) 654-8434, **website:** www.saw.org

Napa Valley Music Festival, P.O. Box 10227, Napa, CA 94581, **website:** www.napafest.com

Pacific Song Contest, P.O. Box 349, Surfers Paradise, Queensland 4217 Australia, **website:**www.pacificsongcontest.com

Portland Songwriters Association Annual Song Contest, 1920 N. Vancouver Avenue, Portland, OR 97227, **website:** www.teleport.com/~psa

Sisters Folk Festival, P.O. Box 1168, Sisters, OR 97759, **website:** www.informat.com/bz /folkfest/songwriting.html

Tucson Folk Festival Songwriting Competition, P.O. Box 26531, Tucson, AZ 85726, **website:** www.rtd.com/ ~dsimpson/con_song.htm

USA Songwriting Competition, Dept. AW98, Box 15711, Boston, MA 02215, (617) 576-9732, **website:** www.tiac.net/ users/asn/songcontest.html

Unisong, 7095 Hollywood Boulevard, #1015, Hollywood, CA 90028, **website:** www.unisong.com

Additional information regarding international song festivals can be obtained by contacting:

FIDOF, 4230 Stansbury Avenue # 05, Sherman Oaks, CA 91423

SONG PERMISSIONS

"Achy Breaky Heart"
Written by Don Von Tress.
© 1991 Millhouse Music.
All Rights Reserved. Used by
Permission.

"Back To Your Heart"
Words and music by Gary Baker,
Jason Blume, and Kevin
Richardson.
© 1999 Zomba Songs, Inc.,
Zomba Enterprises, Inc., Swear
By It Music, and Trek Inc. All
rights on behalf of Swear By It
Music and Trek Inc. adminis-
tered by Zomba Enterprises Inc.
All Rights Reserved. Used by
Permission.

"Because You Loved Me"
Words and music by Diane
Warren.
© 1996 Realsongs and
Touchstone Pictures Song &
Music, Inc. All Rights Reserved.
Used by Permission.

"Better Things To Do"
Words and music by Terri Clark,
Tom Shapiro, Chris Waters.
© Sony/ATV Songs LLC. Dba
Tree Publishing Co.,Warner-
Tamerlane Publishing Corp.,
Hit Haven Music and Hamstein
Cumberland Music. All rights on
behalf of Hit Haven Music
administered by Warner-
Tamerlane Publishing Corp. All
Rights Reserved. Used by
Permission.

"Carried Away"
Words and music by Steve
Bogard and Jeff Stevens.
© 1996 Warner-Tamerlane
Publishing Corp., Rancho Belita
Music and Jeff Stevens Music.
All rights on behalf of Rancho
Belita Music and Jeff Stevens
Music administered by Warner-
Tamerlane Publishing Corp.
All Rights Reserved. Used by
Permission.

"Change My Mind"
Words and music by Jason
Blume and A.J. Masters.
© 1991 Zomba Enterprises and
Bull's Run Music. All Rights
Reserved. Used by Permission.

"Hit Me With Your Best Shot"
Written by Eddie Schwartz
© 1978 Sony/ATV Songs LLC.
All rights administered by
Sony/ATV Music Publishing, 8
Music Square West, Nashville,
TN 37203. All Rights Reserved.
Used by Permission.

"How Can I Help You Say Goodbye"
Words and music by Karen
Taylor-Good and Burton Collins.
© 1993 W.B.M. Music Corp.,
K.T.Good Music, Burton B.
Collins Publishing, Reynsong
Publishing Corp. and Howe
Sound Music. All rights on
behalf of K.T. Good Music
administered by W.B.M. Music
Corp. All Rights Reserved. Used
by Permission.

"How Do I Live"
Words and music by Diane
Warren.
© Realsongs. All Rights Reserved.
Used by Permission.

"I Can Love You Like That"
Words and music by Steve
Diamond, Maribeth Derry and
Jennifer Kimball.
© 1995 Diamond Cuts, Criterion
Music Corp., Windswept Music,
Second Wave Music and Friends
and Angels Music. Diamond
Cuts administered by
Wonderland Music Company,
Inc. Friends and Angels Music
administered by Windswept
Music. All Rights Reserved. Used
by Permission.

"I Swear"
Words and music by Frank J.
Myers and Gary Baker.
© Morganactive Songs, Inc and
Rick Hall Music, Inc. All rights
on behalf of Morganactive
Songs, Inc. for the World ex Usa
and Canada administered by WB
Music Corp. All Rights Reserved.
Used by Permission.

"I Wanna Dance With Somebody (Who Loves Me)"
Words and music by George
Merrill and Shannon Rubicam.
© 1986 Irving Music, Inc. (BMI)
and Boy Meets Girl Music. All
Rights Reserved. Used by
Permission.

"One Of Us"
Words and music by Eric
Bazilian.
©1995 Human Boy Music.
All rights on behalf of Human
Boy Music administered by WB
Music Corp. All Rights Reserved.
Used by Permission.

"Over The Rainbow"
Music by Harold Arlen.
lyric by E.Y. Harburg.
© 1938 (Renewed 1966) Metro-
Goldwyn-Mayer Inc.
© 1939 (Renewed 1967) EMI
Feist Catalog Inc. Rights
throughout the world controlled
by EMI Feist Catalog Inc.
(Publishing)
and Warner Bros. Publications
U.S. Inc. (Print). All Rights
Reserved. Used by Permission.

"Saving All My Love For You"
Words by Gerry Goffin,
music by Michael Masser.
© 1978 Screen Gems-EMI Music
Inc. and Prince Street Music.
All rights administered jointly.
All Rights Reserved. Used by
Permission.

"Send In The Clowns"
Music and lyrics by Stephen
Sondheim.
© 1973 Rilting Music, Inc.
(Ascap). All rights administered
by WB Music Corp. All Rights
Reserved. Used by Permission.

"She's Not The Cheatin' Kind"
Written by Ronnie Dunn.
© 1994 Sony/ATV Songs LLC.
All rights administered by
Sony/ATV Music Publishing
8 Music Square West, Nashville,
TN 37203. All Rights Reserved.
Used by Permission.

"Strawberry Wine"
Words and music by Matraca
Berg and Gary Harrison.
© 1996 Windswept Pacific
Songs, August Wind Music,
Great Broad Music and Georgian
Hills Music. All Rights adminis-
tered by Windswept Pacific
Songs. All Rights Reserved. Used
by Permission.

"Walkin' Away"
Words and music by Annie
Roboff and Craig Wiseman.
© 1996 Almo Music Corp., Anwa
Music and Daddy Rabbit Music.
All Rights Reserved. Used by
Permission.

INDEX

A & R (Artists and Repertoires), 208–209, 218–219, 220
A cappella, 95–97
Action, 37–44
ADATS (Alesis Digital Audio Technology), 151
Alliteration, 57, 58–59
Almodovar, Diane, 89
Altering range, for title, 99–100
Alternate mixes, 149
American Federation of Musicians (AFM), 130
American Federation of Television and Radio Artists (AFTRA), 145
American Society of Composers, Authors and Publishers (ASCAP), xii, xiii, 63, 87, 90, 162–163, 164, 216, 217
Analog vs. digital, 152–153
Answering lyrics, 107, 108–109
Arrangement, deciding on, 138–141
Artist demos, song demos versus, 126–128
Artists
  collaborating with, 198
  pitching to, 210–211, 218–219, 220
Artists' managers, pitching to, 211–212, 218–219, 220
Ascending notes, 114, 115
Aschmann, Lisa, 210
Ask-A-Pro, 196
Assonance, 57–58, 59
Audio cassettes, 149–150, 214, 216

Baker, Gary, 30, 32, 100, 105, 172, 234
Bazilian, Eric, 5
The Beatles, 243
Berg, Matraca, 39, 40–41
Berlin, Irving, 84
Bias, cassette, 150
Big break, hanging in until, 233–237
Big critic inside head, 250–252
The Big Lie, 125–126
Blackwell, Dewayne, 117
Blanket licenses, 163
Blazy, Kent, 248
Blume, Jason, 6, 44, 105, 137, 138, 257
Board, mixing, 149
Bogard, Steve, 9
Books, 185
Bowie, David, 114
Break, hanging in until, 233–237
Breaking lines, 111–112
Bridge, 7–8
Broadcast Music International (BMI), 88, 90, 162–163, 164, 216, 217

Brooks, Garth, 116, 142, 153–154, 211, 248
Brown, Tony, 249
Budgets, demo, 130–132
Buffett, Jimmy, 62, 211
Building song, 8–15
Business, 157–229, 254
Byrd, Tracy, 249

Cabaret songs, 86–88
Call and Response, 107, 108–109
Cameron, Julia, 237
Carey, Kathleen, 64
Carey, Mariah, 145
Carlton, Jeff, 24
Cassettes, 149–150, 214, 216
Casting, 207–208
Casting lists, 205
Catchy melodies, lyrics for, 108–109
Catchy phrases, 104–107
CDs (compact discs), 151
Cerney, Todd, 66, 200–201
Chamberlain, Carson, 104–105
Chapman, Tracy, 81–82
Charts, chord, 136–138
Checklists
  business, 229
  demo, 155
  lyric, 91
  melody, 119
  persistence, 253
  song structure, 17
Child, Desmond, 27, 57
Children's songs, 72–74, 263
  for melodic inspiration, 99
Chord, unexpected, 116–117
Chord charts, 136–138
Chorus, 4–7
Christian music, 74–77, 263–264
Christmas & Holiday Music, 85–86
Christmas songs, 83–86
Chudacoff, Rick, 15, 127, 244
Clark, Terri, 55
Cohen, Leonard, 66
Collaborating, 197–202
Collaborators Network, 196, 202
Collins, Burton, 13, 140
Colvin, Shawn, 81–82
Comedy songs, 77–80
Competitions. *See* Contests
Components, of song, 3–8
Connections, 194–228
Conrad, Jack, 65–66
Consistent tense and tone, 33–35
Contests, 224–226, 265
Continuity, 36–37
Contracts, 184–193
Controlled composition clause, 161
Conversational lyrics, 44

Coping with rejection, 243–246
Co-publishing, 192–193
Copyright, 162, 202–203, 216, 226, 264
Copyright Management Inc., 160
Corfield, Gemma, 44
Cover letters, 214, 215, 220
Craft, 254
Creativity, making time for, 236–237
Critic, inside head, 250–252
Cumming, Bryan, 63–64, 135, 225
Custom session, 127

DAT (digital audio tape), 151
Davis, Linda, 26
Dean, Billy, 100
Demos
  preparing to record, 135–147
  producing of, 121–155
  song versus artist, 126–128
  when and how to record, 122–134
Demo services, self-producing versus, 132–134
Derry, Maribeth, 5
Descending notes, 114, 115
Detail, 37–44
Determination, increasing of, 245
Diamond, Steve, 5, 60, 62, 94, 176
Dictionaries, rhyming, 54–55
Digital, analog vs., 152–153
Directories, 134
Discipline, through collaboration, 198
Domestic royalties, 161–162
Dunn, Ronnie, 5

Effects, 130
Elliott, Carol, 81
EMI Christian Music Group, 75
Emotion, evoking one, 32–33
Emotional support, through collaboration, 198
End credit theme, 167
Engvall, Bill, 79
Enjoying process, 245–246, 254
Eq levels, 149
Evans, Ray, 95
Evoking one emotion, 32–33
Existing hit song, rewriting lyric to, 69
Expectations, realistic, 234–236, 245
Experience, learning from, 245
Exploitation, 169

Feelings, telling story versus, 38
Female vocalist, for demo, 146–147
Feminine rhymes, 53
Fenster, Jeff, 39, 98